D0018101

THE BERLITZ SELF-TEACHER:

SPANISH

NAFEA FAA IPOIPO by Paul Gauguin

This Book Belongs to

William Carr

1991

THE BERLITZ
SELF-TEACHER:
SPANISH

BY THE EDITORIAL STAFF OF
THE BERLITZ SCHOOLS
OF LANGUAGES OF AMERICA, INC.

A Perigee Book

Perigee Books
are published by
The Putnam Publishing Group
200 Madison Avenue
New York, NY 10016

Copyright © 1949 by The Berlitz Schools of Languages of America, Inc.
All rights reserved. This book, or parts thereof,
may not be reproduced in any form without permission.
Published simultaneously in Canada by
General Publishing Co. Limited, Toronto
First Perigee printing 1987

Library of Congress Cataloging-in-Publication Data

The Berlitz self-teacher, Spanish.

  Reprint. Originally published: New York: Grosset &
Dunlap, 1949.
  1. Spanish language—Self-instruction.   I. Berlitz
Schools of Languages of America.
PC4112.5.B48   1987   468.3'421   86-16864
ISBN 0-399-51324-8

Printed in the United States of America

11 12 13 14 15

INTRODUCTION

A very strange paradox exists in connection with languages and the learning of them. On the one hand, the ability to speak two or more languages reasonably well is *prima facie* evidence of better-than-average intelligence. On the other hand, learning a language is a very easy business. The proof of it is that every living human being who is not an utter idiot speaks one!

The trick lies in how you go about it. It would seem reasonable to use somewhat the same system to learn a new language as you did to acquire your own. This idea built up the Berlitz Schools of Languages from a one-room studio in Providence, Rhode Island, to a globe-circling institution with over 300 branches.

In a word, you learn to *speak* a language *by speaking it*—and in no other way. That is how the Spaniards do it, and that is how you learned English.

You will succeed with the BERLITZ SELF-TEACHER to the extent that you *speak*. Do not deceive yourself into thinking you have "arrived" when you find yourself able to read or translate the Spanish text. You master Spanish only in the degree to which you can express *your* ideas in it. The ability to interpret the thoughts of others is only the first step.

One way of using the BERLITZ SELF-TEACHER is to pair off with someone else, or to organize a small group. After reading over the lesson in advance for meaning and pronunciation, each student then reads aloud, direct from the Spanish text. The lesson is divided into convenient portions by agreement among the students. After each student has practiced reading aloud, one of them assumes the role of instructor and questions the others from the exercises called THINKING IN SPANISH. When all can answer these questions without hesitation, each student should invent ten or twelve new questions, based on the same or preceding lessons, and then put these questions to the others. Afterwards, answers to the exercise questions should be written out and corrected from the keys in the appendix.

When a group of you are learning together, do not succumb to the "community-sing" temptation. Each student must speak individually, so that he can hear himself and the others, and profit thereby.

Make no mistake, however! This book is designed primarily for the student working alone. He must do exactly what pairs or groups do, covering each operation for himself. If you are embarrassed by the sound of your own voice, hide in the pantry! Put a sack over your head! No matter what form of defense mechanism you set up, see to it that you *speak out!* Do not mumble or whisper.

Your attention is directed to the glossary in the back of the book. Use it sparingly, if at all. With few exceptions, all the words are made clear in the lesson texts, and only occasionally have we sneaked a new one into the THINKING IN SPANISH exercises, just to keep you on your toes.

The authors have enjoyed preparing the BERLITZ SELF TEACHER, because they are confident that, properly used, it can provide you with a flying start toward a working knowledge of Spanish—and an extra dividend of good, clean fun.

NOTE ON PRONUNCIATION

THE BERLITZ SELF-TEACHER: SPANISH presents a pronunciation system which eliminates completely the bothersome diacritical marks
found in many language books. Each Spanish word is respelled in
the closest approximation to the most common values of English
vowels and consonants. The stressed syllable is printed in SMALL
CAPITALS. Thus, for the word sombrero (hat) the following pronunciation is given:

*sohm-*BREH-*roh*

Say it aloud and place emphasis on the capitalized syllable. The
word pronounces itself!

THE BERLITZ SELF-TEACHER:

SPANISH

PRIMERA LECCIÓN

¿Qué es esto?
Keh ess ESS-*toh?*
What is this?

El libro
Ell LEE-*broh*
The book

la pluma
lah PLOO-*mah*
the pen

¿Qué es esto?
Keh ess ESS-*toh?*
What is this?

el lápiz
ell LAH-*peeth*
the pencil

la caja
lah KAH-*hah*
the box

Es el libro.
Ess ell LEE-*broh.*
It is the book.

el papel
*ell pah-*PEHL
the paper

la llave
*lah l'*YAH-*veh*
the key

¿Es esto el lápiz?
Ess ESS-*toh ell* LAH-*peeth?*
Is this the pencil?

Sí, es el lápiz.
See, ess ell LAH-*peeth.*
Yes, it is the pencil.

¿Es esto la caja, señor?
Ess ESS-*toh lah* KAH-*hah, sehn-*YOHR?
Is this the box, sir?

No, señor, no es la caja, sino la pluma.
*Noh, sehn-*YOHR, *noh ess lah* KAH-*hah,* SEE-*noh lah* PLOO-*mah.*
No, sir, it is not the box, but the pen.

1

NOTE to Student: All nouns are either masculine or feminine. If the word has *el* before it, it is masculine; if it has *la*, it is feminine.

The word *es* means "it is". The "it" is understood. *"Esto"* means "this" when you are indicating an object without specifying whether it is masculine or feminine.

Señor, (sir), *señora* (madam) and *señorita* (miss), are used more frequently in Spanish than we use their equivalents in English. Spanish speaking people are, at least in their language, more polite than we are.

La silla
Lah SEEL-*yah*
The chair

la mesa
lah MEH-*sah*
the table

la lámpara
lah LAHM-*pah-rah*
the lamp

la puerta
lah PWEHR-*tah*
the door

la ventana
*lah vehn-*TAH-*nah*
the window

el cuadro
ell KWAH-*droh*
the picture

Señorita, ¿es esto la lámpara o la silla?
*Sehn-yoh-*REE-*tah, ess* ESS-*toh lah* LAHM-*pah-rah oh lah* SEEL-*yah?*
Miss, is this the lamp or the chair?

Es la silla, señor.
Ess lah SEEL-*yah, sehn-*YOHR.
It is the chair, sir.

¿Qué es esto?
Keh ess ESS-*toh?*
What is this?

Es la pared
*Ess lah pah-*REHD
It is the wall

el piso
ell PEE-*soh*
the floor

el cielo raso
*ell th'*YEH-*loh* RAH-*soh*
the ceiling

¡Muy bien!
*¡Mwee b'*YEHN!
Very well!

¿	2	3	4	5
uno	dos	tres	cuatro	cinco
oo-*noh*	*dohs*	*trehs*	k'WAH-*troh*	THEEN-*koh*

HINTS on Pronunciation: Spanish pronunciation is easy; but the *stress* on the syllable is sometimes a bit worrisome. The stress usually comes on the syllable before the last. We have indicated stress by separating the syllables in our approximate pronunciation, and setting in small capitals the one stressed.

DO NOT FORGET: Spanish uses an upside-down question mark *before* a question to show you that a question is coming.

THINKING IN SPANISH

See whether you can identify the following articles *in Spanish*. Answers may be found on page 253.

1. ¿Qué es esto?
2. ¿Es esto el libro?
3. ¿Es esto la caja?

4. ¿Es esto la mesa?
5. ¿Es esto el papel?
6. ¿Qué es esto?

7. ¿Es esto la lámpara?
8. ¿Es esto la silla?
9. ¿Qué es esto?

10. ¿Qué es esto?
11. ¿Es esto la caja?
12. ¿Es esto la llave?

13. ¿Qué es esto?
14. ¿Es esto el libro?
15. ¿Es esto la pared?

LECCIÓN 2

La ropa
Lah ROH-*pah*
Clothing

El saco
Ell SAH-*koh*
The jacket

el sombrero
*ell sohm-*BREH-*roh*
the hat

el pantalón
*ell pahn-tah-*LOHN
the trousers

el abrigo
*ell ah-*BREE-*goh*
the overcoat

el traje
ell TRAH-*heh*
the suit or dress

la falda
lah FAHL-*dah*
the skirt

la cartera
*lah kahr-*TEH-*rah*
the pocket-book

¿Es esto el sombrero?
Ess ESS-*toh ell sohm-*BREH-*roh?*
Is this the hat?

Sí, señor, es el sombrero.
*See, sehn-*YOHR, *ess ell sohm-*BREH-*roh.*
Yes, sir, it is the hat.

¿Es esto el saco o el pantalón?
Ess ESS-*toh ell* SAH-*koh oh ell pahn-tah-*LOHN?
Is this the jacket or the trousers?

Es el saco.
Ess ell SAH-*koh.*
It is the jacket.

4

NOTE to Student: *Sr., Sra.,* and *Srta.* are abbreviations often found in print for *Señor, Señora,* or *Señorita.* The abbreviation is capitalized.
Traje: means either "dress" or "suit."
Media: can mean either "sock" or "stocking."

el dinero
ell dee-NEH-roh
the money

el reloj
ell reh-LOH
the watch

la media
lah MEHD-yah
the stocking

la corbata
lah kohr-BAH-tah
the tie

la camisa
lah kah-MEE-sah
the shirt

el guante
ell gw'AHN-teh
the glove

el pañuelo
ell pahn-yoo-EH-loh
the handkerchief

¿Qué es esto, la cartera o el dinero?
Keh ess ESS-toh, lah kahr-TEH-rah oh ell dee-NEH-roh?
What is this, the pocket-book or the money?

Es el dinero.	**¡Excelente!**	**¡Hasta mañana!**
Ess ell dee-NEH-roh.	*Ehk-theh-LEHN-teh!*	*AHS-tah mahn-YAH-nah!*
It is the money.	Excellent!	Until tomorrow!

HINTS on Pronunciation: You have probably heard something about the difference between "Castillian" and "South American" Spanish. This is a misconception inasmuch as the name of the language is *castellano,* as well as *español.*
However, there are certain differences in pronunciation between the spoken language in Spain and in most of Spanish America, although the spoken idiom may be said to be more uniform than American English and British English. The two principal differences in accent are detailed below:

LETTER	LATIN AMERICA	SPAIN
z:	*lápiz—LAH-pees*	LAH-peeth
Soft c:	*cinco—SEEN-koh*	THEEN-koh

THINKING IN SPANISH
(Answers on page 253)

1. ¿Qué es esto?
2. ¿Es el guante o el zapato?
3. ¿Es la corbata o el pañuelo?

4. ¿Qué es esto?
5. ¿Es el pañuelo o el guante?
6. ¿Es el lápiz?

7. ¿Que es esto?
8. ¿Es el traje?
9. ¿Es el abrigo?
10. ¿Es el saco o el pantalón?
11. ¿Es el sombrero?
12. ¿Es la camisa?

LECCIÓN 3

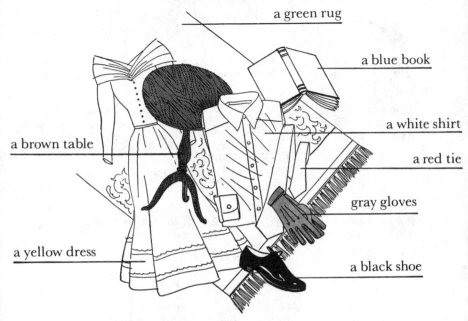

a green rug

a blue book

a white shirt

a red tie

gray gloves

a black shoe

a yellow dress

a brown table

¿De qué color es esto?
*Deh keh koh-*LOHR *ess* ESS-*toh?*
What color is this?

negro	**rojo**	**amarillo**	**gris**
NEH-*groh*	ROH-*hoh*	*ah-mah-*REEL-*yoh*	*greess*
black	red	yellow	grey
blanco	**pardo**	**verde**	**azul**
BLAHN-*koh*	PAHR-*doh*	VEHR-*deh*	*ah-*THOOL
white	brown	green	blue

El lápiz es pardo.
Ell LAH-*peeth ess* PAHR-*doh.*
The pencil is brown.

El libro es azul.
Ell LEE-*broh ess ah-*THOOL.
The book is blue.

El cielo raso es blanco.
*El th'*YEH-*loh* RAH-*soh ess* BLAHN-*coh.*
The ceiling is white.

El teléfono es negro.
*Ell teh-*LEH-*foh-noh ess* NEH-*groh.*
The telephone is black.

El papel es blanco.
*Ell pah-*PEHL *ess* BLAHN-*coh.*
The paper is white.

El sombrero es verde.
*Ell sohm-*BREH-*roh ess* VEHR-*deh.*
The hat is green.

NOTE: Adjectives of color, like other adjectives, must agree with their nouns in gender. Ex: *El libro es rojo, la pluma es roja.*

Some adjectives have the same form for masculine and feminine such as *verde, gris, azul.* Ex: *El lápiz es azul, la caja es azul.*

¿Qué es esto? Es el libro.	¿De qué color es el libro?
Keh ess ESS-*toh? Ess ell* LEE-*broh.*	*Deh keh koh-*LOHR *ess ell* LEE-*broh?*
What is this? It is the book.	What color is the book?

El libro es azul.
Ell LEE-*broh ess ah-*THOOL.
The book is blue.

¿Qué es esto?	Es el cielo raso.
Keh ess ESS-*toh?*	*Ess ell th'*YEH-*loh* RAH-*soh.*
What is this?	It is the ceiling.

¿De qué color el cielo raso?
*Deh keh koh-*LOHR *ess ell th'*YEH-*loh* RAH-*soh?*
What color is the ceiling?

El cielo raso es blanco.
*Ell th'*YEH-*loh* RAH-*soh ess* BLAHN-*koh.*
The ceiling is white.

¿De qué color es el sombrero? Es verde.
*Deh keh koh-*LOHR *ess ell sohm-*BREH-*roh? Ess* VEHR-*deh.*
What color is the hat? It is green.

¿Es pardo el lápiz?	Sí, señor, el lápiz es pardo.
Ess PAHR-*doh ell* LAH-*peeth?*	*See, sehn-*YOHR, *ell* LAH-*peeth ess* PAHR-*doh.*
Is the pencil brown?	Yes, sir, the pencil is brown.

¿Es verde el lápiz?
Ess VEHR-*deh ell* LAH-*peeth?*
Is the pencil green?

No, señor, el lápiz no es verde.
*Noh, sehn-*YOHR, *ell* LAH-*peeth noh ess* VEHR-*deh.*
No, sir, the pencil is not green.

¿Es negro el lápiz?	No, no es negro.
Ess NEH-*groh ell* LAH-*peeth?*	*Noh, noh ess* NEH-*groh.*
Is the pencil black?	No, it is not black.

¿De qué color es el lápiz?	El lápiz es pardo.
*Deh keh koh-*LOHR *ess ell* LAH-*peeth?*	*Ell* LAH-*peeth ess* PAHR-*doh.*
What color is the pencil?	The pencil is brown.

¿Es pardo el libro?
Ehs PAHR-*doh ell* LEE-*broh?*
Is the book brown?

No, el libro no es pardo.
Noh, ell LEE-*broh noh ess* PAHR-*doh.*
No, the book is not brown.

¿De qué color es el libro?
*Deh keh koh-*LOHR *ess ell* LEE-*broh?*
What color is the book?

El libro es azul.
Ell LEE-*broh ess ah-*THOOL.
The book is blue.

¿De qué color es el sombrero?
*Deh keh koh-*LOHR *ess ell sohm-*BREH-*roh?*
What color is the hat?

El sombrero es verde.
*Ell sohm-*BREH-*roh ess* VEHR-*deh.*
The hat is green.

¿De qué color es el teléfono?
*Deh keh koh-*LOHR *ess ell teh-*LEH-*foh-noh?*
What color is the telephone?

El teléfono es negro.
*Ell teh-*LEH-*foh-noh ess* NEH-*groh.*
The telephone is black.

¿De qué color es la pluma?
*Deh keh koh-*LOHR *ess lah* PLOO-*mah?*
What color is the pen?

La pluma es negra.
Lah PLOO-*mah ess* NEH-*grah·*
The pen is black.

¿De qué color es la corbata?
*Deh keh koh-*LOHR *ess lah kohr-*BAH-*tah?*
What color is the tie?

Es roja.
Ess ROH-*hah.*
It is red.

El libro es azul.
Ell LEE-*broh ess ah-*THOOL.
The book is blue.

La caja es gris.
Lah KAH-*hah ess greess.*
The box is grey.

El lápiz es azul.
Ell LAH-*peeth ess ah-*THOOL.
The pencil is blue.

La pluma es azul.
Lah PLOO-*mah ess ah-*THOOL.
The pen is blue.

La corbata es roja.
*Lah kohr-*BAH-*tah ess* ROH-*hah.*
The tie is red.

El sombrero es verde.
*Ell sohm-*BREH-*roh ess* VEHR-*deh*
The hat is green.

¿De qué color es el papel?
*Deh keh koh-*LOHR *ess ell pah-*PEHL?
What color is the paper?

Es blanco.
Ess BLAHN-*koh.*
It is white.

¿De qué color es la regla?
*Deh keh koh-*LOHR *ess lah* REH-*glah?*
What color is the ruler?

Es negra.
Ess NEH-*grah.*
It is black.

¿De qué color es el lápiz?
*Deh keh koh-*LOHR *ess ell* LAH-*peeth?*
What color is the pencil?

Es azul.
*Ess ah-*THOOL.
It is blue.

¿De qué color es la pluma?
*Deh keh koh-*LOHR *ess lah* PLOO-*mah?*
What color is the pen?

Es azul.
*Ess ah-*THOOL.
It is blue.

¿De qué color es el teléfono?
*Deh keh koh-*LOHR *ess ell teh-*LEH-*foh-noh?*
What color is the telephone?

Es negro.
Ess NEH-*groh.*
It is black.

¿De qué color es la corbata?
*Deh keh koh-*LOHR *ess lah kohr-*BAH-*tah?*
What color is the tie?

Es roja.
Ess ROH-*hah.*
It is red.

¿De qué color es el papel?
*Deh keh koh-*LOHR *ess ell pah-*PEHL?
What color is the paper?

Es blanco y amarillo.
Ess BLAHN-*koh ee ah-mah-*REEL-*yoh*
It is white and yellow.

6	7	8	9	10
seis	siete	ocho	nueve	diez
SEH-*ees*	s'YEH-*teh*	OH-*choh*	NWEH-*veh*	d'YEHTH

¡Buenos días!
BWEH-*nohs* DEE-*ahs!*
Good morning!

¡Adios!
*Ahd-*YOHS!
Goodbye!

¡Buenas noches!
BWEH-*nahs* NOH-*chehs!*
Good night! (Good evening!)

THINKING IN SPANISH
(Answers on page 253)

1. ¿Es la pluma azul?
2. ¿Es la pluma gris?
3. ¿De qué color es la pluma?
4. ¿Es roja la pluma?
5. ¿Es la pluma blanca o verde?

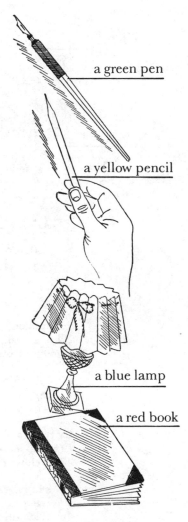

a green pen

a yellow pencil

6. ¿Qué es esto?
7. ¿Es el lápiz?
8. ¿Es el lápiz rojo?
9. ¿Es el lápiz blanco?
10. ¿De qué color es el lápiz?

11. ¿Es la mesa?
12. ¿Es la puerta?
13. ¿Qué es esto?
14. ¿Es la lámpara?
15. ¿De qué color es la lámpara?

a blue lamp

a red book

16. ¿Qué es esto?
17. ¿Es amarillo el libro?
18. ¿Es negro el libro?
19. ¿Es blanco el libro?
20. ¿De qué color es el libro?

LECCIÓN 4

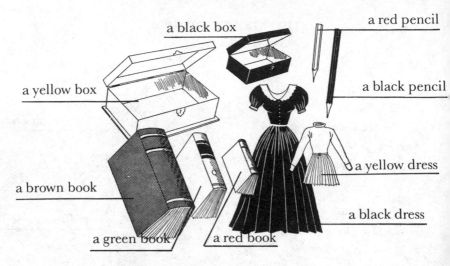

a black box

a red pencil

a yellow box

a black pencil

a brown book

a yellow dress

a black dress

a green book

a red book

Las dimensiones
*Lahs dee-mehns-*YOH*-nehs*
The dimensions

El lápiz negro es largo.
Ell LAH-*peeth* NEH-*groh ess* LAHR-*goh.*
The black pencil is long.

El lápiz rojo no es largo; es corto.
Ell LAH-*peeth* ROH-*hoh noh ess* LAHR-*goh; ess* KOHR-*toh.*
The red pencil is not long; it is short.

La regla amarilla es larga;
Lah REH-*glah ah-mah-*REEL-*yah ess* LAHR-*gah;*
The yellow ruler is long;

la regla negra es corta.
lah REH-*glah* NEH-*grah ess* KOHR-*tah.*
the black ruler is short.

¿Es largo el lápiz negro?
Ess LAHR-*goh ell* LAH-*peeth* NEH-*groh?*
Is the black pencil long?

¿Es corto el lápiz negro?
Ess KOHR-*toh ell* LAH-*peeth* NEH-*groh?*
Is the black pencil short?

12

¿Es corto el lápiz rojo?
Ess KOHR-*toh ell* LAH-*peeth* ROH-*hoh?*
Is the red pencil short?

¿Es largo o corto el lápiz negro?
Ess LAHR-*goh oh* KOHR-*toh eil* LAH-*peeth* NEH-*groh?*
Is the black pencil short or long?

El libro pardo es ancho;
Ell LEE-*broh* PAHR-*doh ess* AHN-*choh;*
The brown book is wide;

el libro rojo no es ancho, es estrecho.
ell LEE-*broh* ROH-*hoh noh ess* AHN-*choh, ess ess*-TREH-*choh.*
the red book is not wide, it is narrow.

La avenida es ancha;	la calle es estrecha.
*Lah ah-veh-*NEE-*dah ess* AHN-*chah;*	*lah* KAHL-*yeh ess ess*-TREH-*chah.*
The avenue is wide;	the street is narrow.
¿Es ancha la avenida?	¿Es estrecha la calle?
Ess AHN-*chah lah ah-veh-*NEE-*dah?*	*Ess ess*-TREH-*chah lah* KAHL-*yeh?*
Is the avenue wide?	Is the street narrow?

El libro pardo es largo y ancho,   es grande.
Ell LEE-*broh* PAHR-*doh ess* LAHR-*goh ee* AHN-*choh,*   *ess* GRAHN-*deh.*
The brown book is long and wide,   it is large.

El libro rojo es corto y estrecho,   es pequeño.
Ell LEE-*broh* ROH-*hoh es* KOHR-*toh ee ess*-TREH-*choh,*   *ess peh-*KEHN-*yoh.*
The red book is short and narrow,   it is small.

La ventana es grande,   la mesa es pequeña.
*Lah vehn-*TAH-*nah ess* GRAHN-*deh,*   *lah* MEH-*sah ess peh-*KEHN-*yah.*
The window is large,   the table is small.

¿Es grande el libro verde?
Ess GRAHN-*deh ell* LEE-*broh* VEHR-*deh?*
Is the green book large?

¿De qué color es el libro pequeño?
*Deh keh koh-*LOHR *ess ell* LEE-*broh peh-*KEHN-*yoh?*
What color is the small book?

¿De qué color es el libro grande?
*Deh keh koh-*LOHR *ess ell* LEE-*broh* GRAHN-*deh?*
What color is the large book?

¿Es grande la mesa?	¿Es pequeña la puerta?
Ess GRAHN-*deh lah* MEH-*sah?*	*Ess peh-*KEHN-*yah lah* PWEHR-*tah?*
Is the table large?	Is the door small?

¿Es grande el papel rojo?
Ess GRAHN-*deh ell pah*-PEHL ROH-*hoh?*
Is the red paper large?

¿De qué color es el libro pequeño?
Deh keh koh-LOHR *ess ell* LEE-*broh peh*-KEHN-*yoh?*
What color is the small book?

¿De qué color es el libro grande?
Deh keh koh-LOHR *ess ell* LEE-*broh* GRAHN-*deh?*
What color is the large book?

¿Es grande el Brasil?
Ess GRAHN-*deh ell Brah*-SEEL?
Is Brazil large?

¿Es Cuba grande o pequeña?
Ess KOO-*bah* GRAHN-*deh oh peh*-KEHN-*yah?*
Is Cuba large or small?

¿Es México grande o pequeño?
Ess MEH-*hee-koh* GRAHN-*deh or peh*-KEHN-*yoh?*
Is Mexico large or small?

11	12	13	14	15
once	doce	trece	catorce	quince
OHN-*theh*	DOH-*theh*	TREH-*theh*	kah-TOHR-*theh*	KEEN-*theh*

¡Buenas tardes!
BWEH-*nahs* TAHR-*dehs!*
Good afternoon!

THINKING IN SPANISH
(Answers on page 254)

1. ¿Es largo el libro rojo?
2. ¿Es ancho?
3. ¿Es grande?
4. ¿Es corto el libro verde?
5. ¿Es estrecho?
6. ¿Es pequeño?
7. ¿De qué color es el libro grande?
8. ¿De qué color es el libro pequeño?

9. ¿De qué color es el traje largo?
10. ¿Es rojo?
11. ¿Es largo el traje negro?
12. ¿Es corto?
13. ¿De qué color es el traje corto?
14. ¿Es negro o verde?

15. ¿Es la ventana larga azul o parda?
16. ¿De qué color es la ventana ancha?
17. ¿Es gris?
18. ¿Es larga la ventana roja?
19. ¿Es ancha o estrecha la ventana azul?

20. ¿Es grande la ventana azul?
21. ¿Es pequeña la ventana roja?
22. ¿Es parda o roja la ventana pequeña?
23. ¿Es azul o verde la ventana grande?

a red book

a green book

a black dress

a yellow dress

a blue window

a red window

LECCIÓN 5

¿Quién es?
*K'*YEHN *ess?*
Who is it?

Un señor (un caballero),
*Oon sehn-*YOHR *(oon kah-bahl-*YEH-*roh),*
A gentleman,

una señora,
OO-*nah sehn-*YOH-*rah,*
a lady,

una señorita.
OO-*nah sehn-yoh-*REE-*tah.*
a young lady.

Este caballero es el señor Berlitz;
Ess-*teh kah-bahl-*YEH-*roh ess ell sehn-*YOHR BEHR-*leets;*
This gentleman is Mr. Berlitz;

esta señora es la señora Berlitz;
ESS-*tah sehn-*YOH-*rah ess lah sehn-*YOH-*rah* BEHR-*leets;*
this lady is Mrs. Berlitz;

esta señorita es la señorita Berlitz.
ESS-*tah sehn-yoh-*REE-*tah ess lah sehn-yoh-*REE-*tah* BEHR-*leets.*
this young lady is Miss Berlitz.

¿Es este caballero el Sr. Berlitz?
Ess ESS-*teh kah-bahl-*YEH-*roh ell sehn-*YOHR BEHR-*leets?*
Is this gentleman Mr. Berlitz?

16

Sí, él es.
See, ell ess.
Yes, he is.

No, (él) no es.
Noh, (ell) noh ess.
No, he is not.

¿Es esta señora la Sra. Berlitz?
Ess ESS-tah sehn-YOH-rah lah sehn-YOH-rah BEHR-leets?
Is this lady Mrs. Berlitz?

Sí, señor, ella es.
See, sehn-YOHR, EHL-*yah ess.*
Yes, sir, she is.

No, (ella) no es.
Noh, (EHL-yah) noh ess.
No, she is not.

¿Es este señor el Sr. López?
Ess ESS-teh sehn-YOHR ell sehn-YOHR LOH-pehth?
Is this gentleman Mr. Lopez?

No...
Noh...
No...

¿Es el Sr. Galdós?
Ess ell sehn-YOHR Gahl-DOHS?
Is he Mr. Galdos?

No...
Noh...
No...

¿Es el Sr. Méndez?
Ess ell sehn-YOHR MEHN-dehth?
Is he Mr. Méndez?

No...
Noh...
No...

¿Quién es este señor?
K'YEHN ess ESS-teh sehn-YOHR?
Who is this gentleman?

¿Quién es esta señora?
K'YEHN ess ESS-tah sehn-YOH-rah?
Who is this lady?

Este señor es el Sr. Pérez.
Ess-*teh sehn-YOHR ess ell sehn-YOHR PEH-rehth.*
This gentleman is Mr. Perez.

Esta señora es la Sra. Villa.
Ess-*tah sehn-YOH-rah ess lah sehn-YOH-rah VEEL-yah.*
This lady is Mrs. Villa.

Esta señorita es la Srta. Fuentes.
Ess-*tah sehn-yoh-REE-tah ess lah sehn-yoh REE-tah FWEHN-tehs.*
This young lady is Miss Fuentes.

Usted es el Sr. Fulano.
Oos-TEHD ess ell sehn-YOHR Foo-LAH-noh.
You are Mr. Fulano.

Yo soy el Sr. Berlitz.
Yoh soy ell sehn-YOHR BEHR-leets.
I am Mr. Berlitz.

Usted es el alumno.
Oos-TEHD ess ell ah-LOOM-noh.
You are the pupil.

Yo soy el profesor.
Yoh soy ell proh-feh-SOHR.
I am the teacher.

¿Es Ud. el Sr. Ortiz?
*Ess oos-*TEHD *ell sehn-*YOHR *Ohr-*TEETH?
Are you Mr. Ortiz?

Sí, yo soy el Sr. Ortiz.
*See, yoh soy ell sehn-*YOHR *Ohr-*TEETH.
Yes, I am Mr. Ortiz.

¿Soy yo el Sr. Jiménez?
*Soy yoh ell sehn-*YOHR *Hee-*MEH*-nehth?*
Am I Mr. Jimenez?

No, Ud. no es el Sr. Jiménez.
*Noh, oos-*TEHD *noh ess ell sehn-*YOHR *Hee-*MEH*-nehth.*
No, you are not Mr. Jimenez.

¿Quién soy yo?	¿Quién es Ud.?
*K'*YEHN *soy yoh?*	*K-*YEHN *ess oos-*TEHD?
Who am I?	Who are you?

REMEMBER: *Ud.* is the abbreviation for *usted.*
You must preface the word *Sr.* and *Sra.* with *el* or *la* unless
you are talking directly to someone. Ex.: "Good morning,
Mr. Parra." *Buenos días, Sr. Parra.* "She is Mrs. Oritz."
Ella es la Sra. Ortiz.

¿Quién es esta señora?	Es la Sra. Córdoba.
*K'*YEHN *ess* ESS*-lah sehn-*YOH*-rah?*	*Ess lah sehn-*YOH*-rah* KOHR*-doh-bah.*
Who is this lady?	She is Mrs. Córdoba.

¿Quién es el Sr. Cucalón?	Ud. es.
*K'*YEHN *ess ell sehn-*YOHR *Koo-kah-*LOHN?	*Oos-*TEHD *ess.*
Who is Mr. Cucalón?	You are.

¿Quién es la Srta. Quevedo?
*K'*YEHN *ess lah sehn-yoh-*REE*-tah Keh-*VEH*-doh?*
Who is Miss Quevedo?

Yo soy la Srta. Quevedo.
*Yoh soy lah sehn-yoh-*REE*-tah Keh-*VEH*-doh.*
I am Miss Quevedo.

¿Quién soy yo?	Ud. es el Sr. Berlitz.
*K'*YEHN *soy yoh?*	*Oos-*TEHD *ess ell sehn-*YOHR *Behr-*BEHR*-leets.*
Who am I?	You are Mr. Berlitz.

¿Quién es este caballero?	Es el Sr. Pérez.
*K'*YEHN *ess* ESS*-teh kah-bahl-*YEH*-roh?*	*Ess ell sehn-*YOHR *Peh-*PEH*-rehth.*
Who is this gentleman?	He is Mr. Pérez.

¿Quién es esta señora?
K'YEHN *ess* ESS-*tah sehn-*YOHR-*ah?*
Who is this lady?

Es la Sra. Villa.
*Ess lah sehn-*YOH-*rah* VEEL-*yah.*
She is Mrs. Villa.

¿Quién es esta señorita?
K'YEHN *ess* ESS-*tah sehn-yoh-*REE-*tah?*
Who is this young lady?

Es la Srta. Fuentes.
*Ess lah sehn-yoh-*REE-*tah* FWEHN-*teh..*
She is Miss Fuentes.

Yo soy español.
*Yoh soy ess-pahn-*YOHL.
I am Spanish.

Ud. es norteamericano.
*Oos-*TEHD *ess* NOHR-*teh-ah-meh-ree-*KAH-*noh.*
You are North American.

El Sr. Rivera es mexicano.
*Ell sehn-*YOHR *Ree-*VEH-*rah ess meh-hee-*KAH-*noh.*
Mr. Rivera is Mexican.

El Sr. Torres es peruano.
*Ell sehn-*YOHR *Toh-*rrehs *ess pehr-*WAH-*noh.*
Mr. Torres is Peruvian.

NOTE to Student: It is not necessary in Spanish to use the personal pronoun. To say "I am Mexican", you may say, *Yo soy mexicano* or *Soy mexicano*. It is the verb form that shows who is speaking. This is very convenient for abbreviated speech.

¿Soy yo norteamericano?
Soy yoh NOHR-*teh-ah-meh-ree-*KAH-*noh?*
Am I North American?

No, señor, Ud. no es norteamericano;
*Noh, sehn-*YOHR, *oos-*TEHD *noh ess* NOHR-*teh-ah-meh-ree-*KAH-*noh;*
No, sir, you are not North American;

Ud. es español.
*oos-*TEHD *ess ess-pahn-*YOHL.
you are Spanish.

¿Es Ud. español?
*Ess oos-*TEHD *ess-pahn-*YOHL?
Are you Spanish?

No, señor, yo no soy español;
*Noh, sehn-*YOHR, *yoh noh soy ess-pahn-*YOHL;
No, sir, I am not Spanish;

yo soy norteamericano.
yoh soy NOHR-*teh-ah-meh-ree-*KAH-*noh.*
I am North American.

¿Es el Sr. Rivera argentino?
*Ess ell sehn-*YOHR *Ree-*VEH-*rah ahr-hehn-*TEE-*noh?*
Is Mr. Rivera Argentinian?

No, señor, él no es argentino;
*Noh, sehn-*YOHR, *ell noh ess ahr-hehn-*TEE-*noh;*
No, sir, he is not Argentinian;

es mexicano.
*ess meh-hee-*KAH-*noh.*
he is Mexican.

16	17	18
diez y seis	diez y siete	diez y ocho
d'yehth ee SEH-*ess*	*d'yehth ee* S'YEH-*teh*	*d'yehth ee* OH-*choh*

19	20
diez y nueve	veinte
d'yehth ee NWEH-*veh*	VAIN-*teh*

An Old Spanish Custom: You have noticed above that we have used the word *norteamericano* (North American) to mean an inhabitant of the United States. Latin Americans are inclined to resent the United States monopolizing the word "American." They feel, with justice, that they are as truly American as anyone else. Therefore for politeness sake, U. S. citizens should call themselves *norteamericanos.*

To say "Mrs. Ortiz" we have used *la Sra. Ortiz.* But you will hear very often *la Sra. de Ortiz.* This means the *Señora* of Ortiz or belonging to Ortiz. Both forms are current.

"A gentleman" is *un señor* or *un caballero. Caballero,* with its connotation of "horseman" or "knight" is even more polite than *señor.* The title in front of the name, however, is always *Sr.*

THINKING IN SPANISH
(Answers on page 254)

1. ¿Quién es Ud.?
2. ¿Es Ud. norteamericano?
3. ¿Es Ud. el profesor?
4. ¿Es Ud. cubano?
5. ¿Soy yo el Sr. Berlitz?
6. ¿Soy yo el profesor?
7. ¿Soy yo mexicano?
8. ¿Soy yo norteamericano?
9. ¿Es Carmen Miranda brasilera?
10. ¿Es mexicana Dolores del Río?
11. ¿Es Maurice Chevalier cubano?
12. ¿Quién es norteamericano, Maurice Chevalier o el general MacArthur?
13. ¿Es el Sr. Churchill alemán o inglés?
14. ¿La Sra. de Perón, es argentina o china?
15. ¿Es el profesor español?

LECCIÓN 6

¿Cuál es?
Kwahl ess?
Which one is it?

Este sombrero es negro;
Ess-teh sohm-BREH-roh ess NEH-groh;
This hat is black;

ese sombrero es verde;
ESS-eh sohm-BREH-roh ess VEHR-deh;
that hat is green;

aquel sombrero es gris.
ah-KEHL sohm-BREH-roh ess greess.
that hat is grey.

¿Qué sombrero es negro?
Keh sohm-BREH-roh ess NEH-groh?
Which hat is black?

Éste.
Ess-teh.
This one.

¿Qué sombrero es verde?
Keh sohm-BREH-roh ess VEHR-deh?
Which hat is green?

Ése.
Ess-seh.
That one.

¿Qué sombrero es gris?
Keh sohm-BREH-roh ess greess?
Which hat is grey?

Aquél.
Ah-KEHL.
That one.

Esta regla es negra;
Ess-*tah* REH-*glah ess* NEH-*grah;*
This ruler is black;

esa regla es amarilla,
ESS-*ah* REH-*glah ess ah-mah-*REEL-*yah,*
that ruler is yellow,

aquella regla es blanca.
*ah-*KEHL-*yah* REH-*glah ess* BLAHN-*kah.*
that ruler is white.

¿Qué regla es negra?
Keh REH-*glah ess* NEH-*grah?*
Which ruler is black?

Ésta.
Ess-*tah.*
This one.

¿Qué regla es amarilla?
Keh REH-*glah ess ah-mah-*REEL-*yah?*
Which ruler is yellow?

Ésa.
Ess-*ah.*
That one.

¿Qué regla es blanca?
Keh REH-*glah ess* BLAHN-*kah?*
Which ruler is white?

Aquélla.
*Ah-*KEHL-*yah.*
That one.

Éste es mi libro,
Ess-*teh ess mee* LEE-*broh,*
This is my book,

su libro de Ud.,
soo LEE-*broh deh* oos-TEHD,
your book,

el libro del Sr.......(su libro)
ell LEE-*broh dehl sehn-*YOHR...... (*soo* LEE-*broh*)
the book of Mr....... (his book)

Ésta es mi pluma,
Ess-*tah ess mee* PLOO-*mah,*
This is my pen,

su pluma,
soo PLOO-*mah,*
your pen,

la pluma de la Sra. Calderón,
lah PLOO-*mah deh lah sehn-*YOH-*rah Kahl-deh-*ROHN,
Mrs. Calderon's pen,

(su pluma),
(*soo* PLOO-*mah*),
(her pen),

su sombrero de Ud.,
*soo sohm-*BREH-*roh deh* oos-TEHD,
your hat,

el sombrero del Sr........
*ell sohm-*BREH-*roh dehl sehn-*YOHR....
the hat of Mr........

¿Qué es esto?
Keh ess ESS-*toh?*
What is this?

Es mi libro.
Ess *mee* LEE-*broh.*
It is my book.

¿Es éste el guante del Sr. Mena?
Ess ESS-*teh ell* GWAHN-*teh dehl sehn-*YOHR MEH-*nah?*
Is this Mr. Mena's glove?

Sí, es su guante (de él).
See, ess soo GWAHN-*teh (deh ell).*
Yes, it is his glove.

¿Es éste mi libro?
Ess ESS-*teh mee* LEE-*broh?*
Is this my book?

Sí, señor, es su libro de Ud.
*See, sehn-*YOHR, *ess soo* LEE-*broh deh* oos-TEHD.
Yes, sir, it is your book.

¿Es éste su traje o su cuello?
Ess ESS-*teh soo* TRAH-*heh oh soo* KWÉHL-*yoh?*
Is this your suit or your collar?

No es mi traje ni mi cuello; es mi pañuelo.
Noh ess mee TRAH-*heh nee mee* KWEHL-*yoh; ess mee pahn-yoo-*EH-*loh.*
It is neither my suit nor my collar; it is my handkerchief.

NOTE to Student: The possessives "his," "her" and "your" are all expressed by *su*. If there is any confusion about whose hat or book you mean, you can always qualify it by adding *de Ud., de él,* or *de ella,* after the article in question.

Do not be confused by the extra demonstrative adjectives and pronouns in Spanish. In English we have two: "this" and "that". But in Spanish there are three: *este, ese, aquel* ("this", "that" and "that over there", respectively). They also have their feminine forms, *esta, esa,* and *aquella*. When they are used alone, without a noun, they have an accent over the "e". *Este sombrero es azul.* "This hat is blue." *¿Es éste su sombrero?* "Is this your hat?"

¿De quién es este sombrero?
*Deh k'*YEHN *ess* ESS-*teh sohm-*BREH-*roh?*
Whose is this hat?

Es del Sr. Mena.	Es de la Sra. Díaz.
*Ess dehl sehn-*YOHR MEH-*nah.*	*Ess deh lah sehn-*YOH-*rah* DEE-*ahth.*
It is Mr. Mena's.	It is Mrs. Díaz'.

¿Es éste su lápiz de Ud.?	No, señor.
Ess ESS-*teh soo* LAH-*peeth deh oos-*TEHD?	*Noh, sehn-*YOHR.
Is this your pencil?	No, sir.

¿Cuál es su lápiz de Ud.?	Ése.
Kwahl ess soo LAH-*peeth deh oos-*TEHD?	*Ess-eh.*
Which is your pencil?	That one.

¿Es ésta mi pluma?	No, señora.
Ess ESS-*tah mee* PLOO-*mah?*	*Noh, sehn-*YOH-*rah.*
Is this my pen?	No, madam.

¿Cuál es mi pluma?	Ésa es.
Kwahl ess mee PLOO-*mah?*	*Ess-ah ess.*
Which is my pen?	That is.

¿Es éste el sombrero del Sr. Méndez?
Ess ESS-*teh ell sohm-*BREH-*roh dehl sehn-*YOHR MEHN-*dehth?*
Is this Mr. Mendez' hat?

No, no es su sombrero.
*Noh, noh ess soo sohm-*BREH-*roh.*
No, it is not his hat.

¿Cuál es el sombrero del Sr. Méndez?
*Kwahl ess ell sohm-*BREH*-roh dehl sehn-*YOHR MEHN*-dehth?*
Which is Mr. Mendez's hat?

Aquél.	¿Cuál es mi lápiz?	Éste.
*Ah-*KEHL.	*Kwahl ess mee* LAH*-peeth?*	Ess-*teh.*
That one.	Which is my pencil?	This one.

¿Cuál es su guante de Ud.? Ése.
Kwahl ess soo GWAHN*-teh deh oos-*TEHD? Ess-*eh.*
Which is your glove? That one.

¿Cuál es el guante de la señorita González?
Kwahl ess ell GWAHN*-teh deh lah sehn-yoh-*REE*-tah Gohn-*THAH*-lehth?*
Which is Miss Gonzalez' glove?

Aquél es.
*Ah-*KEHL *ess.*
That is.

¿Qué libro es rojo? Éste.
Keh LEE*-broh ess* ROH*-hoh?* Ess-*teh.*
Which book is red? This one.

¿Es éste el libro rojo? Sí, señor.
Ess ESS*-teh ell* LEE*-broh* ROH*-hoh?* *See, sehn-*YOHR.
Is this the red book? Yes, sir.

¿Cuál es el libro azul?
Kwahl ess ell LEE*-broh ah-*THOOL?
Which is the blue book?

21	22	23
veintiuno	veintidós	veintitrés
*vain-tee-*OO*-noh*	*vain-tee-*DOHS	*vain-tee-*TREHS

24	25
veinticuatro	veinticinco
*vain-tee-*KWAH*-troh*	*vain-tee-*THEEN*-koh*

REMEMBER: *Qué* and *cuál* both mean "what" or "which". *Cuál* must be used alone. Ex: "Which tie is red?" *¿Qué corbata es roja?* "Which pencil is red?" *¿Qué lápiz es rojo?* "Which is blue?" *¿Cuál es azul?* "What is the capital of Perú?" *¿Cual es la capital del Perú?* "What is this?" *¿Qué es esto?*

When *de* and *el* come together, they become *del*. Ex: "This is Mr. Govea's house." *Ésta es la casa del Sr. Govea.* But notice, "This is his house." *Ésta es su casa de él.* Here *él* (note accent) is a pronoun, not an article, and hence does not combine with *de*.

THINKING IN SPANISH
(Answers on page 254)

el Profesor

Pablo

1. ¿Es negro el sombrero del profesor?
2. ¿Es negro el sombrero de Pablo?
3. ¿De qué color es su sombrero de Ud.?
4. ¿Es mi sombrero verde?

5. ¿Es pequeña la cartera de Doña Felicidad?
6. Y la cartera de Chiquita, ¿es grande?
7. Este lápiz es azul, ése es verde, y aquél es amarillo. ¿Es este lápiz azul?
8. ¿Es aquel lápiz gris?   9. ¿De qué color es su pañuelo de Ud.?
10. ¿Es su casa grande o pequeña?   11. ¿Es ése su libro?
12. ¿De qué color es el sombrero del profesor?
13. ¿Es larga la falda de Doña Felicidad?
14. ¿Es corta la falda de Chiquita?

Doña Felicidad

Chiquita

LECCIÓN 7

¿Dónde está?

DOHN-*deh ess*-TAH?

Where is it?

El libro está encima de la mesa.
Ell LEE-*broh ess*-TAH *enn*-THEE-*mah deh lah* MEH-*sah.*
The book is on the table.

La caja está debajo de la mesa.
Lah KAH-*hah ess*-TAH *deh*-BAH-*hoh deh lah* MEH-*sah.*
The box is under the table.

El libro es rojo.
Ell LEE-*broh ess* ROH-*hoh.*
The book is red.

El lápiz es largo.
Ell LAH-*peeth ess* LAHR-*goh.*
The pencil is long.

El lápiz está debajo de la mesa.
Ell LAH-*peeth ess*-TAH *deh*-BAH-*hoh deh lah* MEH-*sah.*
The pencil is under the table.

Yo soy el profesor.
*Yoh soy ell proh-feh-*SOHR.
I am the teacher.

Yo estoy delante de la puerta.
*Yoh ess-*TOY *deh* LAHN-*teh deh lah* PWEHR-*tah.*
I am in front of the door.

Ud. es el alumno.
*Oos-*TEHD *ess ell ah-*LOOM-*noh.*
You are the pupil.

Ud. está detrás de la mesa.
*Oos-*TEHD *ess-*TAH *deh-*TRAHS *deh lah* MEH-*sah.*
You are behind the table.

El Sr. Pérez es español.
*Ell sehn-*YOHR PEH-*rehth ess ess-puhn-*YOHL.
Mr. Pérez is Spanish.

El está entre Ud. y yo.
*Ell ess-*TAH ENN-*treh oos-*TEHD *ee yoh.*
He is between you and me.

Esta señora es española.
Ess-*tah sehn-*YOH-*rah ess ess-pahn-*YOH-*lah.*
This lady is Spanish.

Ella está sentada.
EHL-*yah ess-*TAH *sehn-*TAH-*dah.*
She is seated.

Esta señorita es francesa.
Ess-*tah sehn-yoh-*REE-*tah ess frahn-*THEH-*sah.*
This young lady is French.

Está de pié.
Ess-TAH *deh pee-*EH.
She is standing.

 NOTE to Student: Spanish has two entirely distinct verbs for the verb "to be". For the present, simply remember that *estoy* and *está* are used for the position or location of objects and persons, and *soy* and *es* are used for description or identification.

For position, note the following: Ex: "The dog is under the automobile"— *El perro está debajo del automóvil.* "Is Caracas in Venezuela?"—*¿Está Caracas en Venezuela?* "Where am I?"—*¿Dónde estoy?* And for description:— "I am the professor": *Soy el profesor.* "Mexico is beautiful". *México es hermoso.*

El libro está encima de la mesa.
Ell LEE-*broh ess-*TAH *enn-*THEE-*mah deh lah* MEH-*sah.*
The book is on the table.

El lápiz está debajo de la mesa.
Ell LAH-*peeth ess-*TAH *deh-*BAH-*hoh deh lah* MEH-*sah.*
The pencil is under the table.

El sombrero está sobre la silla.
*Ell sohm-*BREH-*roh ess-*TAH SOH-*breh lah* SEEL-*yah.*
The hat is on the chair.

La caja está debajo de la mesa.
Lah KAH-*hah ess-*TAH *deh-*BAH-*hoh deh lah* MEH-*sah.*
The box is under the table.

La pluma está dentro de la caja.
Lah PLOO-*mah ess-*TAH DEHN-*troh deh lah* KAH-*hah.*
The pen is in the box.

El papel está dentro del libro.
*Ell pah-*PEHL *ess-*TAH DEHN-*troh dehl* LEE-*broh.*
The paper is in the book.

¿Está el libro encima de la silla?
*Ess-*TAH *ell* LEE-*broh enn-*THEE-*mah deh lah* SEEL-*yah?*
Is the book on the chair?

No, no está encima de la silla.
*Noh, noh ess-*TAH *enn-*THEE-*mah deh lah* SEEL-*yah.*
No, it is not on the chair.

¿Está debajo de la mesa?   No ......
*Ess-*TAH *deh-*BAH-*hoh deh lah* MEH-*sah?*   *Noh* ......
Is it under the table?   No ......

¿Dónde está el libro?   Está encima de la mesa.
DOHN-*deh ess-*TAH *ell* LEE-*broh?*   *Ess-*TAH *enn-*THEE-*mah deh lah* MEH-*sah.*
Where is the book?   It is on the table.

¿Dónde está la caja?   Debajo de la mesa.
DOHN-*deh ess-*TAH *lah* KAH-*hah?*   *Deh-*BAH-*hoh deh lah* MEH-*sah.*
Where is the box?   Under the table.

¿Dónde está la pluma?   Dentro de la caja.
DOHN-*deh ess-*TAH *lah* PLOO-*mah?*   DEHN-*troh deh lah* KAH-*hah.*
Where is the pen?   Inside the box.

¿Dónde está el libro?   Sobre la silla.
DOHN-*deh ess-*TAH *ell* LEE-*bro?*   SOH-*breh lah* SEEL-*yah.*
Where is the book?   On the chair.

¿Dónde está su sombrero de Ud.?
DOHN-*deh ess-*TAH *soo sohm-*BREH-*roh deh* ŋos-TEHD?
Where is your hat?

Mi sombrero está encima de la mesa.
*Mee sohm-*BREH-*roh ess-*TAH *enn-*THEE-*mah deh lah* MEH-*sah.*
My hat is on the table.

La puerta está delante de mí.
Lah PWEHR-*tah ess-*TAH *deh-*LAHN-*teh deh mee.*
The door is in front of me.

La ventana está detrás de mí.
*Lah vehn-*TAH*-nah ess-*TAH *deh-*TRAHS *deh mee.*
The window is behind me.

La mesa está delante de Ud.
Lah MEH*-sah ess-*TAH *deh-*LAHN*-teh deh* oos-TEHD.
The table is in front of you.

La pared está detrás de mí.
*Lah pah-*REHD *ess-*TAH *deh-*TRAHS *deh mee.*
The wall is behind me.

¿Dónde está la puerta?
DOHN*-deh ess-*TAH *lah* PWEHR*-tah?*
Where is the door?

Delante de Ud.
*Deh-*LAHN*-teh deh* oos-TEHD.
In front of you.

¿Dónde está la ventana?
DOHN*-deh ess-*TAH *lah vehn-*TAH*-nah?*
Where is the window?

Detrás de mí.
*Deh-*TRAHS *deh mee.*
Behind me.

¿Dónde está la mesa?
DOHN*-deh ess-*TAH *lah* MEH*-sah?*
Where is the table?

La mesa está entre Ud. y yo.
Lah MEH*-sah ess-*TAH ENN*-treh* oos-TEHD *ee yoh.*
The table is between you and me.

¿Está la silla detrás de mí?
*Ess-*TAH *lah* SEEL*-yan deh-*TRAHS *deh mee?*
Is the chair behind me?

No, señor, la silla no está detrás de Ud.,
*Noh, sehn-*YOHR*, lah* SEEL*-yah noh ess-*TAH *deh-*TRAHS *deh* oos-TEHD,
No, sir, the chair is not behind you,

sino entre Ud. y yo.
SEE*-noh* ENN*-treh* oos-TEHD *ee yoh.*
but between you and me.

¿Dónde está el Sr. Méndez?
DOHN*-deh ess-*TAH *ell sehn-*YOHR MEHN*-dehth?*
Where is Mr. Méndez?

Está entre la Sra. Vásquez y la Srta. Rambaldo.
*Ess-*TAH ENN*-treh lah sehn-*YOH*-rah* VAHTH*-kehth ee lah sehn-yoh-*REE*-tah*
*Rahm-*BAHL*-doh.*
He is between Mrs. Vázquez and Miss Rambaldo.

¿Está el Sr. Toro entre la puerta y la ventana?
*Ess-*TAH *ell sehn-*YOHR TOH-*roh* ENN-*treh la?*: PWEHR-*tah ee lah vehn-*
TAH-*nah?*
Is Mr. Toro between the door and the window?

No, señor, no está.
*Noh, sehn-*YOHR, *noh ess-*TAH.
No, sir, he is not.

¿Dónde está?
DOHN-*deh ess-*TAH?
Where is he?

Yo soy el profesor;
*Yoh soy ell proh-feh-*SOHR;
I am the teacher;

yo estoy de pié delante de la puerta.
*yoh ess-*TOY *deh p'*YEH *deh-*LAHN-*teh deh lah* PWEHR-*tah.*
I am standing in front of the door.

Ud. es el alumno;
*Oos-*TEHD *ess ell ah-*LOOM-*noh;*
You are the pupil;

Ud. está sentado detrás de la mesa.
*oos-*TEHD *ess-*TAH *sehn-*TAH-*doh deh-*TRAHS *deh lah* MEH-*sah.*
you are sitting behind the table.

La señora Gómez es española;
*Lah sehn-*YOH-*rah* GOH-*mehth ess ess-pahn-*YOH-*lah;*
Mrs. Gómez is Spanish;

está sentada delante de la ventana.
*ess-*TAH *sehn-*TAH-*dah deh-*LAHN-*teh deh lah vehn-*TAH-*nah.*
she is sitting in front of the window.

¿Quién soy yo?
K'YEHN *soy yoh?*
Who am I?

Ud. es el profesor.
*Oos-*TEHD *ess ell proh-feh-*SOHR
You are the teacher.

¿Dónde estoy yo?
DOHN-*deh ess-*TOY *yoh?*
Where am I?

Ud. está delante de la puerta.
*Oos-*TEHD *ess-*TAH *deh-*LAHN-*teh deh lah* PWEHR-*tah.*
You are in front of the door.

¿Estoy yo de pié o sentado?
Ess-TOY *yoh deh p'*YEH *oh sehn*-TAH-*doh?*
Am I standing or sitting?

Ud. está de pié.
Oos-TEHD *ess*-TAH *deh p'*YEH.
You are standing.

¿Quién es Ud.?
*K'*YEHN *ess oos*-TEHD?
Who are you?

Yo soy el alumno.
Yoh soy ell ah-LOOM-*noh.*
I am the pupil.

¿Dónde está Ud.?
DOHN-*deh ess*-TAH *oos*-TEHD?
Where are you?

Estoy dentro de la clase.
Ess-TOY DEHN-*troh deh lah* KLAH-*seh.*
I am inside the classroom.

¿Está Ud. de pié?
Ess-TAH *oos*-TEHD *deh p'*YEH?
Are you standing?

No, señor, no estoy de pié sino sentado.
Noh, sehn-YOHR, *noh ess*-TOY *deh p'*YEH, SEE-*noh sehn*-TAH-*doh.*
No, sir, I am not standing but sitting.

¿Dónde está Ud. sentado?
DOHN-*deh ess*-TAH *oos*-TEHD *sehn*-TAH-*doh?*
Where are you sitting?

Estoy sentado detrás de la mesa.
Ess-*toy sehn*-TAH-*doh deh*-TRAHS *deh lah* MEH-*sah.*
I am sitting behind the table.

¿Está la señorita de pié?
Ess-TAH *lah sehn-yoh*-REE-*tah deh p'*YEH?
Is the young lady standing?

No, no está de pié, está sentada.
Noh, noh ess-TAH *deh p'*YEH, *ess*-TAH *sehn*-TAH-*dah.*
No, she is not standing, she is sitting.

¿Dónde estoy yo?
DOHN-*deh ess*-TOY *yoh?*
Where am I?

Ud. está en el pasillo.
Oos-TEHD *ess*-TAH *enn ell pah*-SEEL-*yoh.*
You are in the corridor.

¿Estoy yo dentro del cuarto?
Ess-TOY *yoh* DEHN-*troh dehl* KWAHR-*toh?*
Am I inside of the room?

No, Ud. no está dentro del cuarto, sino fuera del cuarto.
Noh, oos-TEHD *noh ess*-TAH DEHN-*tron dehl* KWAHR-*toh,* SEE-*noh* FWEH-*ral dehl* KWAHR-*toh.*
No, you are not inside the room, but outside the room.

REMEMBER: Many prepositions use *de* as a part of their constructions. Do not forget to use it. Ex: "He is outside of the house":—*Está fuera de la casa.*

La Habana está en Cuba.
Lah Ah-BAH-nah ess-TAH enn Koo-bah.
Havana is in Cuba.

Madrid está en España.
Mah-DREED ess-TAH enn Ess-PAHN-yah.
Madrid is in Spain.

Londres está en Inglaterra.
LOHN-drehs ess-TAH enn Een-glah-TEH-rrah.
London is in England.

¿Está Madrid en España?
Ess-TAH Mah-DREED enn Ess-PAHN-yah?
Is Madrid in Spain?

Sí, está en España.
See, ess-TAH enn Ess-PAHN-yah.
Yes, it is in Spain.

¿Está París en Inglaterra?
Ess-TAH Pah-REES enn Een-glah-TEH-rrah?
Is Paris in England?

No, París no está en Inglaterra, sino en Francia.
Noh, Pah-REES noh ess-TAH enn Een-glah-TEH-rrah, SEE-noh enn FRAHNTH-yah.
No, Paris is not in England, but in France.

¿Está la Srta. Díaz en este cuarto?
Ess-TAH lah sehn-yoh-REE-tah DEE-ahth enn ESS-teh KWAHR-toh?
Is Miss Díaz in this room?

Sí, aquí está.
See, ah-KEE ess-TAH.
Yes, here she is.

¿Está el Sr. Zorrilla en el pasillo?
Ess-TAH ell sehn-YOHR Thoh-RREEL-yah enn ell pah-SEEL-yoh?
Is Mr. Zorrilla in the corridor?

No, señor, no está allí.
Noh, sehn-YOHR, noh ess-TAH ahl-YEE.
No, sir, he is not there.

¿Dónde está su libro de Ud.?
DOHN-*deh* ess-TAH *soo* LEE-*broh deh oos*-TEHD?
Where is your book?

Aquí está.
Ah-KEE *ess*-TAH.
Here it is.

¿Dónde está la ventana?
DOHN-*deh* ess-TAH *lah vehn*-TAH-*nah?*
Where is the window?

Allí está.
Ahl-YEE *ess*-TAH.
There it is.

¿Dónde está mi sombrero?
DOHN-*deh* ess-TAH *mee sohm* BREH-*roh?*
Where is my hat?

Aquí está.
Ah-KEE *ess*-TAH.
Here it is.

¿Está el Sr. Berlitz aquí?
Ess-TAH *ell sehn*-YOHR BEHR-*leets ah*-KEE?
Is Mr. Berlitz here?

No, no está aquí,
Noh, noh ess-TAH *ah*-KEE,
No, he is not here,

está en México.
ess-TAH *enn* MEH-*hee-koh*.
he is in Mexico.

26	27	28
veintiséis	veintisiete	veintiocho
vain-tee-SEH-*ees*	*vain-tees*-YEH-*teh*	*vain-tee*-OH-*choh*

29	30
veintinueve	treinta
vain-tee-NWEH-*veh*	TRAIN-*tah*

WATCH OUT! Words with more than one meaning are sometimes given accents to show which meaning is intended. Accents should be left off capital letters except in textbooks.

él: he or him.
el: the

THINKING IN SPANISH
(Answers on page 255)

1. ¿Dónde está el libro? 2. ¿Está el libro encima de la mesa?

3. ¿Está el libro debajo de la silla? 4. ¿Dónde está la pluma?

5. ¿Está la pluma delante de la mesa? 6. ¿Dónde está la silla?

7. ¿Dónde está el profesor? 8. ¿Está el profesor debajo de la mesa?

9. ¿Está el profesor de pié detrás de la mesa?

10. ¿Está Ud. sentado en la silla?

11. ¿Está Ud. de pié delante de la puerta?

12. ¿Está el papel dentro del libro? 13. ¿Está el papel dentro de la caja?

14. ¿Dónde está la caja? 15. ¿Está la pluma dentro de la caja?

16. ¿Está la llave debajo de la silla?

17. Este lápiz es rojo, ese lápiz es negro. ¿De qué color es ese lápiz?

18. ¿Es negro ese lápiz? 19. ¿De qué color es este lápiz?

20. ¿Es este libro grande o pequeño?

LECCIÓN 8

¿Qué hace el profesor?
Keh AH-*theh ell proh-feh-*SOHR?
What does the professor do?

El profesor toma el libro.
*Ell proh-feh-*SOHR TOH-*mah ell* LEE-*broh.*
The teacher takes the book.

El profesor pone el libro encima de la silla.
*Ell proh-feh-*SOHR POH-*neh ell* LEE-*broh enn-*THEE-*mah deh lah* SEEL-*yah.*
The teacher puts the book on the chair.

El profesor toma la regla.
*Ell proh-feh-*SOHR TOH-*mah lah* REH-*glah.*
The teacher takes the ruler.

Pone la regla debajo de la mesa.
POH-*neh lah* REH-*glah deh-*BAH-*hoh deh lah* MEH-*sah.*
He puts the ruler under the table.

El profesor lleva la silla a la ventana.
*Ell proh-feh-*SOHR *l'*YEH-*vah lah* SEEL-*yah ah lah vehn-*TAH-*nah.*
The teacher takes the chair to the window.

¿Toma el profesor el libro?
TOH-*mah ell proh-feh*-SOHR *ell* LEE-*broh?*
Does the teacher take the book?

No, no toma el libro;
Noh, noh TOH-*mah ell* LEE-*broh;*
No, he does not take the book;

¿Toma la caja?
TOH-*mah lah* KAH-*hah?*
Does he take the box?

¿Toma la regla?
TOH-*mah lah* REH-*glah?*
Does he take the ruler?

¿Qué toma?
Keh TOH-*mah?*
What does he take?

toma el lápiz.
TOH-*mah ell* LAH-*peeth.*
he takes the pencil.

No, no toma la caja.
Noh, noh TOH-*mah lah* KAH-*hah.*
No, he does not take the box.

No.
Noh.
No.

Toma la pluma.
TOH-*mah lah* PLOO-*mah.*
He takes the pen.

¿Pone el profesor la pluma encima de la mesa?
POH-*neh ell proh-feh*-SOHR *lah* PLOO-*mah enn*-THEE-*mah deh lah* MEH-*sah?*
Does the teacher put the pen on the table?

Sí, pone la pluma encima de la mesa.
See, POH-*neh lah* PLOO-*mah enn*-THEE-*mah deh lah* MEH-*sah.*
Yes, he puts the pen on the table.

¿Abre el profesor el libro?
AH-*breh ell proh-feh*-SOHR *ell* LEE-*broh?*
Does the teacher open the book?

¿Abre la puerta?
AH-*breh lah* PWEHR-*tah?*
Does he open the door?

Sí, abre el libro.
See, AH-*breh ell* LEE-*broh.*
Yes, he opens the book.

Sí, abre la puerta.
See, AH-*breh lah* PWEHR-*tah.*
Yes, he opens the door.

¿Cierra el profesor la puerta?
*Th'*YEH-*rrah ell proh-feh*-SOHR *lah* PWEHR-*tah?*
Does the teacher close the door?

No, no cierra la puerta.
*Noh, noh th'*YEH-*rrah lah* PWEHR-*tah.*
No, he does not close the door.

¿Qué hace el profesor?
Keh AH-*theh ell proh-feh*-SOHR?
What does the teacher do?

Abre la ventana.
AH-*breh lah vehn*-TAH-*nah.*
He opens the window.

¿Lleva el profesor la silla al pasillo?
*L'*YEH-*vah ell proh-feh*-SOHR *lah* SEEL-*yah ahl pah*-SEEL-*yoh?*
Does the teacher take the chair to the corridor?

¿Qué hace el profesor?
Keh AH-*theh ell proh-feh-*SOHR?
What does the teacher do?

Lleva la silla al pasillo.
*L'*YEH-*vah lah* SEEL-*yah ahl pah-*SEEL-*yoh.*
He takes the chair to the corridor.

¿Trae el profesor el libro a este cuarto?
TRAH-*eh ell proh-feh-*SOHR *ell* LEE-*broh ah* ESS-*teh* KWAHR-*toh?*
Does the teacher bring the book to this room?

No, señor, no trae el libro.
*Noh, sehn-*YOHR, *noh* TRAH-*eh ell* LEE-*broh.*
No, sir, he does not bring the book.

¿Qué trae el profesor?
Keh TRAH-*eh ell proh-feh-*SOHR?
What does the teacher bring?

Trae la silla.
TRAH-*eh lah* SEEL-*yah.*
He brings the chair.

El profesor va a la puerta.
*Ell proh-feh-*SOHR *vah ah lah* PWEHR-*tah.*
The teacher goes to the door.

El viene a la mesa.
*Ell v'*YEH-*neh ah lah* MEH-*sah*
He comes to the table.

¿Va el profesor a la ventana?
*Vah ell proh-feh-*SOHR *ah lah vehn-*TAH-*nah?*
Does the teacher go to the window?

¿Adónde va?
*Ah-*DOHN-*deh vah?*
Where does he go?

Va a la puerta.
Vah ah lah PWEHR-*tah.*
He goes to the door.

¿Viene el profesor a este cuarto?
*V'*YEH-*neh ell proh-feh-*SOHR *ah* ESS-*teh* KWAHR-*toh?*
Does the teacher come to this room?

Sí, viene a este cuarto.
*See, v'*YEH-*neh ah* ESS-*teh* KWAHR-*toh.*
Yes, he comes to this room.

El profesor cierra la puerta.
*Ell proh-feh-*SOHR *th'*YEH-*rrah lah* PWEHR-*tah.*
The teacher closes the door.

El profesor abre la ventana.
*Ell proh-feh-*SOHR AH-*breh lah vehn-*TAH-*nah.*
The teacher opens the window.

NOTE to Student: You have seen that the spelling of the verb changes, especially the ending, according to the subject. The verb itself, however, is usually referred to in the infinitive mood, which corresponds to our English "to be", "to take", "to put", etc. Therefore, when you look up a verb in the dictionary, you will find it in the infinitive. In Spanish you can identify this by the word having a final *r*. The infinitive forms for the verbs we have studied up to now are *ser, estar, venir, ir, llevar, traer, poner, tomar.*

¿Qué hace el profesor?
Keh AH-theh ell proh-feh-SOHR?
What does the teacher do?

Él toma el libro.
Ell TOH-mah ell LEE-broh.
He takes the book.

Él pone el libro sobre la mesa.
Ell POH-neh ell LEE-broh SOH-breh lah MEH-sah.
He puts the book on the table.

Él abre la puerta.   Él cierra la ventana.
Ell AH-breh lah PWEHR-tah.   *Ell th'YEH-rrah lah vehn-TAH-nah.*
He opens the door.   He closes the window.

Él lleva el periódico a la puerta.
Ell l'YEH-vah ell pehr-YOH-dee-koh ah lah PWEHR-tah.
He takes the paper to the door.

Él trae la pluma a la mesa.
Ell TRAH-eh lah PLOO-mah ah lah MEH-sah.
He brings the pen to the table.

Él va a la puerta.   Él viene a este cuarto.
Ell vah ah lah PWEHR-tah.   *Ell v'YEH-neh ah ESS-teh KWAHR-toñ.*
He goes to the door.   He comes to this room.

Yo soy el profesor.   Yo tomo el libro.
Yoh soy ell proh-feh-SOHR.   *Yoh TOH-moh ell LEE-broh.*
I am the teacher.   I take the book.

Sr. Mena, tome Ud. el libro.
Sehn-YOHR MEH-nah, TOH-meh oos-TEHD ell LEE-broh.
Mr. Mena, take the book.

Ud. toma el libro.   Él toma el libro.
Oos-TEHD TOH-mah ell LEE-broh.   *Ell TOH-mah ell LEE-broh.*
You take the book.   He takes the book.

Yo pongo el libro sobre la silla.
Yoh POHN-goh ell LEE-broh SOH-breh lah SEEL-yah.
I put the book on the chair.

Señorita Fernández, ponga Ud. el libro sobre la mesa.
*Sehn-yoh-REE-tah Fehr-NAHN-dehth, POHN-gah oos-TEHD ell LEE-broh
SOH-breh lah MEH-sah.*
Miss Fernández, put the book on the table.

¿Qué hago yo?   ¿Toma Ud. el libro?
Keh AH-goh yoh?   *TOH-mah oos-TEHD ell LEE-broh?*
What do I do?   Do you take the book?

Sí, yo tomo el libro.
See, yoh TOH-*moh ell* LEE-*broh.*
Yes, I take the book.

¿Tomo yo la caja?   No, Ud. no toma la caja.
TOH-*moh yoh lah* KAH-*hah?*   *Noh, oos-*TEHD *noh* TOH-*mah lah* KAH-*hah*
Do I take the box?   No, you do not take the box.

¿Pone Ud. el libro encima de la silla?
POH-*neh oos-*TEHD *ell* LEE-*broh enn-*THEE-*mah deh lah* SEEL-*yah?*
Do you put the book on the chair?

Sí, pongo el libro encima de la silla.
See, POHN-*goh ell* LEE-*broh enn-*THEE-*mah deh lah* SEEL-*yah.*
Yes, I put the book on the chair.

No, no pongo el libro encima de la silla.
Noh, noh POHN-*goh ell* LEE-*broh enn-*THEE-*mah deh lah* SEEL-*yah.*
No, I do not put the book on the chair.

¿Pongo yo el dinero dentro de mi bolsillo?
POHN-*goh yoh ell dee-*NEH-*roh* DEHN-*troh deh mee bohl-*SEEL-*yoh?*
Do I put the money in my pocket?

No, Ud. no pone el dinero dentro de su bolsillo.
*Noh, oos-*TEHD *noh* POH-*neh ell dee-*NEH-*roh* DEHN-*troh
deh soo bohl-*SEEL-*yoh.*
No, you do not put the money in your pocket.

¿Qué hago yo?   Ud. toma el libro.
Keh AH-*goh yoh?*   *Oos-*TEHD TOH-*mah ell* LEE-*broh.*
What do I do?   You take the book.

Tome Ud. el lápiz.   Gracias.
TOH-*meh oos-*TEHD *ell* LAH-*peeth.* GRAHTH-*yahs.*
Take the pencil.   Thank you.

REMEMBER the Imperative: Verbs whose second and third persons end in *a* form their imperative in *e*, and vice versa. Ex: "He takes": *toma.* "Please take": *Tome por favor.* If the first person ends in *go*, the *g* is retained in the imperative. Ex: "Come here": *Venga aquí.*

Por favor is just one way of saying "please". You will learn several others.

¿Qué hace Ud.?   Tomo el lápiz.
Keh AH-*theh oos-*TEHD?   TOH-*moh ell* LAH-*peeth.*
What do you do?   I take the pencil.

¿Abro yo la ventana?
AH-*broh yoh lah vehn-*TAH-*nah?*
Do I open the window?

Sí, señor, Ud. abre la ventana.
*See, sehn-*YOHR, *oos-*TEHD AH-*breh lah vehn-*TAH-*nah.*
Yes, sir, you open the window.

No, Ud. no abre la ventana.
*Noh, oos-*TEHD *noh* AH-*breh lah vehn-*TAH-*nah.*
No, you do not open the window.

¿Cierra Ud. la puerta?
*Th'*YEH-*rrah oos-*TEHD *lah* PWEHR-*tah?*
Do you close the door?

Sí, cierro la puerta.
*See, th'*YEH-*rroh lah* PWEHR-*tah.*
Yes, I close the door.

Abra Ud. la caja.
AH-*brah oos-*TEHD *lah* KAH-*hah.*
Open the box.

¿Qué hace Ud.?
Keh AH-*theh oos-*TEHD?
What do you do?

(Yo) abro la caja.
(Yoh) AH-*broh lah* KAH-*hah.*
I open the box.

Cierre Ud. la caja, por favor.
*Th'*YEH-*rreh oos-*TEHD *lah* KAH-*hah, pohr fah-*VOHR.
Close the box, please.

¿Qué hace Ud.?
Keh AH-*theh oos-*TEHD?
What do you do?

Cierro la caja.
*Th'*YEH-*rroh lah* KAH-*hah.*
I close the box.

Yo voy a la puerta.
Yoh voy ah lah PWEHR-*tah.*
I go to the door.

Sr. Díaz, vaya Ud. a la ventana, por favor.
*Sehn-*YOHR DEE-*ahth,* VAH-*yah oos-*TEHD *ah lah vehn-*TAH-*nah,*
*pohr fah-*VOHR.
Mr. Diaz, go to the window, please.

Ud. va a la ventana.
*Oos-*TEHD *vah ah lah vehn-*TAH-*nah.*
You go to the window.

El Sr. Díaz va a la ventana.
*Ell sehn-*YOHR DEE-*ahth vah ah lah vehn-*TAH-*nah.*
Mr. Díaz goes to the window.

¿Voy yo a la puerta?
Voy yoh ah lah PWEHR-*tah?*
Do I go to the door?

Sí, señor, Ud. va a la puerta.
*See, sehn-*YOHR, *oos-*TEHD *vah ah lah* PWEHR-*tah.*
Yes, sir, you go to the door.

¿Adónde va el Sr. Díaz?
*Ah-*DOHN-*deh vah ell sehn-*YOHR DEE-*ahth?*
Where does Mr. Díaz go?

El va a la ventana.
*Ell vah ah lah vehn-*TAH-*nah*
He goes to the window.

Sr. Díaz, ¿adónde va Ud.?
*Sehn-*YOHR DEE-*ahth, ah-*DOHN-*deh vah oos-*TEHD?
Mr. Díaz, where do you go?

Voy a Madrid.
*Voy ah Mah-*DREED.
I go to Madrid.

¿Va Ud. a la Habana?
*Vah oos-*TEHD *ah lah Ah-*BAH-*nah?*
Do you go to Havana?

No, no voy a la Habana.
*Noh, noh voy ah lah Ah-*BAH-*nah.*
No. I do not go to Havana.

¿Quién va a la Habana?
*K'*YEHN *vah ah lah Ah-*BAH-*nah?*
Who goes to Havana?

La Srta. Quevedo va allí.
*Lah sehn-yoh-*REE-*tah Keh-*VEH-*doh vah ahl-*YEE.
Miss Quevado goes there.

Yo vengo del pasillo al cuarto.
Yoh VEHN-*goh dehl pah-*SEEL-*yoh ahl* KWAHR-*toh.*
I come from the corridor to the room.

¿Voy yo hacia Ud.?
Voy yoh AHTH-*yah oos-*TEHD?
Do I go towards you?

No, señor, Ud. no viene hacia mí.
*Noh, sehn-*YOHR, *oos-*TEHD *noh v'*YEH-*neh* AHTH-*yah mee.*
No, sir, you do not come towards me.

¿Hacia quién voy yo?
AHTH-*yah k'*YEHN *voy yoh?*
Towards whom do I go?

Ud. va hacia el Sr. Moreno.
*Oos-*TEHD *vah* AHTH-*yah ell sehn-*YOHR Moh-*REH-*noh.*
You go towards Mr. Moreno.

Venga Ud. aquí.
VEHN-*gah oos-*TEHD *ah-*KEE.
Come here.

¿De dónde viene Ud.?
Deh DOHN-*deh v'*YEH-*neh oos-*TEHD?
Where do you come from?

Vengo de la puerta.
VEHN-*goh deh lah* PWEHR-*tah.*
I come from the door.

Señor, tome Ud. el papel, por favor.
*Sehn-*YOHR, TOH-*meh oos-*TEHD *ell pah-*PEHL, *pohr fah-*VOHR.
Sir, take the paper, please.

Gracias.
GRAHTH-*yahs.*
Thank you.

Ponga Ud. el papel encima de esta mesa.
POHN-*gah oos*-TEHD *ell pah*-PEHL *enn*-THEE-*mah deh* ESS-*tah* MEH-*sah.*
Put the paper on this table.

Lleve Ud. esta silla al pasillo.
L'YEH-*veh oos*-TEHD ESS-*tah* SEEL-*yah ahl pah*-SEEL-*yoh.*
Take this chair to the corridor.

Traiga Ud. ese libro a la mesa.
TRY-*gah oos*-TEHD ESS-*eh* LEE-*broh ah lah* MEH-*sah.*
Bring that book to the table.

Abra Ud. su libro.	**Cierre Ud. su libro.**
AH-*brah oos*-TEHD *soo* LEE-*broh.*	*Th'*YEH-*rreh oos*-TEHD *soo* LEE-*broh.*
Open your book.	Close your book.
¿Toma Ud. el libro?	**Sí, (yo) lo tomo.**
TOH-*mah oos*-TEHD *ell* LEE-*broh?*	*See, (yoh) loh* TOH-*moh.*
Do you take the book?	Yes, I take it.

No, no lo tomo.
Noh, noh loh TOH-*moh.*
No, I do not take it.

¿Pongo yo la caja encima de la mesa?
POHN-*goh yoh lah* KAH-*hah enn*-THEE-*mah deh lah* MEH-*sah?*
Do I put the box on the table?

Sí, Ud. la pone encima de la mesa.
See, oos-TEHD *lah* POH-*neh enn*-THEE-*mah deh lah* MEH-*sah.*
Yes, you put it on the table.

¿Abre Ud. su libro?	**No, no lo abro.**
AH-*breh oos*-TEHD *soo* LEE-*broh?*	*Noh, noh loh* AH-*broh.*
Do you open your book?	No, I do not open it.
¿Cierro yo mi libro?	**Sí, Ud. lo cierra.**
*Th'*YEH-*rroh yoh mee* LEE-*broh?*	*See, oos*-TEHD *loh th'*YEH-*rrah.*
Do I close my book?	Yes, you close it.

No, Ud. no lo cierra.
Noh, oos-TEHD *noh loh th'*YEH-*rrah.*
No, you do not close it.

¿Lleva Ud. su sombrero al pasillo?
L'YEH-*vah oos*-TEHD *soo sohm*-BREH-*roh ahl pah*-SEEL-*yoh?*
Do you take your hat to the corridor?

No, no lo llevo.
*Noh, noh loh l'*YEH-*voh.*
No, ʃ do not take it.

¿Traigo yo mi silla al cuarto?
TRY-*goh yoh mee* SEEL-*yah ahl* KWAHR-*toh?*
Do I bring my chair to the room?

Sí, Ud. la trae.
*See, oos-*TEHD *lah* TRAH-*eh*
Yes, you bring it.

Yo soy mexicano.
*Yoh soy meh-hee-*KAH-*noh.*
I am Mexican.

El Sr. Churchill es inglés.
*Ell sehn-*YOHR CHOOR-*cheel ess een-*GLEHS.
Mr. Churchill is English.

Viene de Inglaterra.
*V'*YEH-*neh deh Een-glah-*TEH-*rrah.*
He comes from England.

Viene el Sr. García de Francia?
*V'*YEH-*neh ell sehn-*YOHR *Gahr-*THEE-*ah deh* FRAHNTH-*yah?*
Does Mr. García come from France?

No, él no viene de Francia, sino del Perú.
*Noh, ell noh v'*YEH-*neh deh* FRAHNTH-*yah,* SEE-*noh dehl Peh-*ROO.
No, he does not come from France, but from Peru.

31	32	33
treinta y uno	treinta y dos	treinta y tres
TRAIN-*tah ee* OO-*noh*	TRAIN-*tah ee dohs*	TRAIN-*tah ee trehs*

34	35
treinta y cuatro	treinta y cinco
TRAIN-*tah ee* KWAH-*troh*	TRAIN-*tah ee* THEEN-*koh*

IMPORTANT NOTE: *Lo* and *la* mean "it" when used as a direct object. Ex: "Take it": ¡*Tómelo!* "Aʳ you bringing the box?" "Yes, I am bringing it":¡*Trae Ud. la caja? Sí, yo la traigo.* Observe in the above that when *lo* or *la* follow the verb, they are written as a part of it.

To say, "What do I do?" you say ¿*Qué hago yo?* What you are literally saying is "What make I?" Spanish has no auxiliary corresponding to our "do".

THINKING IN SPANISH

(Answers on page 255)

1 ¿Qué hace el profesor?
2. ¿Toma el profesor el libro?
3. ¿Pone el libro encima de la mesa?
4. ¿Toma el profesor la caja?
5. ¿Está el profesor de pié o sentado?

6. ¿Cierra el profesor la ventana?
7. ¿Qué hace el profesor?
8. ¿Abre el profesor la ventana o la puerta?
9. ¿Abre Ud. la puerta?
10. ¿Abre el profesor la puerta?

11. ¿Va el profesor a Nueva York?
12. ¿Va a Paris?
13. ¿Adónde va el profesor?
14. ¿Es la Habana grande o pequeña?
15. ¿Va Ud. a la Habana?
16. ¿Quién va a la Habana, Ud. o el profesor?

LECCIÓN 9

Contando
Kohn-TAHN-*doh*
Counting

1	5	9	13
uno	**cinco**	**nueve**	**trece**
oo-noh	THEEN-*koh*	NWEH-*ueh*	TREH-*theh*
one	five	nine	thirteen
2	6	10	14
dos	**seis**	**diez**	**catorce**
dohs	SEH-*ees*	*d'*YEHTH	*kah*-TOHR-*theh*
two	six	ten	fourteen
3	7	11	15
tres	**siete**	**once**	**quince**
trehs	*s'*YEH-*teh*	OHN-*theh*	KEEN-*theh*
three	seven	eleven	fifteen
4	8	12	16
cuatro	**ocho**	**doce**	**diez y seis**
KWAH-*troh*	OH-*choh*	DOH-*theh*	*d'*YEHTH-*ee*-SEH-*ees*
four	eight	twelve	sixteen

17 diez y siete d'YEHTH-*ee-s'*YEH-*teh* seventeen	**40** cuarenta *kwah*-REHN-*tah* forty	**90** noventa *noh*-VEHN-*tah* ninety
18 diez y ocho d'YEHTH-*ee*-OH-*choh* eighteen	**41** cuarenta y uno *kwah*-REHN-*tah-ee*-OO-*noh* forty-one	**91** noventa y uno *noh*-VEHN-*tah-ee*-OO-*noh* ninety-one
19 diez y nueve d'YEHTH-*ee*-NWEH-*veh* nineteen	**50** cincuenta *theen*-KWEHN-*tah* fifty	**100** ciento (cien) *th'*YEHN-*toh* (*th'*YEHN) one hundred
20 veinte VAIN-*teh* twenty	**51** cincuenta y uno *theen*-KWEHN-*tah-ee*-OO-*noh* fifty-one	**200** doscientos *dohs-th'*YEHN-*tohs* two hundred
21 veintiuno *vaint-ee*-OO-*noh* twenty-one	**60** sesenta *seh*-SEHN-*tah* sixty	**300** trescientos *trehs-th'*YEHN-*tohs* three hundred
22 veintidós *vain-tee*-DOHS twenty-two	**61** sesenta y uno *seh*-SEHN-*tah-ee*-OO-*noh* SIXTY-one	**400** cuatrocientos KWAH-*troh-th'*YEHN-*tohs* four hundred
23 veintitrés *vain-tee*-TREHS twenty-three	**70** setenta *seh*-TEHN-*tah* seventy	**500** quinientos *keen*-YEHN-*tos* five hundred
30 treinta TRAIN-*tah* thirty	**71** setenta y uno *seh*-TEHN-*tah-ee*-OO-*noh* seventy-one	**600** seiscientos SEH-*ees-th'*YEHN-*tohs* six hundred
31 treinta y uno TRAIN-*tah-ee*-OO-*noh* thirty-one	**80** ochenta *oh*-CHEHN-*tah* eighty	**700** setecientos *seh-teh-th'*YEHN-*tohs* seven hundred
32 treinta y dos TRAIN-*tah-ee*-DOHS thirty-two	**81** ochenta y uno *oh*-CHEHN-*tah-ee*-OO-*noh* eighty-one	**800** ochocientos OH-*choh-th'*YEHN-*tohs* eight hundred

900
novecientos
*noh-vehth-*YEHN-*tohs*
nine hundred

1000
mil
meel
one thousand

365
trescientos sesenta y cinco
*trehs-th'*YEHN-*tohs-seh-*SEHN-*tah-ee-*THEEN-*koh*
three hundred and sixty-five

1949
Mil novecientos cuarenta y nueve
*Meel noh-vehth-*YEHN-*tohs-kwah-*REHN-*tah-ee-*NWEH-*vay*
Nineteen hundred forty-nine

Contar: Yo cuento.   Ud. cuenta.   Cuente Ud.
*Kohn-*TAHR: *Yoh* KWEHN-*toh.*   *Oos-*TEHD KWEHN-*tah.*   KWEHN-*teh oos-*TEHD
To count: I count.   You count.   Count.

Uno, dos, tres, cuatro......etc.
Oo-*noh, dohs, trehs,* KWAH-*troh*...... *eht-*THEH-*teh-rah.*
One, two, three, four......etc.

Ud. cuenta desde uno hasta cuatro.
*Oos-*TEHD KWEHN-*tah* DEHS-*deh* OO-*noh* AHS-*tah* KWAH-*troh.*
You count from one to four.

Yo cuento desde diez hasta quince:
Yoh KWEHN-*toh* DEHS-*deh d'*YEHTH AHS-*tah* KEEN-*theh:*
I count from ten to fifteen:

diez	once	doce	trece
*d'*YEHTH	OHN-*theh*	DOH-*theh*	TREH-*theh*
ten	eleven	twelve	thirteen

	catorce	quince	
	*kah-*TOHR-*theh*	KEEN-*theh*	
	fourteen	fifteen	

¿Qué hago yo?
Keh AH-*goh yoh?*
What do I do?

Ud. cuenta.
*Oos-*TEHD KWEHN-*tah.*
You count.

¿Qué hace Ud.?
Keh AH-*theh oos-*TEHD?
What do you do?

Yo cuento.
*Yoh k*WEHN-*toh.*
I count.

Cuente Ud. desde veinte hasta treinta.
KWEHN-*teh oos-*TEHD DEHS-*deh* VAIN-*teh* AHS-*tah* TRAIN-*tah.*
Count from twenty to thirty.

¿Desde qué número cuenta Ud.?
DEHS-*deh keh* NOO-*meh-roh* KWEHN-*tah* OOS-TEHD?
From what number do you count?

¿Hasta qué número cuenta el señor?
AHS-*tah keh* NOO-*meh-roh* KWEHN-*tah ell sehn-*YOHR?
Up to what number does the gentleman count?

Un libro	dos libros	tres libros
Oon LEE-*broh*	*dohs* LEE-*brohs*	*trehs* LEE-*brohs*
A book	two books	three books
una silla	dos sillas	tres sillas
OO-*nah* SEEL-*yah*	*dohs* SEEL-*yahs*	*trehs* SEEL-*yahs*
a chair	two chairs	three chairs

2 y 2 son cuatro.
Dohs ee dohs sohn KWAH-*troh.*
Two and two are four.

¿Cuántos son 2×4?
KWAHN-*tohs sohn dohs pohr* KWAH-*troh?*
How many are 2 × 4?

2 por 4 son 8.
Dohs pohr KWAH-*troh sohn* OH-*choh.*
2 times 4 are 8.

¿Cuántos libros hay en la mesa?
KWAHN-*tohs* LEE-*brohs I enn lah* MEH-*sah?*
How many books are there on the table?

Hay un libro.
I oon LEE-*broh.*
There is one book.

Hay ocho libros.
I OH-*choh* LEE-*brohs.*
There are eight books.

HELPFUL HINTS: *Hay* means "there is", "there are", or "is there", or "are there" if used interrogatively.

Haga el favor de: is another way of saying "please" and is used with the infinitive of the verb. Ex: "Please shut the door."—*Haga el favor de cerrar la puerta.*

¿Cuántas sillas hay en este cuarto?
KWAHN-*tahs* SEEL-*yahs I enn* ESS-*teh* KWAHR-*toh?*
How many chairs are there in this room?

Hay una silla.
I OO-*nan* SEEL-*yah.*
There is one chair.

Hay doce sillas.
I DOH-*theh* SEEL-*yahs.*
There are twelve chairs.

Cuente Ud. los lápices.
KWEHN-*teh* OOS-TEHD *lohs* LAH-*pee-thehs.*
Count the pencils.

¿Cuántos hay?
KWAHN-*tohs I?*
How many are there?

Hay trece.
I TREH-*theh.*
There are thirteen.

Haga el favor de contar los libros.
AH-*gah ell fah*-VOHR *deh kohn*-TAHR *lohs* LEE-*brohs.*
Please, count the books.

¿Cuántos libros hay aquí?
KWAHN-*tohs* LEE-*brohs I ah*-KEE?
How many books are there here?

Hay doce libros.
I DOH-*theh* LEE-*brohs.*
There are twelve books.

¿Cuántas personas hay?
KWAHN-*tahs pehr*-SOH-*nahs I?*
How many persons are there?

Hay veinte.
I VAIN-*teh.*
There are twenty.

 NOTE TO STUDENT: The plural of nouns is fortunately very simple in Spanish. *Libro* becomes *libros* in the plural. However, if the final letter of the noun is a consonant, then the plural is *es.* Ex: *Un reloj, dos relojes.* Numbers in the hundreds also vary in number and gender with the noun. Ex: "Two hundred Mexican girls": *Doscientas muchachas mexicanas.*

¿Cuántos kilómetros hay entre Buenos Aires y Santiago?
KWAHN-*tohs kee*-LOH-*meh-trohs I* ENN-*treh* BWEH-*nohs* AH-*ee-rehs ee Sahnt*-YAH-*goh?*
How many kilometers are there between Buenos Aires and Santiago?

Hay 1118 (mil ciento diez y ocho).
*I meel th'*YEHN-*toh d'*YEHTH-*ee-*OH-*choh.*
There are 1118.

El periódico cuesta 5 centavos.
Ell pehr-YOH-*dee-koh* KWEHS-*tah.* THEEN-*koh thehn*-TAH-*vohs.*
The newspaper costs 5 cents.

El reloj cuesta 50 pesos.
Ell reh-LOH KWEHS-*tah theen*-KWEHN-*tah* PEH-*sohs.*
The watch costs 50 pesos.

¿Cuánto cuesta el libro?
KWAHN-*toh* KWEHS-*tah ell* LEE-*broh?*
How much does the book cost?

3 pesos.
trehs PEH-*sohs.*
3 pesos.

¿Cuánto cuesta su reloj?
KWAHN-*toh* KWEHS-*tah soo reh*-LOH?
How much does your watch cost?

Mi reloj cuesta 75 pesos.
Mee reh-LOH KWEHS-*tah seh*-TEHN-*tah ee* THEEN-*koh* PEH-*sohs*
My watch costs 75 pesos.

THINKING IN SPANISH
(Answers on page 255)

1. ¿Hay libros encima de la mesa?
2. ¿Cuenta el profesor?
3. ¿Qué cuenta el profesor?
4. ¿Hay una caja encima de la silla grande?
5. ¿Hay una mesa aquí?
6. ¿Cuántas cajas hay encima de la mesa?
7. ¿Hay cuadros en la pared?
8. ¿Hay 2 sombreros encima de la silla?
9. ¿Cuántos son 2 y 8?
10. ¿Cuántos son 5 por 6?
11. ¿Cuánto cuesta este libro?
12. ¿Cuánto cuesta su sombrero?
13. ¿Cuánto cuesta la revista "Life"?
14. ¿Cuántas millas hay entre Los Ángeles y Nueva York? (3000)
15. ¿Cuántas millas hay entre Nueva York y París? (3000)
16. Cuente desde 20 hasta 25. ¿Qué hace Ud.?

LECCIÓN 10

El cuerpo humano
Ell KWEHR-*poh* oo-MAH-*noh*
The human body

La cabeza	**el pelo**	**el ojo**	**la nariz**
Lah kan-BEH-*thah*	*ell* PEH-*loh*	*ell* OH-*hoh*	*lah nah*-REETH
The head	the hair	the eye	the nose
la frente	**la oreja**	**la boca**	**el cuello**
lah FREHN-*teh*	*lah oh*-REH-*hah*	*lah* BOH-*kah*	*ell* KWEHL-*yoh*
the forehead	the ear	the mouth	the neck (or the collar)
la espalda	**el pecho**	**el hombro**	**el brazo**
lah ess-PAHL-*dah*	*ell* PEH-*choh*	*ell* OHM-*broh*	*ell* BRAH-*thoh*
the back	the chest	the shoulder	the arm
el dedo	**la mano**	**el pié**	**la pierna**
ell DEH-*doh*	*lah* MAH-*noh*	*ell* p'YEH	*lah* p'YEHR-*nah*
the finger	the hand	the foot	the leg

el brazo derecho
ell BRAH-*thoh deh*-REH-*choh*
the right arm

el brazo izquierdo
ell BRAH-*thoh eethk*-YEHR-*doh*
the left arm

52

la mano derecha
lah MAH-*noh deh-*REH-*chah*
the right hand

la mano izquierda
lah MAH-*noh eethk-*YEHR-*dah*
the left hand

¿Qué brazo es éste?
Keh BRAH-*thoh ess* ESS-*teh?*
What arm is this?

Es el brazo derecho (izquierdo).
Ess ell BRAH-*thoh deh-*REH-*choh* (*eethk-*YEHR-*doh*).
It is the right arm (left).

¿Qué mano es ésta?
Keh MAH-*noh ess* ESS-*tah?*
Which hand is this?

Es la mano izquierda (derecha).
Ess lah MAH-*noh eethk-*YEHR-*dah* (*deh-*REH-*chah*).
It is the left hand (right).

¿Cuál es su brazo izquierdo?   Éste.
Kwahl ess soo BRAH-*thoh eethk-*YEHR-*doh?*   Ess-*teh.*
Which is your left arm?   This one.

¿Cuál es su mano derecha?   Ésta.
Kwahl ess soo MAH-*noh deh-*REH-*chah?*   Ess-*tah.*
Which is your right hand?   This one.

¿Es éste mi pié derecho o izquierdo?
Ess ESS-*teh mee p'*YEH *deh-*REH-*choh oh eethk-*YEHR-*doh?*
Is this my right or left foot?

Éstos son los dos piés.
Ess-*tohs sohn lohs dohs p'*YEHS.
These are the two feet.

Ésta es la mano derecha y ésta la izquierda.
Ess-*tah ess lah* MAH-*noh deh-*REH-*chah ee* ESS-*tah lah eethk-*YEHR-*dah.*
This is the right hand and this one the left.

Éstas son las 2 manos.
Ess-*tahs sohn lahs dohs* MAH-*nohs.*
These are the two hands.

¿De qué color es este libro?   Este libro es rojo.
*Deh keh koh-*LOHR *ess* ESS-*teh* LEE-*broh?*   Ess-*teh* LEE-*broh ess* ROH-*hoh.*
What color is this book?   This book is red.

¿De qué color son estos libros?
*Deh keh koh-*LOHR *sohn* ESS-*tohs* LEE-*brohs?*
What color are these books?

Estos libros son rojos.
Ess-tohs LEE-*brohs sohn* ROH-*hohs.*
These books are red.

¿De qué color es esta silla?
*Deh keh koh-*LOHR *ess* ESS-*tah* SEEL-*yah?*
What color is this chair?

Esta silla es amarilla.
Ess-tah SEEL-*yah ess ah-mah-*REEL-*yah.*
This chair is yellow.

¿De qué color son estas sillas?
*Deh keh koh-*LOHR *sohn* ESS-*tahs* SEEL-*yahs?*
What color are these chairs?

Estas sillas son amarillas.
Ess-tahs SEEL-*yahs sohn ah-mah-*REEL-*yahs.*
These chairs are yellow.

El lápiz negro no es largo, es corto.
Ell LAH-*peeth* NEH-*groh noh ess* LAHR-*goh, ess* KOHR-*toh.*
The black pencil is not long, it is short.

Los lápices negros no son largos, son cortos.
Lohs LAH-*pee-thehs* NEH-*grohs noh sohn* LAHR-*gohs, soh* KOHR-*tohs.*
The black pencils are not long, they are short.

La puerta no es ancha, es estrecha.
Lah PWEHR-*tah noh ess* AHN-*chah, ess ess-*TREH-*chah.*
The door is not wide, it is narrow.

Las puertas no son anchas, son estrechas.
Lahs PWEHR-*tahs noh sohn* AHN-*chahs, sohn ess-*TREH-*chahs.*
The doors are not wide, they are narrow.

NOTE TO STUDENT: Adjectives agree in number and gender with the nouns they modify. Ex: "The red pocketbook": *La cartera roja.* "The red pocket-books": *Las carteras rojas.* Verbs also change their forms when they are used in the plural. Ex: "He is Cuban": *Él es cubano.* "They are Cubans": *Ellos son cubanos.*

¿Quién es este señor?
*K'*YEHN *ess* ESS-*teh sehn-*YOHR?
Who is this gentleman?

Es el Sr. Quintana.
*Ess ell sehn-*YOHR *Keen-*TAH-*nah.*
He is Mr. Quintana.

¿Quiénes son estos señores?
*K'*YEH-*nehs sohn* ESS-*tohs sehn-*YOH-*rehs?*
Who are these gentlemen?

Son los Sres. Quintana y Gómez.
*Sohn lohs sehn-*YOH-*rehs Keen-*TAH-*nah ee* GOH-*mehth.*
They are Messrs. Quintana and Gómez.

¿Quién es Ud.?   Yo soy la señorita Rodríguez.
*K'*YEHN *ess oos-*TEHD?   *Yoh soy lah sehn-yoh-*REE-*tah Roh-*DREE-*ggehth.*
Who are you?   I am Miss Rodriguez.

Ud. es el señor Berlitz.   ¿Quiénes somos nosotros?
*Oos-*TEHD *ess ell sehn-*YOHR BEHR-*leets. K'*YEH-*nehs* SOH-*mohs noh-*SOH-*trohs?*
You are Mr. Berlitz.   Who are we?

Nosotras somos las señoritas Rodríguez.
*Noh-*SOH-*trahs* SOH-*mohs lahs sehn-yoh-*REE-*tahs Roh-*DREE-*ggehth.*
We are the Misses Rodriguez.

¿Quién es esta señora?   Es la señora Jiménez.
*K'*YEHN *ess* ESS-*tah sehn-*YOH-*rah?*   *Ess lah sehn-*YOH-*rah Hee-*MEH-*nehth.*
Who is this lady?   She is Mrs. Jimenez.

¿Quiénes son estas señoras?
*K'*YEHN-*nehs sohn* ESS-*tahs sehn-*YOH-*rahs?*
Who are these ladies?

Son las Sras. Jiménez y Rivas.
*Sohn lahs sehn-*YOH-*rahs Hee-*MEH-*nehth ee* REE-*vahs.*
They are Mrs. Jimenez and Mrs. Rivas.

El Sr. Quintana está de pié,
*Ell sehn-*YOHR *Keen-*TAH-*nah ess-*TAH *deh p'*YEH,
Mr. Quintana is standing,

el señor Gómez está de pié,
*ell sehn-*YOHR GOH-*mehth ess-*TAH *deh p'*YEH,
Mr. Gómez is standing,

estos señores están de pié,
ESS-*tohs sehn-*YOH-*rehs ess-*TAHN *deh p'*YEH,
these gentlemen are standing,

Ud. está de pié,   yo estoy de pié,
*oos-*TEHD *ess-*TAH *deh p'*YEH,   *yoh ess-*TOY *deh p'*YEH,
you are standing,   I am standing,

la Srta. Pidal está sentada;
*lah sehn-yoh-*REE-*tah Pee-*DAHL *ess-*TAH *sehn-*TAH-*dah;*
Miss Pidal is sitting;

la Srta. Rivas está sentada;
*lah sehn-yoh-*REE-*tah* REE-*vahs ess-*TAH *sehn-*TAH-*dah;*
Miss Rivas is sitting;

estas señoras están sentadas.
ESS-*tahs sehn*-YOH-*rahs ess*-TAHN *sehn*-TAH-*dahs.*
these ladies are sitting.

¿Están los señores sentados a la mesa?
Ess-TAHN *lohs sehn*-YOH-*rehs sehn*-TAH-*dohs ah lah* MEH-*sah?*
Are the gentlemen sitting at the table?

No, (ellos) están de pié delante de la ventana.
Noh, (EHL-*yohs*) *ess*-TAHN *deh p'*YEH *deh*-LAHN-*teh deh lah vehn*-TAH-*nah.*
No, they are standing in front of the window.

¿Están las señoras de pié en el pasillo?
Ess-TAHN *lahs sehn*-YOH-*rahs deh p'*YEH *enn ell pah*-SEEL-*yoh?*
Are the ladies standing in the corridor?

No, (ellas) están sentadas en el cuarto.
Noh, (EHL-*yahs*) *ess*-TAHN *sehn*-TAH-*dahs enn ell* KWAHR-*toh.*
No, they are sitting in the room.

Éste es mi sombrero.	**Éstos son mis guantes.**
Ess-*teh ess mee sohm*-BREH-*roh.*	Ess-*tohs sohn mees* GWAHN-*tehs.*
This is my hat.	These are my gloves.

Esta corbata es su corbata de Ud.
Ess-*tah kohr*-BAH-*tah ess soo kohr*-BAH-*tah deh oos*-TEHD.
This tie is your tie.

Estos zapatos son sus zapatos.
Ess-*tohs thah*-PAH-*tohs sohn soos thah*-PAH-*tohs.*
These shoes are your shoes.

¿Cuál es mi sombrero?	**Éste.**
KWAHL *ess mee sohm*-BREH-*roh?*	Ess-*teh.*
Which is my hat?	This one.

¿Cuáles son mis guantes?	**Éstos.**
KWAH-*lehs sohn mees* GWAHN-*tehs?*	Ess-*tohs.*
Which are my gloves?	These.

¿Cuál es su corbata?	**Ésta.**
KWAHL *ess soo kohr*-BAH-*tah?*	Ess-*tah.*
Which is your tie?	This one.

¿Cuáles son sus plumas?	**Éstas.**
KWAH-*lehs sohn soos* PLOO-*mahs?*	Ess-*tahs.*
Which are your pens?	These.

¿De quién es ese sombrero?	**Es del Sr. Fernández.**
*Deh k'*YEHN *ess* ESS-*eh sohm*-BREH-*roh?*	*Ess dehl sehn*-YOHR *Fehr*-NAHN-*dehth.*
Whose is that hat?	It is Mr. Fernández'.

¿De quiénes son esos sombreros?
Deh k'YEH-nehs sohn ESS-ohs sohm-BREH-rohs?
Whose are those hats?

Son de los alumnos.
Sohn deh lohs ah-LOOM-nohs.
They are the pupils'.

¿Cuáles son los libros de los alumnos?
KWAH-*lehs sohn lohs* LEE-*brohs deh lohs* ah-LOOM-*nohs?*
Which are the pupils' books?

Son aquéllos.
*Sohn ah-*KEHL*-yohs.*
Those are.

¿Cuáles son las sillas de las señoritas?
KWAH-*lehs sohn lahs* SEEL-*yahs deh lahs sehn-yoh-*REE-*tahs?*
Which are the young ladies' chairs?

Son aquéllas.	¿De quién es esta silla?
*Sohn ah-*KEHL*-yahs.*	*Deh k'YEHN ess* ESS-*tah* SEEL-*yah?*
Those are.	Whose is this chair?
Es de Juan.	¿De quiénes son esas sillas?
Ess deh HWAHN.	*Deh k'YEH-nehs sohn* ESS-*ahs* SEEL-*yahs?*
It is John's.	Whose are those chairs?

Son de los señores Berlitz y Romero.
*Sohn deh lohs sehn-*YOH-*rehs* BEHR-*leets ee Roh-*MEH-*roh.*
They are Messrs. Berlitz' and Romero's.

HELPFUL HINTS: When "who", "what", "when", "where", "to where" and "how" are used in questions, they carry an accent to show they are interrogatives. They are written *¿Quién?*, *¿Qué?*, *¿Cuándo?*, *¿Dónde?*, *¿Adónde?*, *¿Cómo?*.

THINKING IN SPANISH
(Answers on page 256)

1. ¿Qué hay debajo del brazo izquierdo del profesor?
2. ¿Hay un periódico debajo de su brazo izquierdo?
3. ¿Está la pipa dentro del bolsillo del profesor?
4. ¿Dónde está el papel?
5. ¿Está la regla debajo del pié derecho?
6. ¿Qué hay en la mano derecha del profesor?
7. ¿Hay plumas en su mano derecha?
8. ¿Hay lápices dentro de la caja?
9. ¿Hay llaves encima de la mesa?
10. ¿Dónde están los libros?
11. ¿Hay cuadros en la pared?
12. ¿Hay un sombrero en la cabeza del profesor?
13. ¿Hay dos perros debajo de la mesa?
14. ¿Están de pié?
15. ¿Cuántos libros hay encima de la mesa?

LECCIÓN 11

Escribo el alfabeto.
*Ess-*KREE-*boh ell ahl-fah-*BEH-*toh.*
I write the alphabet.

El profesor toma la tiza;
*Ell proh-feh-*SOHR TOH-*mah lah* TEE-*thah;*
The teacher takes the chalk;

el profesor escribe en la pizarra.
*ell proh-feh-*SOHR *ess-*KREE-*beh enn lah* pee-THAH-*rrah.*
the teacher writes on the blackboard.

Escribe el alfabeto.
*Ess-*KREE-*beh ell ahl-fah-*BEH-*toh.*
He writes the alphabet.

¿Qué hace el profesor?
Keh AH-*theh ell proh-feh-*SOHR?
What does the teacher do?

Toma la tiza y escribe.
TOH-*mah lah* TEE-*thah ee ess-*KPEE-*beh.*
He takes the chalk and writes.

¿En dónde escribe el profesor?
Enn DOHN-*deh ess-*KREE-*beh ell proh-feh-*SOHR?
Where does the teacher write?

Escribe en la pizarra.
*Ess-*KREE-*beh enn lah* pee-THAH-*rrah.*
He writes on the blackboard

¿Qué escribe?
*Keh ess-*KREE-*beh?*
What does he write?

Escribe el alfabeto.
Ess-KREE-beh ell ahl-fah-BEH-toh.
He writes the alphabet.

¿Quién escribe en la pizarra?
K'YEHN ess-KREE-beh enn lah pee-THAH-rrah?
Who writes on the blackboard?

El profesor escribe en la pizarra.
Ell proh-feh-SOHR ess-KREE-beh enn lah pee-THAH-rrah.
The teacher writes on the blackboard.

Sr. Peralta, tome Ud. un lápiz y una hoja de papel.
Sehn-YOHR Peh-RAHL-tah, TOH-meh oos-TEHD oon LAH-peeth er oo-nah OH-hah deh pah-PEHL.
Mr. Peralta, take a pencil and a sheet of paper.

Escriba Ud. el alfabeto.
Ess-KREE-bah oos-TEHD ell ahl-fah-BEH-toh.
Write the alphabet.

Ud. escribe el alfabeto en el papel.
Oos-TEHD ess-KREE-beh ell ahl-fah-BEH-toh enn ell pah-PEHL.
You write the alphabet on the paper.

A es una letra.	**B es una letra.**
Ah ess oo-nah LEH-trah.	*Beh ess oo-nah LEH-trah.*
A is a letter.	B is a letter.

Yo escribo letras en la pizarra.
Yoh ess-KREE-boh LEH-trahs enn lah pee-THAH-rrah.
I write letters on the blackboard.

Ud. escribe letras en su papel.
Oos-TEHD ess-KREE-beh LEH-trahs enn soo pah-PEHL.
You write letters on your paper.

Tomo un libro y leo.
TOH-moh oon LEE-broh ee LEH-oh.
I take a book and read.

Tome Ud. un libro y lea Ud.
TOH-meh oos-TEHD oon LEE-broh er LEH-ah oos-TEHD.
Take a book and read.

Yo leo,	**Ud. lee.**
Yoh LEH-oh,	*oos-TEHD LEH-eh.*
I read,	You read.
¿Qué hace Ud.?	**Yo leo.**
Keh AH-theh oos-TEHD?	*Yoh LEH-oh.*
What do you do?	I read.

¿Qué hago yo?
Keh AH-*guh yoh?*
What do I do?

Ud. toma el libro y lee.
Oos-TEHD TOH-*mah ell* LEE-*broh ee* LEH-*eh.*
You take the book and read.

Yo leo el alfabeto:
Yoh LEH-*oh ell ahl-fah*-BEH-*toh:*
I read the alphabet:

A,	B,	C,	Ch,	D,	etc.
Ah,	*Beh,*	*Theh,*	*Cheh,*	*Deh,*	*eht*-THEH-*teh-rah.*
A,	B,	C,	Ch,	D,	etc.

¿Qué leo yo?
Keh LEH-*oh yoh?*
What do I read?

Ud. lee el alfabeto.
Oos-TEHD LEH-*eh ell ahl-fah*-BEH-*toh.*
You read the alphabet.

Escriba números en la pizarra.
Ess-KREE-*bah* NOO-*meh-rohs enn lah pee*-THAH-*rrah.*
Write numbers on the blackboard.

Lea Ud. estos números.
LEH-*ah oos*-TEHD ESS-*tohs* NOO-*meh-rohs.*
Read these numbers.

¿Qué lee Ud., señor?
Keh LEH-*eh oos*-TEHD, *sehn*-YOHR?
What do you read, sir?

Yo leo el alfabeto castellano.
Yoh LEH-*oh ell ahl-fah-*BEH-*toh kahs-tehl*-YAH-*noh.*
I read the Spanish alphabet.

Sr. Cruz, lea Ud. en el libro.
Sehn-YOHR *Krooth,* LEH-*ah oos*-TEHD *enn ell* LEE-*broh.*
Mr. Cruz, read from the book.

Srta. Miret, lea Ud. en la pizarra.
Sehn-yoh-REE-*tah Mee*-REHT, LEH-*ah oos*-TEHD *enn lah pee*-THAH-*rrah.*
Miss Miret, read from the blackboard.

¿Qué hace Ud.?
Keh AH-*theh oos*-TEHD?
What do you do?

Yo leo en la pizarra.
Yoh LEH-*oh enn lah pee*-THAH-*rrah.*
I read from the blackboard.

¿Qué lee Ud., libros o periódicos?
Keh LEH-*eh oos*-TEHD, LEE-*brohs oh pehr*-YOH-*dee-kohs?*
What do you read, books or newspapers?

Yo no leo ni libros ni periódicos, yo leo
Yoh noh LEH-*oh nee* LEE-*brohs nee pehr*-YOH-*dee-kohs, yoh* LEH-*oh*
I read neither books nor newspapers, I read

el alfabeto en la pizarra.
*ell ahl-fah-*BEH-*toh enn lah pee*-THAH-*rrah.*
the alphabet on the blackboard.

Yo escribo la letra A,   la letra B,
*Yoh ess-*KREE-*boh lah* LEH-*trah Ah,*   *lah* LEH-*trah Beh,*
I write the letter A,   the letter B,

la letra C.
lah LEH-*trah Theh.*
the letter C.

Escribo letras.   ¿Qué es esto?   Es una letra.
*Ess-*KREE-*boh* LEH-*trahs.*   *Keh ess* ESS-*toh?*   *Ess* OO-*nah* LEH-*trah.*
I write letters.   What is this?   It is a letter.

¿Qué letra es ésta?   Es la A,   Es la B,
Keh LEH-*trah ess* ESS-*tah?*   *Ess lah Ah,*   *Ess lah Beh,*
What letter is this?   It is A,   It is B,

Es la C, etc.
*Ess lah Theh, eht-*THEH-*teh-rah.*
It is C, etc.

Escribo palabras.   Aquí hay una palabra: papel.
*Ess-*KREE-*boh pah-*LAH-*brahs.*   *Ah-*KEE *I* OO-*nah pah-*LAH-*brah: pah-*PEHL.
I write words.   Here is a word: paper.

Aquí hay otra palabra: puerta.
*Ah-*KEE *I* OH-*trah pah-*LAH-*brah:* PWEHR-*tah.*
Here is another word: door.

¿Cuántas letras hay en esta palabra?
KWAHN-*tahs* LEH-*trahs I enn* ESS-*tah pah-*LAH-*brah?*
How many letters are there in this word?

Hay cinco letras en la palabra papel.
I THEEN-*koh* LEH-*trahs enn lah pah-*LAH-*brah pah-*PEHL.
There are five letters in the word paper.

¿En ésa?   Hay seis.
Enn ESS-*ah?*   *I* SEH-*ees.*
In that one?   There are six.

"Monsieur" es una palabra francesa.
"Muss-yuh" ess OO-*nah pah-*LAH-*brah frahn-*THEH-*sah.*
"Monsieur" is a French word.

"Mister" es una palabra inglesa.
"Mister" ess OO-*nah pah-*LAH-*brah een-*GLEH-*sah.*
"Mister" is an English word.

"Herr" es una palabra alemana.
"Hehr" ess OO-*nah pah-*LAH-*brah ah-leh-*MAH-*nah.*
"Herr" is a German word.

"Señor" es una palabra española.
"Sehn-YOHR" ess oo-nah pah-LAH-brah ess-pahn-YOHL-ah.
"Señor" is a Spanish word.

¿Es este libro francés o inglés?
Ess ESS-teh LEE-broh frahn-THEHS oh een-GLEHS?
Is this book French or English?

Ese libro no es francés ni inglés, es español.
ESS-eh LEE-broh noh ess frahn-THEHS nee een-GLEHS, ess ess-pahn-YOHL.
That book is neither French nor English, it is Spanish.

Es éste un libro español?
Ess ESS-teh oon LEE-broh ess-pahn-YOHL.
Is this a Spanish book?

Sí, señor, ése es un libro español.
See, sehn-YOHR, ESS-eh ess oon LEE-broh ess-pahn-YOHL.
Yes, sir, that is a Spanish book.

¿Es éste un libro italiano?
Ess ESS-teh oon LEE-broh ee-tahl-YAH-noh?
Is this an Italian book?

No, no es un libro italiano; es un libro español.
Noh, noh ess oon LEE-broh ee-tahl-YAH-noh; ess oon LEE-broh ess-pahn-YOHL.
No, it is not an Italian book; it is a Spanish book.

Yo digo el alfabeto castellano:
Yoh DEE-goh ell ahl-fah-BEH-toh kahs-tehl-YAH-noh:
I say the Spanish alphabet:

A	B	C	Ch	D	E
Ah	*Beh*	*Theh*	*Cheh*	*Deh*	*Eh*
F	G	H	I	J	K
EH-feh	*Heh*	*AH-cheh*	*Ee*	*HOH-tah*	*Kah*
L	Ll	M	N	Ñ	O
EH-leh	*EHL-yeh*	*EH-meh*	*EH-neh*	*EHN-yeh*	*Oh*
P	Q	R	S	T	U
Peh	*Koo*	*EH-reh*	*EH-seh*	*Teh*	*Oo*
V	X	Y	Z		
Veh	*EH-kees*	*Yeh*	*THEH-tah*		

¿Qué dice el profesor?
Keh DEE-theh ell proh-feh-SOHR?
What does the teacher say?

Dice el alfabeto.
DEE-theh ell ahl-fah-BEH-toh.
He says the alphabet.

Sr. Villanueva, diga Ud. el alfabeto.
*Sehn-*YOHR *Veel-yah-*NWEH*-vah, dee-gah oos-*TEHD *ell ahl-fah-*BEH*-toh.*
Mr. Villanueva, say the alphabet.

¿Qué hace Ud.?	**Yo digo el alfabeto.**
Keh AH*-theh oos-*TEHD*?*	*Yoh* DEE*-goh ell ahl-fah-*BEH*-toh.*
What do you do?	I say the alphabet.
¿Qué hace este señor?	**Dice el alfabeto.**
Keh AH*-theh* ESS*-teh sehn-*YOHR*?*	DEE*-theh ell ahl-fah-*BEH*-toh.*
What does this gentleman do?	He says the alphabet.

En francés, la pronunciación de P-A-R-I-S es "París".
*Enn frahn-*THEHS*, lah proh-noonth-yahth-*YOHN *deh Peh Ah* EH*-reh Ee* EH*-seh ess "Pah-*REE*".*
In French, the pronunciation of PARIS is "Pah-ree".

¿Cuál es la pronunciación francesa de "París"?
KWAHL *ess lah proh-noonth-yahth-*YOHN *frahn-*THEH*-sah deh Pah-*REES*?*
What is the French pronunciation of "Paris"?

¿Cuál es la pronunciación de esta palabra
KWAHL *ess lah proh-noonth-yahth-*YOHN *deh* ESS*-tah pah-*LAH*-brah*
en español?
*enn ess-pahn-*YOHL*?*
What is the pronunciation of this word in Spanish?

La pronunciación en español es "Pah-REES".
*Lah proh-noonth-yahth-*YOHN *enn ess-pahn-*YOHL *ess "Pah-*REES*".*
The pronunciation in Spanish is "Pah-REES".

¿Cuál es la pronunciación exacta de "lápiz", de "periódico", de Málaga, en español?
KWAHL *ess lah pro-noonth yahth-*YOHN *ehk-*SAHK*-tah deh "*LAH*-peeth," deh "pehr-*YOH*-dee-koh", deh* MAH*-lah-gah, enn ess-pahn-*YOHL*?*
What is the exact pronunciation of "lápiz", of "periódico", of Málaga, in Spanish?

HINTS on Pronunciation: Remember that words ending in a vowel or in *s* or *n* are usually stressed on the next to last syllable. If, for some reason, this is not so, then an accent must be used to show this change. Without the accent Málaga would be Mah-*lah*-gah instead of *Mah*-lah-gah.

We refer you once more to the note on page 5 relative to pronunciation differences among Spanish-speaking peoples. In this book we show the "z" to have a "th" or lisping sound, but in many places, particularly in Latin America, it is pronounced as an "s", a sibilant sound. The same is true for the soft "c" before "e" or "i". This "s" sound is acceptable to all but the most unreconstructed purist of the old school.

Yo escribo una frase en la pizarra:
*Yoh ess-*KREE-*boh* OO-*nah* FRAH-*seh enn lah pee-*THAH-*rrah:*
I write a sentence on the board:

"El libro está encima de la mesa."
"Ell LEE-*broh ess-*TAH *enn-*THEE-*mah deh lah* MEH-*sah."*
"The book is on the table."

¿Cuántas palabras hay en esta frase?	Hay seis.
KWAHN-*tahs pah-*LAH-*brahs I enn* ESS-*tah* FRAH-*seh?*	*I* SEH-*ees.*
How many words are there in this sentence?	There are six.

Yo leo, escribo y hablo español.
Yoh LEH-*oh, ess-*KREE-*boh ee* AH-*bloh ess-pahn-*YOHL.
I read, write and speak Spanish.

¿Habla Ud. español?	Sí, señor, lo hablo.
AH-*blah oos-*TEHD *ess-pahn-*YOHL?	*See, sehn-*YOHR, *loh* AH-*bloh.*
Do you speak Spanish?	Yes, sir, I speak it.

No lo hablo pero lo leo.
Noh loh AH-*bloh* PEH-*roh loh* LEH-*oh.*
I do not speak it but I read it.

En París se habla francés;
*Enn Pah-*REES *seh* AH-*blah frahn-*THEHS;
In Paris they speak French;

    en Madrid se habla español;
    *enn Mah-*DREED *seh* AH-*blah* .*ess-pahn-*YOHL;
    in Madrid they speak Spanish;

    en Londres se habla inglés;
    enn LOHN-*drehs seh* AH-*blah een-*GLEHS;
    in London they speak English;

    en Berlín se habla alemán.
    *enn Behr-*LEEN *seh* AH-*blah ah-leh-*MAHN.
    in Berlin they speak German.

NOTE to Student: When *se* is used with the third person, it has the sense of "one" or "everyone". You may see signs in some shop-windows in large American cities *"Aquí se habla español"*. This means that "Spanish is spoken here" or, "one speaks Spanish here".

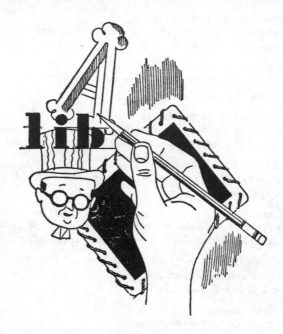

THINKING IN SPANISH
(Answers on page 256)

1. Escriba la letra A en el papel. ¿Qué hace Ud.?

2. Yo escribo la palabra "libertad". ¿Qué escribo yo?

3. El Sr. Campana escribe en la pizarra. ¿Quién escribe el alfabeto en la pizarra?

4. Lea Ud. esta frase: "Yo soy norteamericano." ¿Qué hace Ud.?

5. ¿Cuántas palabras hay en esta frase?   6. ¿Lee Ud. este libro?

7. ¿Lee en español el Sr. Berlitz?   8. ¿Habla inglés el Sr. Padilla?

9. ¿Qué habla Ud., inglés o español?   10. ¿Habla el Sr. Cugat francés?

11. La palabra "book", ¿es española o inglesa?

12. Yo digo A, B, C, Ch, D..., ¿digo el alfabeto?

13. ¿Digo yo el alfabeto ruso?   14. ¿Qué se habla en Nueva York?

15. ¿Se habla español en Buenos Aires?   16. ¿Se habla español en París?

17. ¿Qué se habla en Madrid?

Desde A hasta Z
DEHS-*deh* ah AHS-*tah* THEH-*tah*
From A to Z

El alfabeto castellano empieza por A y acaba en Z.
*Ell ahl-fah-*BEH*-toh kahs-tehl-*YAH*-noh ehmp-*YEH*-thah pohr ah*
*ee ah-*KAH*-bah enn* THEH*-tah.*
The Spanish alphabet begins with A and ends with Z.

A es la primera letra,   **Z es la última.**
*Ah ess lah pree-*MEH*-rah* LEH*-trah,*   THEH*-tah ess lah* OOL*-tee-mah.*
A is the first letter,   Z is the last.

A es la primera letra,
Ah ess lah pree-MEH-*rah* LEH-*trah,*
A is the first letter,

B la segunda,
*Beh lah seh-*GOON-*dah,*
B the second,

C la tercera,
*Theh luh tehr-*THEH-*rah,*
C the third,

Ch la cuarta,
Cheh lah KWAHR-*tah,*
Ch the fourth,

D la quinta,
Deh lah KEEN-*tah,*
D the fifth,

E la sexta,
Eh lah SEHKS-*tah,*
E the sixth,

F la séptima, etc.
EH-*feh lah* SEHP-*tee-mah, eht-*THEH-*teh-rah.*
F the seventh, etc.

¿Cuántas letras hay en el alfabeto castellano?
KWAHN-*tahs* LEH-*trahs I enn ell ahl-fah-*BEH-*toh kahs-tehl-*YAH-*noh?*
How many letters are there in the Spanish alphabet?

Hay 28 letras en el alfabeto castellano.
*I vain-tee-*OH-*choh* LEH-*trahs enn elt ahl-fah-*BEH-*toh kahs-tehl-*YAH-*noh.*
There are 28 letters in the Spanish alphabet.

¿Cuántas vocales hay?
KWAHN-*tahs voh-*KAH-*lehs I?*
How many vowels are there?

Hay cinco:
I THEEN-*koh:*
There are five:

A	E	I	O	U
Ah	*Eh*	*Ee*	*Oh*	*Oo*

¿Cuántas consonantes?
KWAHN-*tahs kohn-soh-*NAHN-*tehs?*
How many consonants?

Hay 23.
*I vain-tee-*TREHS.
There are 23.

¿Qué letra es la D, la cuarta o la quinta?
Keh LEH-*trah ess lah Deh, lah* KWAHR-*tah oh lah* KEEN-*tah?*
What letter is D, the fourth or the fifth?

Es la quinta.
Ess lah KEEN-*tah.*
It is the fifth.

¿Por qué letra empieza el alfabeto?
Pohr keh LEH-*trah ehmp-*YEH-*thah ell ahl-fah-*BEH-*toh?*
With what letter does the alphabet begin?

Empieza por la A.
*Ehmp-*YEH-*thah pohr lah Ah.*
It begins with A.

¿En qué letra acaba?
Enn keh LEH-*trah ah-*KAH-*bah?*
With what letter does it end?

Acaba en Z.
*Ah-*KAH-*bah enn* THEH-*tah.*
It ends with Z.

¿Por qué letra empieza esta frase?
Pohr keh LEH-*trah ehmp-*YEH-*thah* ESS-*tah* FRAH-*seh?*
With what letter does this sentence begin?

Empieza por P.
*Ehmp-*YEH-*thah pohr Peh.*
It begins with P.

¿En qué página acaba la primera lección de su libro?
Enn keh PAH-*hee-nah ah-*KAH-*bah lah pree-*MEH-*rah lehkth-*YOHN *deh soo*
LEE-*broh?*
On what page does the first lesson of your book end?

La primera lección acaba en la página 3.
*Lah pree-*MEH-*rah lehkth-*YOHN *ah-*KAH-*bah enn lah* PAH-*hee-nah 3.*
The first lesson ends on page 3.

¿En qué página empieza la tercera lección?
Enn keh PAH-*hee-nah ehmp-*YEH-*thah lah tehr-*THEH-*rah lehkth-*YOHN?*
On what page does the third lesson begin?

Empieza en la página 7.
*Ehmp-*YEH-*thah enn lah* PAH-*hee-nah 7.*
It begins on page 7.

La letra A está antes de la B.
Lah LEH-*trah Ah ess-*TAH *ahn-tehs deh lah Beh.*
The letter A is before B.

La C está después de la B.
*Lah Theh ess-*TAH *dehs-*PWEHS *deh lah Beh.*
C is after B.

La H está entre la G y la I.
Lah AH-*cheh ess-*TAH ENN-*treh lah Heh ee lah Ee.*
H is between G and I.

¿Dónde está la H,   antes o después de la G?
DOHN-*deh ess-*TAH *lah* AH-*cheh,*   AHN-*tehs oh dehs-*PWEHS *deh lah Heh?*
Where is H,   before or after G?

¿Qué letra está entre la M y la Ñ?
Keh LEH-*trah ess-*TAH ENN-*treh lah* EH-*meh ee lah* EHN-*yeh?*
Which letter is between M and Ñ?

Preguntas *Preh-GOON-tahs* Questions	*Respuestas* *Rehs-PWEHS-tahs* Answers

¿Qué hace Ud.?
Keh AH-theh oos-TEHD?
What do you do?

Leo.
LEH-oh.
I read.

¿Dónde está el libro?
DOHN-deh ess-TAH ell LEE-broh?
Where is the book?

Está encima de la mesa.
Ess-TAH enn-THEE-mah deh lah MEH-sah.
It is on the table.

¿Qué es esto?
Keh ess ESS-toh?
What is this?

Es el libro.
Ess ell LEE-broh.
It is the book.

Yo hago una pregunta:
Yoh AH-goh OO-nah preh-GOON-tah:
I ask a question:

¿Quién es este señor?
K'YEHN ess ESS-teh sehn-YOHR?
Who is this gentleman?

Responda Ud. (Conteste Ud.) a mi pregunta, señora.
Rehs-POHN-dah oos-TEHD (Kohn-tehs-teh oos-TEHD) ah mee preh-GOON-tah, sehn-YOH-rah.
Answer my question, madam.

"Es el Sr. Rios."
Ess ell sehn-YOHR REE-ohs.
"He is Mr. Rios."

¿Qué hace Ud., Sra.?
Keh AH-theh oos-TEHD, sehn-YOH-rah?
What do you do, madam?

Yo contesto (yo respondo) a su pregunta.
Yoh kohn-TEHS-toh (yoh rehs-POHN-doh) ah soo preh-GOON-tah.
I answer your question.

Haga una pregunta al señor.
AH-gah OO-nah preh-GOON-tah ahl sehn-YOHR.
Ask the gentleman a question.

¿Quién hace la pregunta?
K'YEHN AH-theh lah preh-GOON-tah?
Who asks the question?

La señora hace la pregunta.
Lah sehn-YOH-rah AH-theh lah preh-GOON-tah.
The lady asks the question.

Señor, conteste (responda) a la pregunta de la señora.
Sehn-YOHR, kohn-TEHS-teh (rehs-POHN-dah) ah lah preh-GOON-tah deh lah sehn-YOH-rah.
Sir, answer the lady's question.

Antes y después de una pregunta se pone un signo de interrogación.
AHN-*tehs ee dehs*-PWEHS *deh* OO-*nah preh*-GOON-*tah seh* POH-*neh oon*
SEEG-*noh deh een-teh-rroh-gahth*-YOHN.
Before and after a question we put a question mark.

Después de una respuesta se pone un punto final (.)
Dehs-PWEHS *deh* OO-*nah rehs*-PWEHS-*tah seh* POH-*neh oon* POON-*toh*
fee-NAHL (.)
After an answer we put a period (.)

Ésta es la coma (,)
Ess-*tah ess lah* KOH-*mah* (,)
This is the comma (,)

Éstos son los signos de admiración (¡!)
Ess-*tohs sohn lohs* SEEG-*nohs deh ahd-mee-rahth*-YOHN (¡!)
These are the exclamation marks (¡!)

Éste es el guión (-)
Ess-*teh ess ell ggee*-OHN (-)
This is the hyphen (-)

Éste es el acento (')
Ess-*teh ess ell ah*-THEHN-*toh* (')
This is the accent (')

THINKING IN SPANISH

(Answers on page 256)

1. ¿Quién escribe en la pizarra?
2. ¿Escribe Doña Felicidad?
3. ¿Qué periódico lee?
4. ¿Qué libro lee Chiquita?
5. ¿Qué palabra escribe el profesor en la pizarra?
6. ¿Escribe el profesor con lápiz o con tiza?
7. ¿Escribe el profesor el alfabeto?
8. ¿Lee Doña Felicidad un periódico español?
9. ¿Habla español el profesor?
10. ¿Habla español el perro de Chiquita?
11. ¿Lee Ud. español?
12. ¿Habla Ud. inglés?
13. ¿Habla francés el Sr. Berlitz?
14. ¿Habla Chiquita inglés?
15. ¿Está Chiquita sentada o de pié?
16. ¿Cuántas letras hay en el alfabeto castellano?
17. ¿Cuántas letras hay en el alfabeto inglés?

LECCIÓN 13

¿Quién tiene más dinero?
*K'*YEHN *t'*YEH-*neh mahs dee-*NEH-*roh?*
Who has more money?

Sr. González, tome Ud. un libro.
*Sehn-*YOHR *Gohn-*THAH-*lehth,* TOH-*meh oos-*TEHD *oon* LEE-*broh*
Mr. Gonzalez, take a book.

Ud. tiene un libro en la mano.
*Oos-*TEHD *t'*YEH-*neh oon* LEE-*broh enn lah* MAH-*noh.*
You have a book in your hand.

Yo tengo dos libros en la mano.
Yoh TEHN-*goh dohs* LEE-*brohs enn lah* MAH-*noh.*
I have two books in my hand.

La Srta. Pérez tiene su sombrero en la cabeza.
*Lah sehn-yoh-*REE-*tah* PEH-*rehth t'*YEH-*neh soo sohm-*BREH-*roh enn lah
kah-*BEH-*thah.*
Miss Perez has her hat on her head.

Este caballero no tiene sombrero.
Ess-*teh kah-bahl-*YEH-*roh noh t'*YEH-*neh sohm-*BREH-*roh.*
This gentleman has no hat.

Ud. tiene guantes.	No tengo guantes.
*Oos-*TEHD *t'*YEH-*neh* GWAHN-*tehs.*	*Noh* TEHN-*goh* GWAHN-*tehs.*
You have gloves.	I have no gloves.

Ud. tiene un traje azul,
*Oos-*TEHD *t'*YEH-*neh oon* TRAH-*heh ah-*THOOL,
You have a blue suit,

la señora tiene un traje gris.
*lah sehn-*YOH-*rah t'*YEH-*neh oon* TRAH-*heh grees.*
the lady has a gray suit.

Ud. tiene un libro y yo tengo un libro;
*Oos-*TEHD *t'*YEH-*neh oon* LEE-*broh ee yoh* TEHN-*goh oon* LEE-*broh;*
You have a book and I have a book;

nosotros tenemos libros.
*noh-*SOH-*trohs teh-*NEH-*mohs* LEE-*brohs.*
we have books.

Tenemos lápices.	No tenemos plumas.
*Teh-*NEH-*mohs* LAH-*pee-thehs.*	*Noh teh-*NEH-*mohs* PLOO-*mahs.*
We have pencils.	We do not have pens.

El profesor tiene un libro;
*Ell proh-feh-*SOHR *t'*YEH-*neh oon* LEE-*broh;*
The teacher has a book;

los alumnos tienen libros.
*lohs ah-*LOOM-*nohs t'*YEH-*nehn* LEE-*brohs.*
the pupils have books.

Las señoras tienen faldas.
*Lahs sehn-*YOH-*rahs t'*YEH-*nehn* FAHL-*dahs.*
Ladies have skirts.

Los señores no tienen faldas.
*Lohs sehn-*YOH-*rehs noh t'*YEH-*nehn* FAHL-*dahs.*
Gentlemen do not have skirts.

Sres. Andrade y Briceño, ¿qué tienen Uds. en las manos?
*Sehn-*YOH-*rehs Ahn-*DRAH-*deh ee Bree-*THEHN-*yoh, keh t'*YEH-*nehn oos-*TEHD-*ehs enn lahs* MAH-*nohs?*
Messrs. Andrade and Briceño, what have you in your hands?

Tenemos libros.
*Teh-*NEH-*mohs* LEE-*brohs.*
We have books.

¿Tienen Uds. lápices?
*T'*YEH-*nehn* oos-TEH-*dehs* LAH-*pee-thehs?*
Have you pencils?

No, señor, no tenemos lápices, sino libros.
*Noh, sehn-*YOHR, *noh teh-*NEH-*mohs* LAH-*pee-thehs,* SEE-*noh* LEE-*brohs.*
No, sir, we haven't pencils, but books.

Yo tengo dos libros;
Yoh TEHN-*goh dohs* LEE-*brohs;*
I have two books;

Ud. tiene cinco (libros).
oos-TEHD *t'*YEH-*neh* THEEN-*koh* (LEE-*brohs*),
you have five (books).

El Sr. Robledo tiene siete libros.
*Ell sehn-*YOHR *Roh-*BLEH-*doh t'*YEH-*neh s'*YEH-*teh* LEE-*brohs.*
Mr. Robledo has seven books.

Yo tengo menos libros que Ud.
Yoh TEHN-*goh* MEH-*nohs* LEE-*brohs keh* oos-TEHD.
I have fewer books than you.

El Sr. Robledo tiene más libros que Ud.
*Ell sehn-*YOHR *Roh-*BLEH-*doh t'*YEH-*neh mahs* LEE-*brohs keh* oos-TEHD.
Mr. Robledo has more books than you.

Ud. y yo juntos tenemos siete libros.
*Oos-*TEHD *ee yoh* HOON-*tohs teh-*NEH-*mohs s'*YEH-*teh* LEE-*brohs.*
You and I together have seven books.

Nosotros juntos tenemos tantos libros como el Sr. Robledo.
*Noh-*SOH-*trohs* HOON-*tohs teh-*NEH-*mohs* TAHN-*tohs* LEE-*brohs* KOH-*moh
ell sehn-*YOHR *Roh-*BLEH-*doh.*
Together we have as many books as Mr. Robledo.

¿Cuántos libros tenemos juntos?
KWAHN-*tohs* LEE-*brohs teh-*NEH-*mohs* HOON-*tohs?*
How many books have we together?

Juntos nosotros tenemos siete libros.
HOON-*tohs noh-*SOH-*trohs teh-*NEH-*mohs s'*YEH-*teh* LEE-*brohs.*
Together we have seven books.

¿Tiene el Sr. Robledo más libros que nosotros?
*T'*YEH-*neh ell sehn-*YOHR *Roh-*BLEH-*doh mahs* LEE-*brohs keh noh-*SOH-*trohs?*
Has Mr. Robledo more books than we?

No, él no tiene más libros;
*Noh, ell noh t'*YEH-*neh mahs* LEE-*brohs;*
No, he has not more book;·

tiene tantos libros como nosotros
*t'*YEH-*neh* TAHN-*tohs* LEE-*brohs* KOH-*moh noh-*SOH-*trohs.*
he has as many books as we.

¿Cuántos libros tiene Ud. más que yo?
KWAHN-*tohs* LEE-*brohs t'*YEH-*neh oos-*TEHD *mahs keh yoh?*
How many more books than I have you?

Yo tengo tres libros más que Ud.
Yoh TEHN-*goh trehs* LEE-*brohs mahs keh oos-*TEHD·
I have three books more than you.

¿Cuántos tengo yo menos que Ud.?
KWAHN-*tohs* TEHN-*goh yoh* MEH-*nohs keh oos·*TEHD?
How many books less than you have I?

Ud. tiene tres menos que yo.
*Oos-*TEHD *t'*YEH-*neh trehs* MEH-*nohs keh yoh.*
You have three less than I.

¿Cuántas plumas tiene la Srta. Miró?
KWAHN-*tahs* PLOO-*mahs t'*YEH-*neh lah sehn-yoh-*REE-*tah Mee-*ROH?
How many pens has Miss Miró?

Tiene tres.
*T'*YEH-*neh trehs.*
She has three.

¿Y cuántas tiene la Srta. Gómez?
Ee KWAHN-*tahs t'*YEH-*neh lah sehn-yoh-*REE-*tah* GOH-*mehth?*
And how many has Miss Gómez?

Ella tiene cinco.
EHL-*yah t'*YEH-*neh* THEEN-*koh.*
She has five.

¿Cuántas tengo yo?
KWAHN-*tahs* TEHN-*goh yoh?*
How many have I?

Ud. tiene dos plumas.
*Oos-*TEHD *t'*YEH-*neh dohs* PLOO-*mahs.*
You have two pens.

¿Tiene la Srta. Gómez menos plumas que nosotros dos?
*T'*YEH-*neh lah sehn-yoh-*REE-*tah* GOH-*mehth* MEH-*nohs* PLOO-*mahs keh noh-*SOH-*trohs dohs?*
Has Miss Gómez fewer pens than we two?

No, no tiene menos, tiene tantas plumas como nosotros.
*Noh, noh t'*YEH-*neh* MEH-*nohs, t'*YEH-*neh* TAHN-*tahs* PLOO-*mahs* KOH-*moh*
*noh-*SOH-*trohs.*
No, she has not fewer, she has as many pens as we.

Ud. tiene veinte pesos, yo tengo quince;
*Oos-*TEHD *t'*YEH-*neh* VAIN-*teh* PEH-*sohs, yoh* TEHN-*goh* KEEN-*theh;*
You have twenty pesos, I have fifteen;

Santos tiene treinta pesos.
SAHN-*tohs t'*YEH-*neh* TRAIN-*tah* PEH-*sohs.*
Santos has thirty pesos.

¿Cuánto dinero tiene Ud.?
KWAHN-*toh dee-*NEH-*roh t'*YEH-*neh oos-*TEHD?
How much money have you?

Yo tengo veinte pesos.   ¿Cuánto tengo yo?
Yoh TEHN-*goh* VAIN-*teh* PEH-*sohs.*   KWAHN-*toh* TEHN-*goh yoh?*
I have twenty pesos.   How much have I?

Ud. tiene quince pesos.
*Oos-*TEHD *t'*YEH-*neh* KEEN-*theh* PEH-*sohs.*
You have fifteen pesos.

¿Cuánto tiene el Sr. Santos?
KWAHN-*toh t'*YEH-*neh el sehn-*YOHR SAHN-*tohs?*
How much has Mr. Santos?

Tiene treinta.   ¿Quién tiene más dinero?
*T'*YEH-*neh* TRAIN-*tah.*   *K'*YEHN *t'*YEH-*neh mahs dee-*NEH-*roh?*
He has thirty.   Who has the most money?

El Sr. Santos tiene más dinero.
*Ell sehn-*YOHR SAHN-*tohs t'*YEH-*neh mahs dee-*NEH-*roh.*
Mr. Santos has the most money.

¿Quién tiene menos?   Ud. tiene menos.
*K'*YEHN *t'*YEH-*neh* MEH-*nohs?*   *Oos-*TEHD *t'*YEH-*neh* MEH-*nohs.*
Who has the least?   You have the least.

En el libro grueso hay 450 páginas;
Enn ell LEE-*broh* GRWEH-*soh I* KWAH-*troh th'*YEHN-*tahs theen-*KWEHN-*tah*
PAH-*hee-nahs;*
In the thick book there are 450 pages;

hay muchas páginas.
I MOO-*chahs* PAH-*hee-nahs.*
there are many pages.

En el libro delgado hay 60 páginas;
Enn ell LEE-*broh* dehl-GAH-*doh I seh-*SEHN-*tah* PAH-*hee-nahs;*
In the thin book there are sixty pages;

no hay muchas páginas, hay pocas páginas.
noh I MOO-*chahs* PAH-*hee-nahs, I* POH-*kahs* PAH-*hee-nahs.*
there are not many pages, there are few pages.

En la mesa del profesor hay muchos libros;
Enn lah MEH-*sah dehl proh-feh-*SOHR *I* MOO-*chohs* LEE-*brohs;*
On the teacher's table there are many books,

en aquella mesa no hay muchos libros, hay pocos.
*enn ah-*KEHL-*yah* MEH-*sah noh I* MOO-*chohs* LEE-*brohs, I* POH-*kohs.*
on that table there are not many books, there are few

¿Hay muchas páginas en el libro grueso?
I MOO-*chahs* PAH-*hee-nahs enn ell* LEE-*broh* GRWEH-*soh?*
Are there many pages in the thick book?

Sí, hay muchas.
See, I MOO-*chahs.*
Yes, there are many.

¿Hay pocas páginas en el libro delgado?
I POH-*kahs* PAH-*hee-nahs enn ell* LEE-*broh dehl-*GAH-*doh?*
Are there few pages in the thin book?

Sí, hay pocas.
See, I POH-*kahs.*
Yes, there are few.

¿Hay muchos alumnos en la clase?
I MOO-*chohs ah-*LOOM-*nohs enn lah* KLAH-*seh?*
Are there many pupils in the class?

No, hay pocos.
Noh, I POH-*kohs.*
No, there are few.

¿Hay muchos fósforos en esta caja?
I MOO-*chohs* FOHS-*foh-rohs enn* ESS-*tah* KAH-*hah?*
Are there many matches in this box?

Sí, hay muchos.
See, I MOO-*chohs.*
Yes, there are many.

¿Tengo yo mucho dinero en mi bolsillo?
TEHN-*goh yoh* MOO-*choh dee-*NEH-*roh enn mee bohl-*SEEL-*yoh?*
Do I have much money in my pocket?

No, no tiene mucho, tiene poco.
*Noh, noh t'*YEH-*neh* MOO-*choh, t'*YEH-*neh* POH-*koh.*
No, you have not much, you have little.

¿Hay dos profesores en esta clase?
*I dohs proh-feh-*SOH-*rehs enn* ESS-*tah* KLAH-*seh?*
Are there two teachers in this class?

No, no hay más que uno.
Noh, noh I mahs keh OO-*noh.*
No, there is only one.

¿No tiene más que un libro?
*Noh t'*YEH-*neh mahs keh oon* LEE-*broh?*
Have you only one book?

No, señor, tengo varios, cuatro, cinco.
*Noh, sehn-*YOHR, TEHN-*goh* VAHR-*yohs,* KWAH-*troh,* THEEN-*koh.*
No, sir, I have several, four, five.

¿Hay varias mesas aquí?
I VAHR-*yahs* MEH-*sahs ah-*KEE?
Are there several tables here?

No, no hay más que una.
Noh, noh I mahs keh OO-*nah.*
No, there is only one.

¿No hay más que una silla aquí?
Noh I mahs keh OO-*nah* SEEL-*yah ah-*KEE?
Is there only one chair here?

No, señor, hay más de una, hay varias.
*Noh, sehn-*YOHR, *I mahs deh* OO-*nah, I* VAHR-*yahs.*
No, sir, there are more than one, there are several.

NOTE to Student:
no más que = "not more than," "only."
más de = "more than."

Este sombrero es negro, este otro es gris.
Ess-*teh sohm-*BREH-*roh ess* NEH-*groh,* ESS-*teh* OH-*troh ess grees.*
This hat is black, this other one is grey.

Esta regla es larga, la otra es corta.
Ess-*tah* REH-*glah ess* LAHR-*gah, lah* OH-*trah ess* KOHR-*tah.*
This ruler is long, the other one is short.

¿Son rojos los sombreros?
Sohn ROH-*hohs lohs sohm-*BREH-*rohs?*
Are the hats red?

No, son de diferentes colores, uno es negro y otro es gris.
*Noh, sohn deh dee-feh-*REHN-*tehs koh-*LOHR-*ehs,* OO-*noh ess* NEH-*groh ee* OH-*troh ess greess.*
No, they are of different colors, one is black and the other is grey.

¿Cuál es la diferencia entre 5 y 8?
KWAHL *ess lah dee-feh-*REHNTH-*yah* ENN-*treh* THEEN-*koh ee* OH-*choh?*
What is the difference between 5 and 8?

Es 3.
Ess trehs.
It is three.

Aquí hay varios libros: uno es rojo,
*Ah-*KEE *I* VAHR-*yohs* LEE-*brohs:* OO-*noh ess* ROH-*hoh,*
Here are several books: one is red,

otro es gris,
OH-*troh ess greess,*
another is grey,

otro verde,
OH-*troh* VEHR-*deh,*
another green,

y otros azules.
ee OH-*trohs ah-*THOOL-*es.*
and others blue.

¿Son todos los libros del mismo color?
Sohn TOH-*dohs lohs* LEE-*brohs dehl* MEES-*moh koh-*LOHR?
Are all the books of the same color?

No, unos son de un color y otros de otros colores.
Noh, OO-*nohs sohn deh oon koh-*LOHR *ee* OH-*trohs deh* OH-*trohs koh-*LOHR-*es.*
No, some are of one color and others of other colors.

¿Son estas cajas del mismo color?
Sohn ESS-*tahs* KAH-*hahs dehl* MEES-*moh koh-*LOHR?
Are these boxes of the same color?

No, unas son negras y otras rojas.
Noh, OO-*nahs sohn* NEH-*grahs ee* OH-*trahs* ROH-*hahs.*
No, some are black and others red.

THINKING IN SPANISH

(Answers on page 257)

1. ¿Cuánto dinero tiene Chiquita?
2. ¿Tiene tanto dinero como el profesor?
3. ¿Quién tiene más dinero, el profesor o Doña Felicidad?
4. ¿Tiene el profesor lápices detrás de su oreja?
5. ¿Tiene más lápices que Chiquita?
6. ¿Tiene Chiquita tantos libros como el profesor?
7. ¿Quién tiene más libros?   8. ¿Quién tiene menos dinero?
9. ¿Tiene Chiquita mucho dinero?   10. ¿Tiene el profesor muchos libros?
11. ¿Leemos muchas palabras españolas?
12. ¿Quién escribe más frases, nosotros o el profesor?
13. ¿Hay muchas páginas en este libro?
14. ¿Hay más páginas en el diccionario que en este libro?
15. ¿Cuánto dinero tiene Doña Felicidad?
16. ¿Cuánto dinero tienen Doña Felicidad y Chiquita juntas?
17. ¿Cuánto dinero tienen el profesor y Doña Felicidad juntos?
18. ¿Tiene sombrero Chiquita?   19. ¿Tiene sombrero Doña Felicidad?
20. ¿Quién no tiene sombrero?

¿Qué hacemos?
*Keh ah-*THEH*-mohs?*
What do we do?

Tome Ud. un libro.
TOH-*meh oos*-TEHD *oon* LEE-*broh.*
Take a book.

Ud. toma un libro.
*Oos-*TEHD TOH-*mah oon* LEE-*broh.*
You take a book.

Yo tomo un libro.
Yoh TOH-*moh oon* LEE-*broh.*
I take a book.

Nosotros (Usted y yo) tomamos un libro.
*Noh-*SOH-*trohs (oos-*TEHD *ee yoh) toh-*MAH-*mohs oon* LEE-*broh.*
We (you and I) take a book.

¿Qué hace Ud.?
Keh AH-*theh oos-*TEHD?
What do you do?

Yo tomo un libro.
Yoh TOH-*moh oon* LEE-*broh.*
I take a book.

¿Qué hago yo?
Keh AH-*goh yoh?*
What do I do?

Ud. toma un libro.
*Oos-*TEHD TOH-*mah oon* LEE-*broh.*
You take a book.

¿Qué hacemos?
*Keh ah-*THEH-*mohs?*
What do we do?

Nosotros tomamos un libro.
*Noh-*SOH-*trohs toh-*MAH-*mohs oon* LEE-*broh.*
We take a book.

OBSERVE: This lesson indicates the plural endings for the verbs you have already studied. Notice that they follow practically the same pattern as *tener* in the preceding lesson.

¿Qué hace el Sr. Valle?
Keh AH-*theh ell sehn-*YOHR VAHL-*yeh?*
What does Mr. Valle do?

El Sr. Valle toma su sombrero.
*Ell sehn-*YOHR VAHL-*yeh* TOH-*mah soo sohm-*BREH-*roh.*
Mr. Valle takes his hat.

¿Qué hacen los alumnos?
Keh AH-*thehn lohs ah-*LOOM-*nohs?*
What do the pupils do?

Ellos toman sus sombreros.
EHL-*yohs* TOH-*mahn soos sohm-*BREH-*rohs.*
They take their hats.

¿Qué hago yo?
Keh AH-*goh yoh?*
What do I do?

Yo pongo mi libro encima de la mesa.
Yoh POHN-*goh mee* LEE-*broh enn-*THEE-*mah deh lah* MEH-*sah.*
I put my book on the table.

Ponga Ud. su libro encima de la mesa.
POHN-*gah oos-*TEHD *soo* LEE-*broh enn-*THEE-*mah deh lah* MEH-*sah.*
Put your book on the table.

¿Qué hace Ud.?
Keh AH-*theh oos-*TEHD?
What do you do?

Yo pongo mi libro encima de la mesa.
Yoh POHN-*goh mee* LEE-*broh enn-*THEE-*mah deh lah* MEH-*sah.*
I put my book on the table.

¿Qué hacemos?
*Keh ah-*THEH-*mohs?*
What do we do?

(Nosotros) ponemos nuestros libros encima de la mesa.
(*Noh-*SOH-*trohs*) *poh-*NEH-*mohs* NWEHS-*trohs* LEE-*brohs enn-*THEE-*mah deh lah* MEH-*sah.*
We put our books on the table.

NOTE on Plural: Possessive adjectives agree in number with the nouns they modify. Ex: "My tie", *Mi corbata;* "My ties", *mis corbatas.*

Abra Ud. su libro.
AH-*brah oos*-TEHD *soo* LEE-*broh.*
Open your book.

¿Qué hace Ud.?
Keh AH-*theh oos*-TEHD?
What do you do?

Yo abro mi libro.
Yoh AH-*broh mee* LEE-*broh.*
I open my book.

(Nosotros) abrimos nuestros libros.
(*Noh*-SOH-*trohs*) *ah*-BREE-*mohs* NWEHS-*trohs* LEE-*brohs.*
We open our books.

¿Qué hacemos?
Keh ah-THEH-*mohs?*
What do we do?

Abrimos nuestros libros.
Ah-BREE-*mohs* NWEHS-*trohs* LEE-*brohs.*
We open our books.

Ud. es un hombre;
Oos-TEHD *ess oon* OHM-*breh;*
You are a man;

yo soy un hombre.
yoh soy oon OHM-*breh.*
I am a man.

¿Qué somos nosotros?
Keh SOH-*mohs noh*-SOH-*trohs?*
What are we?

Somos hombres.
SOH-*mohs* OHM-*brehs.*
We are men.

Ella es una mujer;
EHL-*yah ess* OO-*nah moo*-HEHR;
She is a woman;

ellas son mujeres.
EHL-*yahs sohn moo*-HEH-*rehs.*
they are women.

Los alumnos abren sus libros.
Lohs ah-LOOM-*nohs* AH-*brehn soos* LEE-*brohs.*
The pupils open their books.

¿Qué hacen los alumnos?
Keh AH-*thehn lohs ah*-LOOM-*nohs?*
What do the pupils do?

Abren sus libros.
AH-*brehn soos* LEE-*brohs.*
They open their books.

Nosotros cerramos la ventana.
Noh-SOH-*trohs theh*-RRAH-*mohs lah vehn*-TAH-*nah.*
We close the window.

Los alumnos cierran sus libros.
Lohs ah-LOOM-*nohs th'*YEH-*rrahn soos* LEE-*brohs.*
The pupils close their books.

¿Qué hacen?
Keh AH-*thehn?*
What do they do?

Señores, cierren Uds. sus libros.
Sehn-YOH-*rehs, th'*YEH-*rrehn oos*-TEHD-*ehs soos* LEE-*brohs.*
Gentlemen, close your books.

¿Qué hacen Uds.?
Keh AH-*thehn oos*-TEHD-*ehs?*
What do you do?

Abran Uds. sus libros.
AH-*brahn oos*-TEHD-*ehs soos* LEE-*brohs.*
Open your books.

Abrimos nuestros libros.
Ah-BREE-*mohs* NWEHS-*trohs* LEE-*brohs.*
We open our books.

Tomemos nuestros sombreros.
Toh-MEH-*mohs* NWEHS-*trohs sohm*-BREH-*rohs.*
Let us take our hats.

¿Qué tomamos?
Keh toh-MAH-*mohs?*
What do we take?

¿Tomamos nuestros sombreros?
Toh-MAH-*mohs* NWEHS-*trohs sohm*-BREH-*rohs?*
Do we take our hats?

Sí, señor, los tomamos.
See, sehn-YOHR, *lohs toh*-MAH-*mohs.*
Yes, sir, we take them.

Ud. escribe,
OOS-TEHD *ess*-KREE-*beh,*
you write,

¿Qué hacemos?
Keh ah-THEH-*mohs?*
What do we do?

¿En qué escribimos?
Enn keh ess-kree-BEE-*mohs?*
On what do we write?

Un señor escribe.
Don sehn-YOHR *ess*-KREE-*beh,*
A gentleman writes,

Cierran sus libros.
*Th'*YEH-*rrahn soos* LEE-*brohs.*
They close their books.

Cerramos nuestros libros.
Theh-RRAH-*mohs* NWEHS-*trohs* LEE-*brohs.*
We close our books.

¿Qué hacen?
Keh AH-*thehn?*
What do you do?

Nuestros sombreros.
NWEHS-*trohs sohm*-BREH-*rohs.*
Our hats.

Yo escribo,
Yoh ess-KREE-*boh,*
I write,

nosotros escribimos.
noh-SOH-*trohs ess-kree*-BEE-*mohs.*
we write.

Escribimos.
Ess-kree-BEE-*mohs.*
We write.

En el papel.
Enn ell pah-PEHL.
On the paper.

dos señores escriben.
dohs sehn-YOH-*rehs ess*-KREE-*behn.*
two gentlemen write.

¿En dónde escribe el profesor?
Enn DOHN-*deh* *ess*-KREE-*beh* *ell* *proh-feh*-SOHR?
Where does the teacher write?

En la pizarra.
Enn lah pee-THAH-*rrah.*
On the blackboard.

¿En dónde escriben los alumnos?
Enn DOHN-*deh* *ess*-KREE-*behn lohs ah*-LOOM-*nohs?*
Where do pupils write?

En el papel.
Enn ell pah-PEHL.
On the paper.

Yo leo un libro.
Yoh LEH-*oh oon* LEE-*broh.*
I read a book.

Uds. señores, lean en la pizarra.
Oos-TEH-*dehs sehn*-YOHR-*ehs,* LEH-*ahn enn lah*
pee-THAH-*rrah.*
You gentlemen, read from the blackboard.

Nosotros leemos.
Noh-SOH-*trohs leh*-EH-*mohs.*
We read.

Un señor lee;
Oon sehn-YOHR LEH-*eh;*
A gentleman reads;

dos señores leen.
dohs sehn-YOH-*rehs* LEH-*ehn.*
two gentlemen read.

¿Qué hace el profesor?
Keh AH-*theh ell proh-feh*-SOHR?
What does the teacher do?

Lee.
LEH-*eh,*
He reads.

¿Qué hacen los alumnos?
Keh AH-*thehn lohs ah*-LOOM-*nohs?*
What do the pupils do?

Leen.
LEH-*ehn.*
They read.

Ud. está en la clase.
Oos-TEHD *ess*-TAH *enn lah* KLAH-*seh.*
You are in the class.

¿Dónde estamos nosotros?
DOHN-*deh ess*-TAH-*mohs noh*-SOH-*trohs.*
Where are we?

Estamos en la clase.
Ess-TAH-*mohs enn lah* KLAH-*seh.*
We are in the class.

Yo voy al teatro;
Yoh voy ahl teh-AH-*troh;*
I go to the theater;

Ud. va al teatro;
oos-TEHD *vah ahl teh*-AH-*troh;*
you go to the theater;

nosotros vamos al teatro.
noh-SOH-*trohs* VAH-*mohs ahl teh*-AH-*troh.*
we go to the theater.

El Sr. Quintero va al teatro;
Ell sehn-YOHR *Keen*-TEH-*roh vah ahl teh*-AH-*troh;*
Mr. Quintero goes to the theater;

el Sr. Campana va a la iglesia.
ell sehn-YOHR *Kahm*-PAH-*nah vah ah lah ee*-GLEHS-*yah.*
Mr. Campana goes to the church.

Juan y Pablo van a la escuela.
HWAHN *ee* PAH-*bloh vahn ah lah ess*-KWEH-*lah.*
John and Paul go to the school.

La Sra. de Garrido va a la tienda.
Lah sehn-YOH-*rah deh Gah*-RREE-*doh vah ah lah t'*YEHN-*dah.*
Mrs. Garrido goes to the store.

¿**Voy yo al teatro?**   **Sí, Ud. va al teatro.**
Voy yoh ahl teh-AH-*troh?*   *See, oos*-TEHD *vah ahl teh*-AH-*troh.*
Do I go to the theater?   Yes, you go to the theater.

¿**Va Ud. al teatro?**   **Sí, yo voy al teatro.**
Vah oos-TEHD *ahl teh*-AH-*troh?*   *See, yoh voy ahl teh*-AH-*troh.*
Do you go to the theater?   Yes, I go to the theater.

¿**Adónde va el Sr. Campana?**
Ah-DOHN-*deh vah ell sehn*-YOHR *Kahm*-PAH-*nah?*
Where does Mr. Campana go?

Va a la iglesia.
Vah ah lah ee-GLEHS-*yah.*
He goes to church.

¿**Vamos nosotros al teatro o a la iglesia?**
VAH-*mohs noh*-SOH-*trohs ahl teh*-AH-*troh oh ah lah ee*-GLEHS-*yah?*
De we go to the theater or to church?

Vamos al teatro.
VAH-*mohs ahl teh*-AH-*troh.*
We go to the theater.

¿**Adónde van Juan y Pablo?**   **Van a la escuela.**
Ah-DOHN-*deh vahn* HWAHN *ee* PAH-*bloh?*   *Vahn ah lah ess*-KWEH-*lah.*
Where do John and Paul go?   They go to school.

Sres. Campana y Bertín, ¿van Uds. a Madrid?
Sehn-YOH-*rehs Kahm*-PAH-*nah ee Behr*-TEEN, *vahn oos*-TEHD-*ehs*
ah Mah-DREED?*
Messrs. Campana and Bertin, do you go to Madrid?

Sí, señor, allí vamos.
See, sehn-YOHR, *ahl*-YEE VAH-*mohs.*
Yes, sir, we are going there.

¿**Adónde va la Sra. de Garrido?**
Ah-DOHN-*deh vah la sehn*-YOH-*rah deh Gah*-RREE-*doh?*
Where does Mrs. Garrido go?

Va a la tienda.
Vah ah lah t'YEHN-dah.
She goes to the store.

Venimos aquí.
Veh-NEE-mohs ah-KEE.
We come here.

¿Viene el Sr. Berlitz a la clase?
V'YEH-neh ell sehn-YOHR BEHR-leets ah lah KLAH-seh?
Does Mr. Berlitz come to the class?

Sí, viene a la clase.
See, v'YEH-neh ah lah KLAH-seh.
Yes, he comes to the class.

¿Vienen los alumnos a la clase?
V'YEH-nehn lohs ah-LOOM-nohs ah lah KLAH-seh?
Do the pupils come to the class?

Sí, vienen a la clase.
See, v'YEH-nehn ah lah KLAH-seh.
Yes, they come to the class.

 NOTE: Observe how the imperative with *nosotros* is formed in the following verbs.

pongamos = "let us put"
vengamos = "let us come"
traigamos = "let us bring"
escribamos = "let us write"
hablemos = "let us speak"

Pongamos los lápices encima de la mesa.
Pohn-GAH-mohs lohs LAH-pee-thehs enn-THEE-mah deh lah MEH-sah.
Let us put the pencils on the table.

¿En dónde ponemos los lápices?
Enn DOHN-deh poh-NEH-mohs lohs LAH-pee-thehs?
Where do we put the pencils?

Los ponemos encima de la mesa.
Lohs poh-NEH-mohs enn-THEE-mah deh lah MEH-sah.
We put them on the table.

¿Ponemos nosotros las plumas encima de la mesa?
Poh-NEH-mohs noh-SOH-trohs lahs PLOO-mahs enn-THEE-mah deh lah MEH-sah?
Do we put the pens on the table?

No, señor, no las ponemos.
Noh, sehn-YOHR, noh lahs poh-NEH-mohs.
No, sir, we do not put them (there).

¿Ponen los alumnos sus sombreros en la percha?
POH-*nehn lohs ah-*LOOM-*nohs soos sohm-*BREH-*rohs enn lah* PEHR-*chah?*
Do the pupils put their hats on the hook?

Sí, los ponen.
See, lohs POH-*nehn.*
Yes, they put them (there).

¿Ponen Uds. las cajas dentro de sus bolsillos?
POH-*nehn oos-*TEHD-*ehs lahs* KAH-*hahs* DEHN-*troh deh soos bohl-*SEEL-*yohs?*
Do you put the boxes in your pockets?

No, no las ponemos dentro de nuestros bolsillos.
*Noh, noh lahs poh-*NEH-*mohs* DEHN-*troh deh* NWEHS-*trohs bohl-*SEEL-*yohs.*
No, we do not put them in our pockets.

¿De quién es este libro?   Es mío.
*Deh k'*YEHN *ess* ESS-*teh* LEE-*broh?*   *Ess* MEE-*oh.*
Whose is this book?   It is mine.

¿De quién es esta corbata?   Es mía.
*Deh k'*YEHN *ess* ESS-*tah kohr-*BAH-*tah?*   *Ess* MEE-*ah.*
Whose is this tie?   It is mine.

¿Es éste mi lápiz?   Sí, es suyo.
Ess ESS-*teh mee* LAH-*peeth?*   *See, ess* SOO-*yoh.*
Is this my pencil?   Yes, it is yours.

MORE POSSESSIVES: When the possessive is used alone, or *after* the noun, the forms *el mío, la mía, el suyo, la suya, el nuestro, la nuestra,* and their plurals are used. The articles *el* and *la* are sometimes dropped.

Observe the following: "The red pen is mine": *La pluma roja es mía.* "Which are yours?": *¿Cuáles son las suyas?*

¿Es esta corbata del Sr. Díaz?
Ess ESS-*tah* KOHR-*bah-tah dehl sehn-*YOHR DEE-*ahth?*
Is this tie Mr. Díaz'?

Sí, es suya.
See, ess SOO-*yah.*
Yes, it is his.

¿Es aquél el paraguas de la Sra. García?
*Ess ah-*KEHL *ell pah-*RAH-*gwahs deh lah sehn-*YOH-*rah Gahr-*THEE-*ah?*
Is that umbrella Mrs. García's?

Sí, es el suyo.
See, ess ell SOO-*yoh.*
Yes, it is hers.

¿Quién es este profesor?
K'YEHN ess ESS-teh proh-feh-SOHR?
Who is this teacher?

Es el profesor de español.
Ess ell proh-feh-SOHR deh ess-pahn-YOHL.
He is the Spanish teacher.

¿Qué clase es ésta?
Keh KLAH-seh ess ESS-tah?
What class is this?

Es la nuestra.
Ess lah NWEHS-trah.
It is ours.

¿Son suyos estos paraguas?
Sohn soo-yohs ESS-tohs pah-RAH-gwahs?
Are these umbrellas yours?

No, no son nuestros.
Noh, noh sohn NWEHS-trohs.
No, they are not ours.

¿De quiénes son?
Deh k'YEHN-ehs sohn?
Whose are they?

Son de los Sres. Campana y Bertín.
Sohn deh lohs sehn-YOH-rehs Kahm-PAH-nah ee Behr-TEEN.
They are Messrs. Campana and Bertin's.

Son suyos (de ellos).
Sohn soo-yohs (deh EHL-yohs).
They are theirs.

AN OLD SPANISH CUSTOM: If you admire your host's necktie, automobile, horse or house, he may very likely reply: es suyo (or es suya), signifying that it is yours. This does not usually mean he has really given it to you. You should simply thank him effusively for his kindness.

THINKING IN SPANISH
(Answers on page 257)

1. ¿Van los alumnos a la escuela Berlitz?
2. ¿Llevan sus libros allí?
3. ¿Escriben los profesores en la pizarra?
4. Victor y yo vamos al teatro. ¿Adónde vamos?
5. Guadalupe y Mercedes van a la iglesia. ¿Adónde van ellas?
6. Alberto y Francisco van al cabaret. ¿Adónde van?
7. ¿Tienen los alumnos libros de español?
8. ¿Abren sus libros antes de la clase?
9. Y después de la clase, ¿qué hacen?
10. ¿Qué leen Uds., inglés o español?
11. ¿Qué hablamos nosotros, chino o español?
12. ¿Son suyos los libros azules?
13. Mis libros son verdes, ¿de qué color son mis libros?

LECCIÓN 15

¿Qué hay sobre la mesa?
Keh I soh-*breh lah* MEH-*sah?*
What is on the table?

Sobre la mesa hay un tintero, una caja, unos libros, unos lápices.
Soh-*breh lah* MEH-*sah I oon teen*-TEH-*roh,* OO-*nah* KAH-*hah,*
OO-*nohs* LEE-*brohs,* OO-*nohs* LAH-*pee-thehs.*
On the table there are an inkwell, a box, some books, some pencils.

En mi bolsillo hay un pañuelo.
Enn *mee bohl*-SEEL-*yoh I* OON *pahn-yoo*-EH-*loh.*
In my pocket there is a handkerchief.

En la caja hay plumas.
Enn *lah* KAH-*hah I* PLOO-*mahs.*
In the box there are pens.

En mi mano derecha hay un lápiz.
Enn *mee* MAH-*noh deh*-REH-*chah I oon* LAH-*peeth.*
In my right hand there is a pencil.

En mi mano izquierda no hay nada.
Enn *mee* MAH-*noh eethk*-YEHR-*dah noh I* NAH-*dah.*
In my left hand there is nothing.

92

¿Quién está delante de la pared?
K'YEHN ess-TAH deh-LAHN-teh deh lah pah-REHD?
Who is in front of the wall?

Nadie.
NAHD-yeh.
Nobody.

 NOTE to Student: "Nothing" is *nada*, but when you say "there is nothing on the table" you must really say "there is not nothing on the table" (*No hay nada sobre la mesa*). You must also use the double negative for "nobody" which is *nadie*. Ex. "Nobody is here." *No hay nadie aquí.*

Delante de la pizarra hay alguien;
Deh-LAHN-teh deh lah pee-THAH-rrah I AHLG-yehn;
In front of the blackboard there is somebody;

delante de la ventana hay alguien;
deh-LAHN-teh deh lah vehn-TAH-nah I AHLG yehn;
in front of the window there is someone;

en el pasillo no hay nadie;
enn ell pah-SEEL-yoh noh I NAHD-yeh;
in the corridor there is nobody;

en esta clase hay alguien.
enn ESS-tah KLAH-seh I AHLG-yehn.
in this class there is somebody.

¿Hay más de un libro sobre la mesa?
I mahs deh oon LEE-broh SOH-breh lah MEH-sah?
Is there more than one book on the table?

Sí, señor, hay varios (3, 4, 5).
See, sehn-YOHR, I VAHR-yohs (trehs, kwAH-troh, THEEN-koh).
Yes, sir, there are several (3, 4, 5).

¿Son todos los libros grandes?
Sohn TOH-dohs lohs LEE-brohs GRAHN-dehs?
Are all the books large?

No, todos no son grandes;
Noh, TOH-dohs noh sohn GRAHN-dehs;
No, all (of them) are not large;

algunos son grandes y otros son pequeños.
ahl-GOO-nohs sohn GRAHN-dehs ee OH-trohs sohn peh-KEHN-yohs.
some (of them) are large and others are small.

¿No tiene Ud. más que una corbata?
Noh t'YEH-neh oos-TEHD mahs keh OO-nah kohr-BAH-tah?
Have you only one tie?

No, tengo varias.
Noh, TEHN-goh VAHR-yahs.
No, I have several.

¿Son todas sus corbatas del mismo color?
Sohn TOH-*dahs soos* kohr-BAH-*tahs dehl* MEES-*moh koh*-LOHR?
Are all your ties of the same color?

No, algunas son rojas y otras negras o azules.
Noh, ahl-GOO-*nahs sohn* ROH-*hahs ee* OH-*trahs* NEH-*grahs oh ah*-THOO-*lehs.*
No, some are red and others are black or blue.

¿Escribe el profesor algunas letras en la pizarra?
Ess-KREE-*beh ell proh-feh*-SOHR *ahl*-GOO-*nahs* LEH-*trahs*
enn lah pee-THAH-*rrah?*
Does the teacher write some letters on the blackboard?

Sí, escribe algunas.	No, no escribe ninguna.
See, ess-KREE-*beh ahl*-GOO-*nahs.*	*Noh, noh ess*-KREE-*beh neen*-GOO-*nah.*
Yes, he writes some.	No, he does not write any.
¿Hay algún piano aquí?	No, no hay ninguno.
I ahl-GOON *p'*YAH-*noh ah*-KEE?	*Noh, noh I neen*-GOO-*noh.*
Is there a piano here?	No, there is not any.

OBSERVE: *Unos* and *algunos* both mean "some" or "several".

Ud. está delante de la ventana.
Oos-TEHD *ess*-TAH *deh*-LAHN-*teh deh lah vehn*-TAH-*nah.*
You are in front of the window.

¿Delante de qué está Ud.?
Deh-LAHN-*teh deh keh ess*-TAH *oos*-TEHD?
In front of what are you?

Estoy delante de la ventana.
Ess-TOY *deh*-LAHN-*teh deh lah vehn*-TAH-*nah.*
I am in front of the window.

Ud. está al lado del Sr. Valle.
Oos-TEHD *ess*-TAH *ahl* LAH-*doh dehl Sehn*-YOHR VAHL-*yeh.*
You are beside Mr. Valle.

El Sr. Valle está a su lado.
Ell sehn-YOHR VAHL-*yeh ess*-TAH *ah soo* LAH-*doh.*
Mr. Valle is beside you (at your side).

¿Al lado de quién está Ud.?
Ahl LAH-*doh deh k'*YEHN *ess*-TAH *oos*-TEHD?
Beside whom are you?

Estoy al lado del Sr. Valle.
Ess-TOY *ahl* LAH-*doh dehl Sehn*-YOHR VAHL-*yeh.*
I am beside Mr. Valle.

¿Quién está al lado de Ud.?
K'YEHN ess-TAH ahl LAH-doh deh oos-TEHD?
Who is beside you?

El Sr. Valle.
Ell sehn-YOHR VAHL-yeh.
Mr. Valle.

¿Está Ud. al lado de la ventana o de la puerta?
Ess-TAH oos-TEHD ahl LAH-doh deh lah vehn-TAH-nah oh deh lah PWEHR-tah?
Are you beside the window or the door?

Estoy al lado de la puerta.
Ess-TOY ahl LAH-doh deh lah PWEHR-tah.
I am beside the door.

¿Quién está a su lado derecho (a su derecha)?
K'YEHN ess-TAH ah soo LAH-doh deh-REH-choh (ah soo deh-REH-chah)?
Who is at your right side (at your right)?

Ud. está a mi lado derecho (a mi derecha).
Oos-TEHD ess-TAH ah mee LAH-doh deh-REH-choh (ah mee deh-REH-chah).
You are at my right side (at my right).

¿Quién está a su lado izquierdo (a su izquierda)?
K'YEHN ess-TAH ah soo LAHD-oh eethk-YEHR-doh (ah soo eethk-YEHR-dah)?
Who is at your left side (at your left)?

Nadie.
NAHD-yeh.
Nobody.

¿Hay algo a su lado izquierdo?
I AHL-goh ah soo LAH-doh eethk-YEHR-doh?
Is there something at your left side?

No, no hay nada.
Noh, noh I NAH-dah.
No, there is nothing.

HELPFUL hints: When giving directions in Spanish, *a la derecha* means "to the right" and *a la izquierda*, "to the left". But *derecho*, used by itself as a direction, means "straight ahead".

THINKING IN SPANISH
(Answers on page 257)

1. ¿Tiene el profesor un cigarillo en su mano derecha?
2. ¿Qué hay en la mano izquierda de Doña Felicidad?
3. ¿Tiene Chiquita algo en su mano izquierda?
4. ¿Qué tiene ella en su mano derecha?
5. ¿Quién está al lado del profesor?
6. ¿Hay alguien a la derecha del profesor?
7. ¿Hay alguien entre el profesor y Chiquita?
8. ¿Hay un libro en la mano izquierda de Doña Felicidad?
9. ¿Quién está sentado en la silla?   10. ¿Hay algo encima de la mesa?
11. ¿Qué hay debajo del brazo izquierdo del profesor?
12. ¿Hay alguien a la izquierda de Chiquita?
13. ¿Quién está a su derecha?   14. ¿Qué hay encima de la silla?
15. ¿Está Chiquita al lado del profesor?
16. ¿Hay alguien detrás de la mesa?
17. ¿Tiene el profesor un sombrero en la cabeza?
18. ¿Qué tiene el profesor en la cabeza?

LECCIÓN 16

¡Entre!
EHN-*treh!*
Come in!

(Yo) entro en el cuarto.
(Yoh) ENN-*troh enn ell* KWAHR-*toh.*
I enter the room.

(Yo) tomo una silla.
(Yoh) TOH-*moh* OO-*nah* SEEL-*yah.*
I take a chair.

(Yo) me levanto y salgo del cuarto.
*(Yoh) meh leh-*VAHN-*toh ee* SAHL-*goh dehl* KWAHR-*toh.*
I get up and leave the room.

(Yo) me siento.
*(Yoh) meh s'*YEHN-*toh.*
I sit down.

Sr. González, haga el favor de saliı del cuarto.
*Sehn-*YOHR *Gohn-*THAH-*lehth,* AH-*gah ell fah-*VOHR *deh sah-*LEER
dehl KWAHR-*toh.*
Mr. Gonzalez, please, leave the room.

Ud. sale del cuarto.
*Oos-*TEHD SAH-*leh dehl* KWAHR-*toh.*
You leave the room.

Sr. González, ¿se levanta y sale Ud. del cuarto?
*Sehn-*YOHR *Gohn-*THAH-*lehth, seh leh-*VAHN-*tah ee* SAH-*leh oos-*TEHD
dehl KWAHR-*toh?*
Mr. Gonzalez, do you get up and leave the room?

Sí, señor, me levanto y salgo del cuarto.
*See, sehn-*YOHR, *meh leh-*VAHN-*toh ee* SAHL-*goh dehl* KWAHR-*toh.*
Yes, sir, I get up and leave the room.

¿Qué hace este señor?
Keh AH-*theh* ESS-*teh sehn-*YOHR?
What does this gentleman do?

Se levanta y sale del cuarto.
*Seh leh-*VAHN-*tah ee* SAH-*leh dehl* KWAHR-*toh.*
He gets up and leaves the room.

Entre Ud., por favor.
ENN-*treh oos-*TEHD, *pohr fah-*VOHR.
Come in, please.

¿Qué hace Ud.?
Keh AH-*theh oos-*TEHD?
What do you do?

Siéntese Ud.
S'YEHN-*teh-seh oos-*TEHD.
Sit down.

¿Qué hace Ud.?
Keh AH-*theh oos-*TEHD?
What do you do?

Levántese Ud.
*Leh-*VAHN-*teh-seh oos-*TEHD.
Stand up.

¿Qué hace Ud.?
Keh AH-*theh oos-*TEHD?
What do you do?

¿Qué hago yo?
Keh AH-*goh yoh?*
What do I do?

Ud. sale.
*Oos-*TEHD SAH-*leh.*
You go out.

Ud. entra.
*Oos-*TEHD ENN-*trah.*
You come in.

Ud. se sienta.
*Oos-*TEHD *seh s'*YEHN-*tah.*
You sit down.

Ud. se levanta.
*Oos-*TEHD *seh leh-*VAHN-*tah.*
You stand up.

¿Entramos nosotros en la clase antes de la lección?
Enn-TRAH-mohs noh-SOH-trohs enn lah KLAH-seh AHN-tehs deh lah lehkth-YOHN?
Do we enter the class before the lesson?

Sí, entramos en la clase.
See, enn-TRAH-mohs enn lah KLAH-seh.
Yes, we enter the class.

¿Salimos de la clase después de la lección?
Sah-LEE-mohs deh lah KLAH-seh dehs-PWEHS deh lah lehkth-YOHN?
Do we leave the class after the lesson?

Sí, salimos de la cíase.
See, sah-LEE-mohs deh lah KLAH-seh.
Yes, we leave the class.

¿Nos sentamos (nosotros) en las sillas?
Nohs sehn-TAH-mohs (noh-SOH-trohs) enn lahs SEEL-yahs?
Do we sit on the chairs?

Sí, (nosotros) nos sentamos en las sillas.
See, (noh-SOH-trohs) nohs sehn-TAH-mohs enn lahs SEEL-yahs.
Yes, we sit on the chairs.

¿Entran los alumnos?
ENN-trahn lohs ah-LOOM-nohs?
Do the pupils come in?

Sí, (ellos) entran.
See, (EHL-yohs) ENN-trahn.
Yes, they come in.

¿Se sientan los alumnos?
Seh s'YEHN-tahn loh ah-LOOM-nohs?
Do the pupils sit down?

Se sientan.
Seh s'YEHN-tahn.
They sit down.

¿Se levantan (ellos)?
Seh leh-VAHN-tahn (EHL-yohs)?
Do they stand up?

Se levantan.
Seh leh-VAHN-tahn.
They stand up.

¿Salen?
SAH-lehn?
Do they leave?

Salen.
SAH-lehn.
They leave.

NOTE: *Sentarse* and *levantarse* are called reflexive verbs. The verbs are really *sentar* and *levantar*, and the *se* is affixed to the end of the infinitive to show that *me, se,* and *nos* must be used with the appropriate person when the verb is conjugated.

REMEMBER: While it is not always necessary to use *yo*, *Ud.*, *él*, etc. with the verb, the reflexive pronoun must always be used with a reflexive verb.

Levántese Ud.
*Leh-*VAHN-*teh-seh* oos-TEHD.
Stand up.

Me levanto.
*Meh leh-*VAHN-*toh.*
I stand up.

¿Qué hace Ud.?
Keh AH-*theh* oos-TEHD?
What do you do?

Salga Ud.
SAHL-*gah* oos-TEHD.
Go out.

Salgo.
SAHL-*goh.*
I go out.

¿Qué hace Ud.?
Keh AH-*theh* oos-TEHD?
What do you do?

Señores, levántense Uds.
*Sehn-*YOH-*rehs, leh-*VAHN-*tehn-seh* oos-TEHD-*ehs.*
Gentlemen, stand up.

¿Qué hacen Uds?
Keh AH-*thehn* oos-TEHD-*ehs?*
What do you do?

Siéntense Uds.
S'YEHN-*tehn-seh* oos-TEHD-*ehs.*
Sit down.

Nos sentamos.
*Nohs sehn-*TAH-*mohs.*
We sit down.

¿Qué hacen Uds.?
Keh AH-*thehn* oos-TEHD-*ehs?*
What do you do?

¿Qué hace Ud.?
Keh AH-*theh* oos-TEHD?
What do you do?

Siéntese Ud.
S'YEHN-*teh-seh* oos-TEHD.
Sit down.

Me siento.
*Meh s'*YEHN-*toh.*
I sit down.

¿Qué hace Ud.?
Keh AH-*theh* oos-TEHD?
What do you do?

Entre Ud.
ENN-*treh* oos-TEHD.
Come in.

Entro.
ENN-*troh.*
I come in.

Nos levantamos.
*Nohs leh-vahn-*TAH-*mohs.*
We stand up.

¿Qué hacen Uds.?
Keh AH-*thehn* oos-TEHD-*ehs?*
What do you do?

Señores, salgan Uds.
*Sehn-*YOH-*rehs,* SAHL-*gahn* oos-TEHD-*ehs*
Gentlemen, go out.

Salimos.
*Sah-*LEE-*mohs.*
We go out.

Levantémonos.
*Leh-vahn-*TEH*-moh-nohs.*
Let us stand up.

¿Qué hacemos?
*Keh ah-*THEH*-mohs?*
What do we do?

Nos levantamos.
*Nohs leh-vahn-*TAH*-mohs.*
We stand up.

Sentémonos.
*Sehn-*TEH*-moh-nohs.*
Let us sit down.

Salgamos.
*Sahl-*GAH*-mohs.*
Let us go out.

Entremos.
*Enn-*TREH*-mohs.*
Let us go in.

¿Qué hacemos?
*Keh ah-*THEH*-mohs?*
What do we do?

Nos sentamos; salimos; entramos.
*Nohs sehn-*TAH*-mohs; sah-*LEE*-mohs; enn-*TRAH*-mohs.*
We sit down; we go out; we come in.

NOTE: In the reflexive imperative, such as "get up", *(levántese)* the *se* is affixed to the verb. This *se* has no relation to the *se* in lesson 11.

The system of affixing a reflexive pronoun to the affirmative command is also followed for *nosotros.* Ex: *Levantémonos.* "Let's get up". The *s* which belongs between the first *o* and the *n* is left out for easier pronunciation.

El Profesor   Alfredo   Anita   Elena   Roberto

THINKING IN SPANISH
(Answers on page 258)

1. ¿Quién sale de la clase?
2. ¿Se sienta Anita?
3. ¿Se sienta Alfredo?
4. ¿Quién se levanta?
5. ¿Entra Roberto en la clase?
6. ¿Entra Elena?
7. ¿Sale Roberto?
8. ¿Sale el profesor de la clase?
9. ¿Están Roberto y Elena de pié?
10. ¿Qué hace Alfredo?
11. ¿Está sentado el profesor?
12. ¿Se levanta Ud. después de la clase?
13. ¿Se sienta Ud. en la silla?
14. ¿Me siento yo en la silla o en la mesa?
15. ¿Salen los alumnos después de la lección?
16. ¿Nos sentamos nosotros en el cine?
17. ¿Nos sentamos en el autobús?

LECCIÓN 17

Le doy el libro
Leh doy ell LEE-*broh*
I give you the book

Yo le doy el libro (a Ud.).
Yoh leh doy ell LEE-*broh (ah oos*-TEHD).
I give you the book (to you).

¿Qué hago yo?
Keh AH-*goh yoh?*
What do I do?

Ud. me da el libro.
Oos-TEHD *meh dah ell* LEE-*broh.*
You give me the book.

Deme Ud. el lápiz.
DEH-*meh oos*-TEHD *ell* LAH-*peeth.*
Give me the pencil.

¿Qué hace Ud.?
Kēh AH-*theh oos*-TEHD?
What do you do?

Yo le doy el lápiz (a Ud.).
Yoh leh doy ell LAH-*peeth (ah oos*-TEHD).
I give you the pencil (to you).

Yo doy el papel al Sr. Blanco.
*Yoh doy ell pah-*PEHL *ahl sehn-*YOHR BLAHN-*koh.*
I give the paper to Mr. Blanco.

¿Qué doy yo al Sr. Blanco?   Ud. le da el papel.
*Keh doy yoh ahl sehn-*YOHR BLAHN-*koh?*   Oos-TEHD *leh dah ell pah-*PEHL.
What do I give to Mr. Blanco?   You give him the paper.

Haga Ud. el favor de dar su libro a la señorita.
AH-*gah oos-*TEHD *ell fah-*VOHR *deh dahr soo* LEE-*broh*
*ah iah sehn-yoh-*REE-*tah.*
Please give your book to the young lady.

¿Qué le da Ud. a la señorita?   Yo le doy mi libro.
*Keh leh dah oos-*TEHD *ah lah sehn-yoh-*REE-*tah?*   *Yoh leh doy mee* LEE-*broh.*
What do you give to the young lady?   I give her my book.

Señores, yo les doy la lección.
*Sehn-*YOH-*rehs, yoh lehs doy lah lehkth-*YOHN.
Gentlemen, I give the lesson to you.

¿Qué les doy yo (a Uds.)?   Ud. nos da la lección.
*Keh lehs doy yoh (ah oos-*TEHD-*ehs) ?*   Oos-TEHD *nohs dah lah lehkth-*YOHN
What do I give (to) you?   You give us the lesson.

¿Les doy yo (a Uds.) la lección, señoras?
*Lehs doy yoh (ah oos-*TEH-*dehs) lah lehkth-*YOHN, *sehn-*YOH-*rahs?*
Do I give you the lesson, ladies?

Sí, señor, Ud. nos da la lección.
*See, sehn-*YOHR, *oos-*TEHD *nohs dah lah lehkth-*YOHN.
Yes, sir, you give us the lesson.

¿Les doy yo (a Uds.) la lección?
*Lehs doy yoh (ah oos-*TEH-*dehs) lah lehkth-*YOHN?
Do I give you the lesson?

El profesor da ejercicios a los alumnos.
*Ell proh-feh-*SOHR *dah eh-hehr-*THEETH-*yohs ah lohs ah-*LOOM-*nohs.*
The teacher gives exercises to the pupils.

¿Qué les da el profesor a los alumnos?
*Keh lehs dah ell proh-feh-*SOHR *ah lohs ah-*LOOM-*nohs?*
What does the teacher give the pupils?

Les da ejercicios.
*Lehs dah eh-hehr-*THEETH-*yohs.*
He gives them exercises.

NOTE: *Le* means "to you", "to him", "to her", or "to it". Hence, for precision, when *le* is used, the antecedent may also be used. Ex: *Yo le doy el lápiz al señor.* Literally: "I give him the pencil to the gentleman."

Me and *nos* mean "to me" and "to us" respectively.

When the affirmative imperative is used, these indirect object pronouns are attached to end of verb. Ex: "Give me": ¡*Deme!* But when the negative imperative is used, the pronouns are written separately and precede the verb. Ex: "Don't tell me." *No me diga.*

Yo le hablo (a Ud.).
Yoh leh AH-bloh (ah oos-TEHD).
I speak to you.

Yo le digo algo (a Ud.).
Yoh leh DEE-goh AHL-goh (ah oos-TEHD).
I say something to you.

Ud. me habla.
Oos-TEHD meh AH-blah.
You speak to me.

Ud. me dice algo.
Oos-TEHD meh DEE-theh AHL-goh.
You say something to me.

El Sr. Berlitz nos habla.
Ell sehn-YOHR BEHR-leets noh AH-blah.
Mr. Berlitz speaks to us.

Nos dice algo.
Nohs DEE-theh AHL-goh.
He says something to us.

Nosotros hablamos al Sr. Berlitz.
Noh-SOH-trohs ah-BLAH-mohs ahl sehn-YOHR BEHR-leets.
We speak to Mr. Berlitz.

(Nosotros) le decimos algo.
(Noh-SOH-trohs) leh deh-THEE-mohs AHL-goh.
We tell him something.

Los alumnos hablan al Sr. Berlitz.
Lohs ah-LOOM-nohs AH-blahn ahl sehn-YOHR BEHR-leets.
The pupils speak to Mr. Berlitz.

(Ellos) le dicen algo.
(EHL-yohs) leh DEE-thehn AHL-goh.
They say something to him.

Yo le hablo.
Yoh leh AH-bloh.
I speak to you.

Yo le digo mi nombre.
Yoh leh DEE-goh mee NOHM-breh.
I tell you my name.

¿Qué le digo yo a Ud.?
Keh leh DEE-goh yoh ah oos-TEHD?
What do I say to you?

Ud. me dice su nombre.
Oos-TEHD meh DEE-theh soo NOHM-breh.
You tell me your name.

Haga el favor de decirme su nombre.
AH-gah ell fah-VOHR deh deh-THEER-meh soo NOHM-breh.
Please tell me your name.

Dígame Ud. su nombre.
DEE-*gah-meh* oos-TEHD *soo* NOHM-*breh.*
Tell me your name.

Dígame Ud. lo que hay en la mesa.
DEE-*gah-meh* oos-TEHD *loh keh I enn lah* MEH-*sah.*
Tell me what there is on the table.

Sra., diga Ud. su nombre al Sr. Berlitz.
Sehn-YOH-*rah,* DEE-*gah* oos-TEHD *soo* NOHM-*breh ahl sehn-*YOHR BEHR-*leets*
Madam, tell Mr. Berlitz your name.

¿Qué dice Ud. al Sr. Berlitz?
Keh DEE-*theh* oos-TEHD *ahl sehn-*YOHR BEHR-*leets?*
What do you tell Mr. Berlitz?

Le digo mi nombre.
Leh DEE-*goh mee* NOHM-*breh.*
I tell him my name.

Sr. Berlitz: ¿qué le dice esta señora (a Ud.)?
Sehn-YOHR BEHR-*leets, keh leh* DEE-*theh* ESS-*tah sehn-*YOH-*rah* (*ah* oos-TEHD)*
Mr. Berlitz, what does this lady say to you?

Me dice su nombre.	**¿Qué dice Ud.?**
Meh DEE-*theh soo* NOHM-*breh.*	Keh DEE-*theh* oos-TEHD?
She tells me her name.	What do you say?

No digo nada.
Noh DEE-*goh* NAH-*dah.*
I say nothing.

Dígame dónde está la Habana, señor.
DEE-*gah-meh* DOHN-*deh* ess-TAH *lah* Ah-BAH-*nah, sehn-*YOHR.
Tell me where Havana is, sir.

La Habana está en Cuba.
Lah Ah-BAH-*nah ess-*TAH *enn* Koo-*bah.*
Havana is in Cuba.

Yo doy algo al Sr. Berlitz.	**Yo le doy algo.**
Yoh doy AHL-*goh ahl sehn-*YOHR BEHR-*leets.*	Yoh leh doy AHL-*goh.*
I give something to Mr. Berlitz.	I give him something

Yo le doy algo a Ud.	**Yo le doy algo.**
Yoh leh doy AHL-*goh ah* oos-TEHD.	Yoh leh doy AHL-*goh.*
I give you something.	I give you something.

Yo doy el libro al Sr. Berlitz.	**Yo se lo doy.**
Yoh doy ell LEE-*broh ahl sehn-*YOHR BEHR-*leets.*	Yoh seh loh doy.
I give the book to Mr. Berlitz.	I give it to him.

NOTE: When two pronouns are used together after an imperative, they are both affixed to the verb. Ex: "Tell it to me." *Digamelo.*

Caution: You cannot use *le* and *lo* together because of the awkward pronunciation which would result. Therefore for "tell him it" you must say *digaselo.* The *se* in this construction stands for *le.* Ex: "Don't give it to him": ¡No se lo dé!

This *se* has no connection with the *se* in Lessons 11 and 16.

Ud. me da el libro azul.
*Oos-*TEHD *meh dah ell* LEE-*broh ah-*THOOL.
You give me the blue book.

Ud. me lo da.
*Oos-*TEHD *meh loh dah.*
You give it to me.

¿Nos da algo el Sr. Berlitz?
Nohs dah AHL-*goh ell sehn-*YOHR BEHR-*leets?*
Does Mr. Berlitz give us something?

Sí, señor, nos da algo.
*See, sehn-*YOHR, *nohs dah* AHL-*goh.*
Yes, sir, he gives us something.

¿Nos da el Sr. Berlitz el libro?
*Nohs dah ell sehn-*YOHR BEHR-*leets ell* LEE-*broh?*
Does Mr. Berlitz give us the book?

Nos lo da.
Nohs loh dah.
He gives it to us.

¿Nos da la caja?
Nohs dah lah KAH-*hah?*
Does he give us the box?

Nos la da.
Nohs lah dah.
He gives it to us.

Yo doy a Uds. algo.
*Yoh doy ah oos-*TEHD-*ehs* AHL-*goh.*
I give something to you.

Yo les doy algo.
Yoh lehs doy AHL-*goh.*
I give you something.

Yo les doy mi corbata.
*Yoh lehs doy mee kohr-*BAH-*tah.*
I give you my tie.

Yo se la doy.
Yoh seh lah doy.
I give it to you.

Yo les doy mis libros.
Yoh lehs doy mees LEE-*brohs.*
I give you my books.

Yo se los doy.
Yoh seh lohs doy.
I give them to you.

¿Me da Ud. algo?
*Meh dah oos-*TEHD AHL-*goh?*
Do you give something to me?

No, señor, no le doy nada.
*Noh, sehn-*YOHR, *noh leh doy* NAH-*dah.*
No, sir, I do not give anything to you.

¿Me da Ud. su libro?
*Meh dah oos-*TEHD *soo* LEE-*broh?*
Do you give me your book?

No, señor, no se lo doy.
*Noh, sehn-*YOHR, *noh seh loh doy.*
No, sir, I do not give it to you.

¿Da Ud. algo al Sr. Berlitz?
*Dah oos-*TEHD AHL-*goh ahl sehn-*YOHR BEHR-*leets.*
Do you give something to Mr. Berlitz?

Sí, le doy algo.
See, leh doy AHL-*goh.*
Yes, I give him something.

¿Le da Ud. su libro?
*Leh dah oos-*TEHD *soo* LEE-*broh?*
Do you give him your book?

No, no se lo doy.
Noh, noh seh loh doy.
No, I do not give it to him.

¿Le doy yo algo?
Leh doy yoh AHL-*goh?*
Do I give him something?

¿Qué le doy?
Keh leh doy?
What do I give him?

¿Le doy la pluma?
Leh doy lah PLOO-*mah?*
Do I give you the pen?

Sí, señor, me la da.
*See, sehn-*YOHR, *meh lah dah.*
Yes, sir, you give it to me.

Sres., ¿les digo yo algo?
*Sehn-*YOH-*rehs, lehs* DEE-*goh yoh* AHL-*goh?*
Gentlemen, do I tell you anything?

Sí, señor, nos dice algo.
*See, sehn-*YOHR, *nohs* DEE-*theh* AHL-*goh.*
Yes, sir, you tell us something.

Gracias, Señor

THINKING IN SPANISH
(Answers on page 258)

1. ¿Le da el profesor un libro a Doña Felicidad?
2. ¿Qué le da Chiquita al profesor?
3. ¿Qué hace Doña Felicidad con la mano izquierda?
4. ¿Le dan Chiquita y Doña Felicidad una corbata al profesor?
5. ¿Quién le habla a Chiquita?
6. ¿Qué le da el profesor a Chiquita?
7. ¿Le dice algo Doña Felicidad a Capitán, el perro de Chiquita?
8. ¿Le da algo?   9. ¿Qué dice Capitán?
10. Los alumnos de la clase de español, ¿le hablan al profesor en español?
11. ¿Le dicen "buenos días", antes de la clase?
12. ¿Qué les dice el profesor después de la clase?
13. Dígame lo que hay en la mano izquierda de Doña Felicidad.
14. ¿Qué me dice Ud.?
15. ¿Qué le dice Doña Felicidad al profesor?
16. Yo le doy un chocolate. ¿Qué me dice Ud.?
17. Dígame su nombre, por favor.   18. ¿Qué me dice?

LECCIÓN 18

¿Con qué andamos?
Kohn keh ahn-DAH-mohs?
With what do we walk?

¿Qué hacemos con un lápiz?
Keh ah-THEY-mohs kohn oon LAH-peeth?
What do we do with a pencil?

Escribimos con un lápiz.
Ess-kree-BEE-mohs kohn oon LAH-peeth.
We write with a pencil.

Escribimos con una pluma.
Ess-kree-BEE-mohs kohn OO-nah PLOO-mah.
We write with a pen.

Con un cuchillo cortamos.
Kohn oon koo-CHEEL-yoh kohr-TAH-mohs.
With a knife we cut.

¿Con una pluma?
Kohn OO-nah PLOO-mah?
With a pen?

¿Con un cuchillo?
Kohn oon koo-CHEEL-yoh?
With a knife?

¿Con las manos?
Kohn lahs MAH-nohs?
With our hands?

Con las manos tomamos.
Kohn lahs MAH-nohs toh-MAH-mohs.
With our hands we take.

Con los piés caminamos.
Kohn lohs pee-EHS kah-mee-NAH-mohs.
With our feet we walk.

Con los oidos oímos.
Kohn lohs oh-EE-dohs oh-EE-mohs.
With our ears we hear.

Abro los ojos, veo.
AH-broh lohs OH-hohs, VEH-oh.
I open my eyes, I see.

¿Con los piés?
Kohn lohs pee-EHS?
With our feet?

Con los ojos vemos.
Kohn lohs OH-hohs VEH-mohs.
With our eyes we see.

Cierro los ojos, no veo.
Th'YEH-rroh lohs OH-hohs, noh VEH-oh.
I close my eyes, I do not see.

Ud. está delante de mi, yo le veo.
Oos-TEHD ess-TAH deh-LAHN-teh deh mee, yoh leh VEH-oh.
You are in front of me, I see you.

El Sr. Berlitz no está aquí, no veo al Sr. Berlitz.
Ell sehn-YOHR BEHR-leets noh ess-TAH ah-KEE, no VEH-oh ahl
sehn-YOHR BEHR-leets.
Mr. Berlitz is not here, I do not see Mr. Berlitz.

¿Está la mesa delante de Ud.?
Ess-TAH lah MEH-sah deh-LAHN-teh deh oos-TEHD?
Is the table in front of you?

¿Ve Ud. la mesa?
Veh oos-TEHD lah MEH-sah?
Do you see the table?

¿Está la ventana detrás de Ud.?
Ess-TAH lah vehn-TAH-nah deh-TRAHS deh oos-TEHD?
Is the window behind you?

¿Ve Ud. la ventana?
Veh oos-TEHD lah vehn-TAH-nah?
Do you see the window?

Cierre Ud. los ojos.
Th'YEH-rreh oos-TEHD lohs OH-hohs.
Close your eyes.

¿Ve Ud.?
Veh oos-TEHD?
Do you see?

¿Qué ve Ud. sobre la mesa?
Keh veh oos-TEHD SOH-breh lah MEH-sah?
What do you see on the table?

Yo veo un libro.
Yoh VEH-oh oon LEE-broh.
I see a book.

¿A quién ve Ud. aquí?
Ah k'YEHN veh oos-TEHD ah-KEE?
Whom do you see here?

Yo veo al Sr. Torres.
Yoh VEH-oh ahl sehn-YOHR TOH-rrehs.
I see Mr. Torres.

NOTE to Student: In Spanish you must use the preposition *a* before a word representing a person when it is the direct object of a verb. This is not necessary before words representing places or things. Ex: "I see the table": *Veo la mesa.* "I see the president": *Veo al presidente.* "Do you hear Miss Alvarez?" *¿Oye Ud. a la Srta. Álvarez?*

Yo hablo, Ud. me oye hablar.
Yoh AH-*bloh, oos-*TEHD *meh* OH-*yeh ah-*BLAHR.
I speak, you hear me speak.

¿A quién oye Ud. bablar?
*Ah k'*YEHN OH-*yeh oos-*TEHD *ah-*BLAHR?
Whom do you hear speak?

Yo le oigo.
Yoh leh OY-*goh.*
I hear you.

Yo llamo a la puerta.
*Yoh l'*YAH-*moh ah lah* PWEHR-*tah.*
I knock at the door.

¿Me oye Ud. llamar?
Meh OH-*yeh oos-*TEHD *l'yah-*MAHR?
Do you hear me knocking?

Sí, le oigo llamar.
See, leh OY-*goh l'yah-*MAHR.
Yes, I hear you knocking.

¿Oye Ud. a alguien llamar?
OH-*yeh oos-*TEHD *ah* AHLG-*yehn l'yah-*MAHR?
Do you hear someone knocking?

Sí, oigo llamar.
See, OY-*goh l'yah-*MAHR.
Yes, I hear (someone) knocking.

¿Oímos los automóviles en la calle?
*Oh-*EE-*mohs lohs ah-oo-toh-*MOH-*vee-lehs enn lah* KAHL-*yeh?*
Do we hear the automobiles on the street?

Sí, los oímos.
*See, lohs oh-*EE-*mohs.*
Yes, we near them.

¿Oyen los alumnos hablar al profesor?
OH-*yehn lohs ah-*LOOM-*nohs ah-*BLAHR *ahl proh-feh-*SOHR?
Do the pupils hear the teacher speak?

Sí, ellos le oyen.
See, EHL-*yohs leh* OH-*yehn.*
Yes, they hear him.

¿Qué oye Ud. por radio, música o conversación?
Keh OH-*yeh* oos-TEHD *pohr lah* RAHD-*yoh,* MOO-*see-kah oh*
*kohn-vehr-sahth-*YOHN?
What do you hear on the radio, music or conversation?

Yo oigo música.
Yoh OY-*goh* MOO-*see-kah.*
I hear music.

NOTE: When a double verb construction is used, as in "I hear him speak", *Yo le oigo hablar,* the second verb is put into the infinitive. Also notice "I see him coming". *Yo le veo venir.*

Yo veo un libro, un lápiz, una pluma.
Yoh VEH-*oh oon* LEE-*broh, oon* LAH-*peeth,* OO-*nah* PLOO-*mah.*
I see a book, a pencil, a pen.

Yo veo a un señor, una señora.
Yoh VEH-*oh ah oon sehn-*YOHR, OO-*nah. sehn-*YOH-*rah.*
I see a gentleman, a lady.

¿Qué ve Ud. en la calle?
*Keh veh oos-*TEHD *enn lah* KAHL-*yeh?*
What do you see in the street?

Veo automóviles y a muchas personas.
VEH-*oh ah-oo-toh-*MOH-*vee-lehs ee ah* MOO-*chahs pehr-*SOH-*nahs.*
I see automobiles and many people.

Yo oigo un automóvil.
Yoh OY-*goh oon ah-oo-toh-*MOH-*veel.*
I hear an automobile.

Yo oigo a un señor.
Yoh OY-*goh ah oon sehn-*YOHR.
I hear a gentleman.

Con la nariz olemos.
*Kohn lah nah-*REETH *oh-*LEH-*mohs.*
With our nose we smell.

Las flores huelen bien;
Lahs FLOH-*rehs* WEH-*lehn b'*YEHN;
Flowers smell good;

la tinta no huele bien, huele mal.
lah TEEN-*tah noh* WEH-*leh b'*YEHN, WEH-*leh mahl.*
ink does not smell good, it smells bad.

El gas huele mal.
Ell gahs WEH-*leh mahl.*
Gas smells bad.

Aquí tenemos unas flores: una rosa, un tulipán,
*Ah-*KEE *teh-*NEH-*mohs* OO-*nahs* FLOH-*rehs:* OO-*nah* ROH-*sah, oon too-lee-*PAHN,
Here we have some flowers: a rose, a tulip,

unas violetas, un clavel y un pensamiento.
*oo-nahs v'yoh-*LEH-*tahs, oon klah-*VEHL *ee oon pehn-sahm-*YEHN-*toh.*
some violets, a carnation and a pansy.

¿Huele bien la rosa?
WEH-*leh* b'YEHN *lah* ROH-*sah?*
Does the rose smell good?

Sí, la rosa huele bien.
See, lah ROH-*sah* WEH-*leh* b'YEHN.
Yes, the rose smells good.

Con la boca comemos y bebemos.
Kohn lah BOH-*kah koh*-MEH-*mohs ee beh*-BEH-*mohs.*
With our mouth we eat and drink.

Comemos pan, carne, vegetales y fruta.
Koh-MEH-*mohs pahn,* KAHR-*neh, veh-heh*-TAH-*lehs ee* FROO-*tah.*
We eat bread, meat, vegetables and fruit.

Carnes: El pollo, el bistec, las chuletas
KAHR-*nehs: Ell* POHL-*yoh, el bees*-TEHK, *lahs choo*-LEH-*tahs*
de puerco (de cordero), el filete, el pescado.
deh PWEHR-*koh (deh kohr*-DEH-*roh) , ell fee*-LEH-*teh, ell pehs*-KAH-*doh.*
Meats: Chicken, beef steak, pork chops (lamb), steak, fish.

Frutas: la manzana, la pera, las uvas,
FROO-*tahs: lah mahn*-THAH-*nah, lah* PEH-*rah, lahs* OO-*vahs,*
Fruits: the apple, the pear, grapes,

la fresa, el melocoton, el mango, el plátano, la piña.
lah FREH-*sah, ell meh-loh-koh*-TOHN, *ell* MAHN-*goh, ell* PLAH-*tah-noh,*
lah PEEN-*yah.*
the strawberry, the peach, the mango, the banana, the pineapple.

Vegetales: Las habichuelas, los frijoles,
Veh-heh-TAH-*lehs: Lahs ah-bee*-CHWEH-*lahs, lohs free*-HOH-*lehs,*
Vegetables: Beans, kidney beans,

las judías verdes, los guisantes, la col, las papas,
lahs hoo-DEE-*ahs* VEHR-*dehs, lohs gee*-SAHN-*tehs, lah kohl, lahs* PAH-*pahs*
string beans, peas, cabbage, potatoes,

la coliflor, los espárragos, las zanahorias, el arroz, las cebollas.
lah koh-lee-FLOHR, *lohs ess*-PAH-*rrah-gohs, lahs thah-nah*-OHR-*yahs,*
ell ah-RROHTH, *lahs theh*-BOHL-*yahs.*
cauliflower, asparagus, carrots, rice, onions.

Bebemos agua, vino, cerveza, te, café, leche, chocolate.
Beh-BEH-*mohs* AH-*gwah,* VEE-*noh, thehr*-VEH-*thah, teh, kah*-FEH, LEH-*cheh,*
choh koh-LAH-*teh.*
We drink water, wine, beer, tea, coffee, milk, chocolate.

THINKING IN SPANISH
(Answers on page 258)

1. ¿Con qué huele el profesor la cebolla?
2. ¿Huele bien la cebolla?   3. ¿Huele bien la rosa?
4. ¿Huele Doña Felicidad la rosa o la cebolla?
5. ¿Vemos las cosas que están detrás de nosotros?
6. ¿Vemos las cosas que están delante de nosotros?
7. Oímos a alguien llamar a la puerta?
8. ¿Oímos hablar al presidente por la radio?   9. ¿Comemos pan?
10. ¿Come Ud. pan con mantequilla?   11. ¿Beben los ingleses mucho té?
12. ¿Qué bebe Ud., cerveza o vino?   13. ¿Beben los cubanos ron?
14. ¿Pone Ud. azúcar en su café?
15. ¿Qué pone Ud. en su té, leche o limón?
16. ¿Con qué cortamos la carne?
17. ¿Comemos los guisantes con un cuchillo?
18. ¿Hablamos con nuestros amigos por teléfono?
19. ¿Con qué escribe Ud., con una pluma o con un lápiz?

LECCIÓN 19

¿Con qué comemos?
*Kohn keh koh-*MEH*-mohs?*
With what do we eat?

¿Con qué tomamos la sopa?
*Kohn keh toh-*MAH*-mohs lah* SOH*-pah?*
With what do we eat soup?

Tomamos la sopa con una cuchara.
*Toh-*MAH*-mohs lah* SOH*-pah kohn* OO*-nah koo-*CHAH*-rah.*
We eat soup with a spoon.

¿Con qué cortamos la carne?
*Kohn keh kohr-*TAH*-mohs lah* KAHR*-neh?*
With what do we cut meat?

Cortamos la carne con un cuchillo.
*Kohr-*TAH*-moks lah* KAHR*-neh kohn oon koo-*CHEEL*-yoh.*
We cut meat with a knife.

116

¿Con qué comemos la carne?
Kohn keh koh-MEH-mohs lah KAHR-neh?
With what do we eat meat?

Comemos la carne con un tenedor.
Koh-MEH-mohs lah KAHR-neh kohn oon teh-neh-DOHR.
We eat meat with a fork.

Aquí hay un plato, una fuente.
Ah-KEE I oon PLAH-toh, OO-nah FWEHN-teh.
Here is a plate, a platter.

¿En qué traemos la carne?
Enn keh trah-EH-mohs lah KAHR-neh?
On what do we bring the meat?

La traemos en una fuente.
Lah trah-EH-mohs enn OO-nah FWEHN-teh.
We bring it on a platter.

¿En qué la comemos?
Enn keh luh koh-MEH-mohs?
From what do we eat it?

La comemos en un plato.
Lah koh-MEH-mohs enn oon PLAH-toh.
We eat it from a plate.

La copa, el vaso, la taza.
Lah KOH-pah, ell VAH-soh, lah TAH-thah.
The wine glass, the glass, the cup.

¿En qué bebemos el vino?
Enn keh beh-BEH-mohs ell VEE-noh?
From what do we drink wine?

¿En qué bebemos el té?
Enn keh beh-BEH-mohs ell teh?
From what do we drink tea?

El pan es bueno para comer.
Ell pahn ess BWEH-noh PAH-rah koh-MEHR.
Bread is good to eat.

El papel no es bueno para comer.
Ell pah-PEHL noh ess BWEH-noh PAH-rah koh-MEHR.
Paper is not good to eat.

Es malo.
Ess MAH-loh.
It is bad.

El agua es buena para beber.
Ell AH-gwah ess BWEH-nah PAH-rah beh-BEHR.
Water is good to drink.

La tinta no es buena para beber.
Lah TEEN-tah noh ess BWEH-nah PAH-rah beh-BEHR.
Ink is not good to drink.

Es mala.
Ess MAH-lah.
It is bad.

Este lápiz no escribe bien, no es bueno.
Ess-*teh* LAH-*peeth noh* ess-KREE-*beh b'*YEHN, *noh ess* BWEH-*noh.*
This pencil does not write well, it is not good.

Este cuchillo no corta bien, es malo.
Ess-*teh koo-*CHLEL-*yoh noh* KOHR-*tah b'*YEHN, *ess* MAH-*loh.*
This knife does not cut well, it is bad.

Esta pluma está rota, es mala.
Ess-*tah* PLOO-*mah ess-*TAH ROH-*tah, ess* MAH-*lah.*
This pen is broken, it is bad.

Escribe mal.
Ess-KREE-*beh mahl.*
It writes badly.

La otra pluma es buena, escribe muy bien.
Lah OH-*trah* PLOO-*mah ess* BWEH-*nah, ess-*KREE-*beh mwee b'*YEHN.
The other pen is good, it writes very well.

La rosa huele bien; la rosa tiene buen olor,
Lah ROH-*sah* WEH-*leh b'*YEHN; *lah* ROH-*sah t'*YEH-*neh* BWEHN *oh-*LOHR,
The rose smells good; the rose has a good odor,

tiene un olor agradable.
*t'*YEH-*neh oon oh-*LOHR *ah-grah-*DAH-*bleh.*
it has a pleasant odor.

La tinta huele mal; la tinta tiene mal olor,
Lah TEEN-*tah* WEH-*leh mahl; lah* TEEN-*tah t'*YEH-*neh mahl oh-*LOHR,
Ink smells bad; ink has a bad odor,

tiene un olor desagradable.
*t'*YEH-*neh oon oh-*LOHR *deh-sah-grah-*DAH-*bleh.*
it has an unpleasant odor.

La fresa tiene un olor y un sabor muy agradables.
Lah FREH-*sah t'*YEH-*neh oon oh-*LOHR *ee oon sah-*BOHR
*mwee ah-grah-*DAH-*blehs.*
The strawberry has a very pleasant odor and (a very pleasant) taste.

El café con azúcar tiene un sabor agradable.
*Ell kah-*FEH *kohn ah-*THOO-*kahr t'*YEH-*neh oon sah-*BOHR *ah-grah-*DAH-*bleh.*
Coffee with sugar has a pleasant flavor.

El café con cerveza tiene un sabor desagradable.
*Ell kah-*FEH *kohn thehr-*VEH-*thah t'*YEH-*neh oon sah-*BOHR
*deh-sah-grah-*DAH-*bleh.*
Coffee with beer has an unpleasant flavor.

¿Qué sabor tiene el limón?
*Keh sah-*BOHR *t'*YEH-*neh ell lee-*MOHN?
What taste has lemon?

Un sabor agrio.
*Oon sah-*BOHR AH-*gree-oh.*
A sour taste.

¿Cuál es el sabor del azúcar?   Es dulce.
KWAHL *ess ell sah-*BOHR *dehl ah-*THOO-*kahr?*   *Ess* DOOL-*theh.*
What is the taste of sugar?   It is sweet.

¿Cuál es el gusto de la sopa sin sal?   Es soso.
KWAHL *ess ell* GOOS-*toh deh lah* SOH-*pah seen sahl?*   *Ess* SOH-*soh.*
What is the taste of soup without salt?   It is flat.

¿Qué tal es el gusto del café sin azúcar?   Es amargo.
Keh tahl ess ell GOOS-*toh dehl kah-*FEH *seen ah-*THOO-*kahr?*   *Ess ah-*MAHR-*goh.*
What is the taste of coffee without sugar?   It is bitter.

 A USEFUL IDIOM: *¿Qué tal?* is still another way of saying "how"; you will also hear it used by itself, as a greeting, instead of *"¿Cómo está?"*

Las cosas agradables nos gustan,
Lahs KOH-*sahs ah-grah-*DAH-*blehs nohs* GOOS-*tahn,*
We like pleasant things;

las cosas desagradables no nos gustan.
lahs KOH-*sahs dehs-ah-grah-*DAH-*blehs noh nohs* GOOS-*tahn.*
we do not like unpleasant things.

El olor de la rosa me gusta: es agradable.
*Ell oh-*LOHR *deh lah* ROH-*sah meh* GOOS-*tah: ess ah-grah-*DAH-*bleh.*
I like the odor of the rose; it is pleasant.

El olor del gas no me gusta.
*Ell oh-*LOHR *dehl gahs noh meh* GOOS-*tah.*
I do not like the smell of gas.

El café en el vino no me gusta;
*Ell kah-*FEH *enn ell* VEE-*noh noh meh* GOOS-*tah;*
I do not like coffee in wine;

tiene sabor desagradable.
*t'*YEH-*neh sah-*BOHR *deh-sah-grah-*DAH-*bleh.*
it has an unpleasant taste.

El azúcar en el café me gusta.
*Ell ah-*THOO-*kahr enn ell kah-*FEH *meh* GOOS-*tah.*
I like sugar in coffee.

¿Toma Ud. café sin leche?   Sí, pero no me gusta.
TOH-*mah oos-*TEHD *kah-*FEH *seen* LEH-*cheh?*   *See,* PEH-*roh noh meh* GOOS-*tah.*
Do you take coffee without milk?   Yes, but I do not like it.

 **IMPORTANT NOTE:** To translate "to like" use the impersonal *gustar*.

You are really saying, "it pleases me". Ex: "She likes champagne": *El champán le gusta.* But if the object of your likes is plural, then the verb *gustar* is used in the plural. Ex: "I like beans": *Los frijoles me gustan.* A verb in its infinitive form can also be used with *gustar.* Ex: "Do you like to dance the rumba?": *¿Le gusta a Ud. bailar la rumba?*

¿Les gustan a Uds. las fresas?
Lehs GOOS-tahn ah oos-TEH-dehs lahs FREH-sahs?
Do you like strawberries?

Sí, nos gustan mucho.
See, nohs GOOS-tahn MOO-choh.
Yes, we like them very much.

¿Les gustan las flores a las señoras?
Lehs GOOS-tahn lahs FLOH-rehs ah lahs sehn-YOH-rahs?
Do ladies like flowers?

Sí, les gustan mucho.
See, lehs GOOS-tahn MOO-choh.
Yes, they like them very much.

¿Le gusta a Ud. hablar español?
Leh GOOS-tah ah oos-TEHD ah-BLAHR ess-pahn-YOHL?
Do you like to speak Spanish?

Sí, me gusta mucho.
See, meh GOOS-tah MOO-choh.
Yes, I like it very much.

¿Le gusta bailar?
Leh GOOS-tah bah-ee-LAHR?
Do you like to dance?

Sí, me gusta mucho.
See, meh GOOS-tah MOO-choh.
Yes, I like it very much.

Las cosas que tienen formas
Lahs KOH-sahs keh t'YEH-nehn FOHR-mahs
o colores agradables son hermosas.
oh koh-LOH-rehs ah-grah-DAH-blehs sohn ehr-MOH-sahs.
Things which have pleasant forms or colors are beautiful.

La estatua de Venus es hermosa;
Lah ess-TAH-twah deh VEH-noos ess ehr-MOH-sah;
The statue of Venus is beautiful;

la catedral de México es hermosa.
lah kah-teh-DRAHL deh MEH-hee-koh ess ehr-MOH-sah.
the cathedral of Mexico is beautiful.

En los museos hay cuadros hermosos y estatuas hermosas.
*Enn lohs moo-*SEH*-ohs I* KWAH*-drohs ehr-*MOH*-sohs ee*
*ees-*TAH*-twahs ehr-*MOH*-sahs.*
In the museums there are beautiful pictures and beautiful statues.

Lo que es desagradable a la vista es feo.
*Loh keh ess dehs-ah-grah-*DAH*-bleh ah lah* VEES*-tah ess* FEH*-oh.*
What is unpleasant to the sight is ugly.

La cabeza de Medusa no es agradable para ver: es fea.
*Lah kah-*BEH*-thah deh Meh-*DOO*-sah noh ess ah-grah-*DAH*-bleh* PAH*-rah vehr:*
ess FEH*-ah.*
The head of Medusa is not pleasant to see: it is ugly.

El mono no es hermoso; es feo.
Ell MOH*-noh noh ess ehr-*MOH*-soh; ess* FEH*-oh.*
The monkey is not beautiful; it is ugly.

El caballo es un animal hermoso; el camello es feo.
*Ell kah-*BAHL*-yoh ess oon ah-nee-*MAHL *ehr-*MOH*-soh; ell kah-*MEHL*-yoh*
ess FEH*-oh.*
The horse is a beautiful animal; the camel is ugly.

El pavo real es hermoso; el buho es feo.
Ell PAH*-voh reh-*AHL *ess ehr-*MOH*-soh; ell* BOO*-oh ess* FEH*-oh.*
The peacock is beautiful; the owl is ugly.

THINKING IN SPANISH
(Answers on page 259)

1. ¿Con qué cortamos la carne?   2. ¿Comemos la carne con un tenedor?
3. ¿Con qué tomamos la sopa?   4. ¿Le gusta a Ud. el café sin azúcar?
5. ¿Nos gusta la sopa sin sal?
6. ¿En qué comemos la carne?
7. ¿Nos gusta el olor de la rosa?
8. ¿Les gustan los trajes hermosos a la señoritas?
9. ¿Es Dolores del Río hermosa?
10. ¿Es Boris Karloff hermoso?
11. ¿Habla el profesor el español bien?
12. Y Ud. ¿habla el inglés bien o mal?
13. ¿Baila Ud. bien?
14. ¿Qué tal baila Ud. la rumba?

No puedo ver
Noh PWEH-*doh vehr*
I cannot see

Yo toco la mesa, la silla, el libro, etc.
Yoh TOH-*koh lah* MEH-*sah, lah* SEEL-*yah, el* LEE-*broh, eht-*THEH-*teh-rah.*
I touch the table, the chair, the book, etc.

Toque Ud. la mesa.
TOH-*keh oos-*TEHD *lah* MEH-*sah.*
Touch the table.

Ud. toca la mesa.
*Oos-*TEHD TOH-*kah lah* MEH-*sah.*
You touch the table.

¿Qué hace Ud.?
Keh AH-*theh oos-*TEHD?
What do you do?

Toque Ud. el libro, la silla, la mesa, etc.
TOH-*keh oos-*TEHD *ell* LEE-*broh, lah* SEEL-*yah, lah* MEH-*sah, eht-*THEH-*teh-rah.*
Touch the book, the chair, the table, etc.

Toque Ud. el techo.
Toh-*keh* oos-TEHD *ell* TEH-*choh.*
Touch the roof.

Ud. no puede tocar el techo.
Oos-TEHD *noh* PWEH-*deh* toh-KAHR *ell* TEH-*choh.*
You cannot touch the roof.

Yo no puedo tocar el techo.
Yoh noh PWEH-*doh* toh-KAHR *ell* TEH-*choh.*
I cannot touch the roof.

El señor no puede tocar el techo.
Ell sehn-YOHR *noh* PWEH-*deh* toh-KAHR *ell* TEH-*choh.*
The gentleman cannot touch the roof.

Ud. puede tocar la mesa.
Oos-TEHD PWEH-*deh* toh-KAHR *lah* MEH-*sah.*
You can touch the table.

Yo puedo tocar la silla.
Yoh PWEH-*doh* toh-KAHR *lah* SEEL-*yah.*
I can touch the chair.

El Sr. Petisco puede tocar el libro.
Ell sehn-YOHR *Peh*-TEES-*koh* PWEH-*deh* toh-KAHR *ell* LEE-*broh.*
Mr. Petisco can touch the book.

Yo cierro la puerta, la puerta está cerrada;
*Yoh th'*YEH-*rroh lah* PWEHR-*tah, lah* PWEHR-*tah ess*-TAH *theh*-RRAH-*dah;*
I close the door, the door is closed;

no puedo salir.
noh PWEH-*doh sah*-LEER.
I cannot go out.

Abro la puerta, la puerta está abierta; puedo salir.
AH-*broh lah* PWEHR-*tah, lah* PWEHR-*tah ess*-TAH *ahb*-YEHR-*tah;*
PWEH-*doh sah*-LEER.
I open the door, the door is open; I can go out.

Tengo un lápiz; puedo escribir.
TEHN-*goh oon* LAH-*peeth;* PWEH-*doh ess*-*kree*-BEER.
I have a pencil; I can write.

Este señor no tiene lápiz; no puede escribir.
Ess-*teh sehn*-YOHR *noh t'*YEH-*neh* LAH-*peeth; noh* PWEH-*deh ess*-*kree*-BEER.
This gentleman has no pencil; he cannot write.

El techo está alto, no lo puedo tocar (no puedo tocarlo).
Ell TEH-*choh* ess-TAH AHL-*toh, noh loh* PWEH-*doh toh-*KAHR
(noh PWEH-*doh toh-*KAHR-*loh).*
The roof is high, I cannot touch it. (I cannot touch it.)

La pizarra está baja;
*Lah pee-*THAH-*rrah ess-*TAH BAH-*hah;*
The blackboard is low;

la puedo tocar (puedo tocarla).
lah PWEH-*doh toh-*KAHR (PWEH-*doh toh-*KAHR-*lah).*
I can touch it.

Puedo ver las cosas que están delante de mi;
PWEH-*doh vehr lahs* KOH-*sahs keh ess-*TAHN *deh-*LAHN-*teh deh mee;*
I can see the things which are in front of me;

no puedo ver las cosas que están detrás de mi.
noh PWEH-*doh vehr lahs* KOH-*sahs keh ess-*TAHN *deh-*TRAHS *deh mee.*
I cannot see the things which are behind me.

Cierro los ojos; no puedo ver.
*Th'*YEH-*rroh lohs* OH-*hohs; noh* PWEH-*doh vehr.*
I close my eyes; I cannot see.

Yo no tengo cortaplumas; no puedo cortar el papel.
Yoh noh TEHN-*goh kohr-tah-*PLOO-*mahs;*
noh PWEH-*doh kohr-*TAHR *ell pah-*PEHL.
I have no penknife; I cannot cut the paper.

El Sr. Berlitz lleva anteojos; puede ver con sus anteojos;
*Ell sehn-*YOHR BEHR-*leets l'*YEH-*vah ahn-teh-*OH-*hohs;* PWEH-*deh vehr kohn*
*soos ahn-teh-*OH-*hohs;*
Mr. Berlitz wears glasses; he can see with his glasses;

sin sus anteojos no puede ver.
*seen soos ahn-teh-*OH-*hohs noh* PWEH-*deh vehr.*
without his glasses he cannot see.

NOTE: As we have seen in earlier lessons, all Spanish verbs fall into three conjugations whose infinitives end in *-ar, -er, -ir.*

The verbs *poder* (to be able or can) and *querer* (to wish or want) are used with infinitives of the other verbs. Ex: "She wants to go to the movies": *Ella quiere ir al cine.* "Her mother says she cannot go out": *Su madre dice que no puede salir.*

¿Puedo yo tocar el techo?
PWEH-*doh yoh toh-*KAHR *ell* TEH-*choh?*
Can I touch the roof?

No, Ud. no puede tocar el techo (tocarlo).
*Noh, oos-*TEHD *noh* PWEH-*deh toh-*KAHR *ell* TEH-*choh* (*toh-*KAHR-*loh*).
No, you cannot touch the roof (touch it).

¿Puedo tocar la luz eléctrica?
PWEH-*doh toh-*KAHR *lah looth eh-*LEIIK-*tree-kah?*
Can I touch the electric light?

Sí, Ud. puede tocarla.
*See, oos-*TEHD PWEH-*deh toh-*KAHR-*lah.*
Yes, you can touch it.

¿Puede Ud. contar los libros?
PWEH-*deh oos-*TEHD *kohn-*TAHR *lohs* LEE-*brohs?*
Can you count the books?

Sí, puedo contarlos.   **Cuéntelos.**
See, PWEH-*doh kohn-*TAHR-*lohs.* KWEHN-*teh-lohs.*
Yes, I can count them.   Count them.

¿Podemos romper la llave?
*Poh-*DEH-*mohs rohm-*PEHR *lah l'*YAH-*veh?*
Can we break the key?

No, no podemos romperla.
*Noh, noh poh-*DEH-*mohs rohm-*PEHR-*lah.*
No, we cannot break it.

¿Podemos romper el fósforo?
*Poh-*DEH-*mohs rohm-*PEHR *ell* FOHS-*foh-roh?*
Can we break the match?

Sí, podemos romperlo.
*See, poh-*DEH-*mohs rohm-*PEHR-*loh.*
Yes, we can break it.

Cortamos con un cuchillo.
*Kohr-*TAH-*mohs kohn oon koo-*CHEEL-*yoh.*
We cut with a knife.

¿Podemos cortar sin cuchillo?
*Poh-*DEH-*mohs kohr-*TAHR *seen koo-*CHEEL-*yoh?*
Can we cut without a knife?

¿Podemos comer la carne con un tenedor?
*Poh-*DEH-*mohs koh-*MEHR *lah* KAHR-*neh kohn oon teh-neh-*DOHR?
Can we eat meat with a fork?

¿Podemos leer sin libro?
Poh-DEH-mohs leh-EHR seen LEE-broh?
Can we read without a book?

¿Puede Ud. hablar sin abrir la boca?
PWEH-*deh oos-*TEHD *ah-*BLAHR *seen ah-*BREER *lah* BOH-*kah?*
Can you speak without opening your mouth?

Los alumnos no tienen tiza;
*Lohs ah-*LOOM-*nohs noh t'*YEH-*nehn* TEE-*thah;*
The pupils have no chalk;

¿pueden escribir en la pizarra?
PWEH-*dehn ess-kree-*BEER *enn lah pee-*THAH-*rrah?*
can they write on the blackboard?

No, sin tiza no pueden escribir en la pizarra.
Noh, seen TEE-*thah noh* PWEH-*dehn ess-kree-*BEER *enn lah pee-*THAH-*rrah.*
No, without chalk they cannot write on the blackboard.

Los libros son grandes, los bolsillos son pequeños.
Lohs LEE-*brohs sohn* GRAHN-*dehs, lohs bohl-*SEEL-*yohs sohn peh-*KEHN-*yohs.*
The books are big, the pockets are small.

¿Pueden los alumnos meter sus libros en sus bolsillos?
PWEH-*dehn lohs ah-*LOOM-*nohs meh-*TEHR *soos* LEE-*brohs enn soos bohl-*SEEL-*yohs?*
Can the pupils put their books in their pockets?

No, no pueden meter sus libros en sus bolsillos.
Noh, noh PWEH-*dehn meh-*TEHR *soos* LEE-*brohs enn soos bohl-*SEEL-*yohs.*
No, they cannot put their books in their pockets.

No puedo cortar el papel ... no tengo tijeras.
Noh PWEH-*doh kohr-*TAHR *ell pah-*PEHL ... *noh* TEHN-*goh tee-*HEH-*rahs.*
I cannot cut the paper ... I have no scissors.

No puedo cortar el papel porque no tengo tijeras.
Noh PWEH-*doh kohr-*TAHR *ell pah-*PEHL POHR-*keh noh* TEHN-*goh tee-*HEH-*rahs.*
I cannot cut the paper because I have no scissors.

¿Puedo yo cortar el papel?	No, Ud. no puede.
PWEH-*doh yoh kohr-*TAHR *ell pah-*PEHL?	*Noh, oos-*TEHD *noh* PWEH-*deh.*
Can I cut the paper?	No, you cannot.

¿Por qué?	Porque Ud. no tiene tijeras.
Pohr KEH?	POHR-*keh oos-*TEHD *noh t'*YEH-*neh tee-*HEH-*rahs*
Why?	Because you have no scissors.

¿Por qué no puedo cortar el papel?
Pohr KEH *noh* PWEH-*doh kohr*-TAHR *ell pah*-PEHL?
Why can I not cut the paper?

Porque Ud. no tiene tijeras.
POHR-*keh oos*-TEHD *noh t'*YEH-*neh tee*-HEH-*rahs.*
Because you have no scissors.

La puerta está cerrada.
Lah PWEHR-*tah ess*-TAH *theh*-RRAH-*dah.*
The door is closed.

Ud. no puede salir.
Oos-TEHD *noh* PWEH-*jeh sah*-LEER.
You cannot go out.

¿Por qué no puede Ud. salir?
Pohr KEH *noh* PWEH-*deh oos*-TEHD *sah*-LEER?
Why can you not go out?

Porque la puerta está cerrada.
POHR-*keh lah* PWEHR-*tah ess*-TAH *theh*-RRAH-*dah.*
Because the door is closed.

La caja es pequeña, el libro es grande;
Lah KAH-*hah ess peh*-KEHN-*yah, ell* LEE-*broh ess* GRAHN-*deh;*
The box is small, the book is big;

no podemos meter el libro dentro de la caja.
noh poh-DEH-*mohs meh*-TEHR *ell* LEE-*broh* DEHN-*troh deh lah* KAH-*hah.*
we cannot put the book inside the box.

¿Por qué no podemos meter el libro en la caja?
Pohr KEH *noh poh*-DEH-*mohs meh*-TEHR *ell* LEE-*broh enn lah* KAH *hah?*
Why can we not put the book into the box?

Porque el libro es grande
POHR-*keh ell* LEE-*broh ess* GRAHN-*deh*
Because the book is big

(porque la caja es pequeña).
(POHR-*keh lah* KAH-*hah ess peh*-KEHN-*yah*).
(because the box is small).

Cierre Ud. los ojos; Ud. no puede ver.
*Th'*YEH-*rreh oos*-TEHD *lohs* OH-*hohs; oos*-TEHD *noh* PWEH-*deh vehr.*
Close your eyes; you cannot see.

¿Por qué no puede Ud. ver?
Pohr KEH *noh* PWEH-*deh oos*-TEHD *vehr?*
Why can you not see?

Porque cierro los ojos.
POHR-*keh th'*YEH-*rroh lohs* OH-*hohs.*
Because I close my eyes.

El Sr. Berlitz no está aquí.
*Ell sehn-*YOHR BEHR-*leets noh ess-*TAH *ah-*KEE.
Mr. Berlitz is not here.

¿Por qué no pueden ver los alumnos al Sr. Berlitz?
Pohr KEH *noh* PWEH-*dehn vehr lohs ah-*LOOM-*nohs ahl sehn-*YOHR BEHR-*leets?*
Why can the pupils not see Mr. Berlitz?

Porque no está aquí.
POHR-*keh noh ess-*TAH *ah-*KEE.
Because he is not here.

Tomo su libro.	**¿Puede Ud. leer?**
TOH-*moh soo* LEE-*broh.*	PWEH-*deh oos-*TEHD *leh-*EHR?
I take your book.	Can you read?

No, no puedo.	**¿Por qué?**	**Porque no tengo libro.**
Noh, noh PWEH-*doh.*	*Pohr* KEH?	POHR-*que noh* TEHN-*goh* LEE-*broh.*
No, I cannot.	Why?	Because I have no book.

El Sr. Berlitz no tiene anteojos.
*Ell sehn-*YOHR BEHR-*leets noh t'*YEH-*neh ahn-teh-*OH-*hohs.*
Mr. Berlitz has no glasses.

¿Puede ver sin anteojos?	**No, no puede ver.**
PWEH-*deh vehr seen ahn-teh-*OH-*hohs?*	*Noh, noh* PWEH-*deh vehr.*
Can he see without glasses?	No, he cannot see.

¿Por qué no puede ver?
Pohr KEH *noh* PWEH-*deh vehr?*
Why can he not see?

Porque no tiene anteojos.
POHR-*keh noh t'*YEH-*neh ahn-teh-*OH-*hohs.*
Because he has no glasses.

REMEMBER: Why? = *¿Por qué?* (2 words)
Because = *Porque* (1 word)

La puerta está abierta.	**¿Puede Ud. salir?**
Lah PWEHR-*tah ess-*TAH *ahb-*YEHR-*tah.*	PWEH-*deh oos-*TEHD *sah-*LEER?
The door is open.	Can you go out?

Sí, puedo salir.	**¿Por qué no sale Ud.?**
See, PWEH-*doh sah-*LEER.	*Pohr* KEH *noh* SAH-*leh oos-*TEHD?
Yes, I can go out.	Why do you not go out?

Porque yo no quiero.
POHR-*keh yoh noh k'*YEH-*roh.*
Because I do not want to.

¿Puede Ud. romper su libro?
PWEH-*deh oos-*TEHD *rohm-*PEHR *soo* LEE-*broh?*
Can you tear your book?

Sí, puedo romperlo.
See, PWEH-*doh rohm-*PEHR-*loh.*
Yes, I can tear it.

¿Por qué no lo rompe Ud.?
Pohr KEH *noh loh* ROHM-*peh oos-*TEHD?
Why do you not tear it?

Porque yo no quiero.
POHR-*keh yoh noh k'*YEH-*roh.*
Because I do not want to.

Puedo romper mi reloj, pero no
PWEH-*doh rohm-*PEHR *mee reh-*LOH, PEH-*roh noh*
I can break my watch, but

quiero romperlo.
*k'*YEH-*roh rohm-*PEHR-*loh.*
I do not want to break it.

Puedo romper mi corbata, pero no
PWEH-*doh rohm-*PEHR *mee kohr-*BAH-*tah,* PEH-*roh noh*
I can tear my tie, but

quiero romperla.
*k'*YEH-*roh rohm-*PEHR-*lah.*
I do not want to tear it.

El profesor puede escribir en la pared,
*Ell proh-feh-*SOHR PWEH-*deh ess-kree-*BEER *enn lah pah-*REHD,
The teacher can write on the wall,

pero no quiere escribir en la pared.
PEH-*roh noh k'*YEH-*reh ess-kree-*BEER *enn lah pah-*REHD.
but he does not want to write on the wall.

THINKING IN SPANISH
(Answers on page 259)

1. ¿Toca Chiquita a Capitán?
2. ¿Puede ella tocar la mano derecha del profesor?
3. ¿Puede el profesor tocar el sombrero de Chiquita?
4. ¿Lo toca?
5. ¿Está baja la lámpara?
6. ¿Puede el profesor tocarla?
7. ¿Qué toca el profesor?
8. ¿Lleva anteojos el profesor?
9. ¿Puede ver sin anteojos?
10. La puerta está abierta, ¿podemos salir del cuarto?
11. No tengo pluma ni lápiz, ¿puedo escribir?
12. ¿Podemos nosotros ver las cosas detrás de nosotros?
13. ¿Pueden los alumnos tocar el techo?
14. ¿Podemos romper el fósforo?
15. ¿Puede Ud. romper la llave de la puerta?
16. ¿Podemos tocar nuestro libro?
17. Los alumnos. ¿pueden romper la ventana con una pelota?

LECCIÓN 21

¡Qué debo hacer para salir?

Keh DEH-*boh* ah-THEHR PAH-*rah* sah-LEER?

What must I do to go out?

La puerta está cerrada; la puerta está abierta.
Lah PWEHR-*tah* ess-TAH *theh*-RRAH-*dah; lah* PWEHR-*tah* ess-TAH *ahb*-YEH-*tah.*
The door is closed; the door is open.

La puerta está cerrada; no podemos salir.
Lah PWEHR-*tah* ess-TAH *theh*-RRAH-*dah;* noh *poh*-DEH-*mohs* sah-LEER.
The door is closed; we cannot go out.

Si la puerta está abierta, podemos salir.
See lah PWEHR-*tah* ess-TAH *ahb*-YEHR-*tah, poh*-DEH-*mohs* sah-LEER.
If the door is open, we can go out.

Si cerramos los ojos, no podemos ver.
See theh-RRAH-*mohs lohs* OH-*hohs,* noh *poh*-DEH-*mohs* vehr.
If we close our eyes, we cannot see.

132

Si no tengo tiza, no puedo escribir en la pizarra.
See noh TEHN-*goh* TEE-*thah, noh* PWEH-*doh ess-kree-*BEER
*enn lah pee-*THAH-*rrah.*
If I have no chalk, I cannot write on the blackboard.

Si no tenemos lápices ni plumas, no podemos escribir.
*See noh teh-*NEH-*mohs* LAH-*pee-thehs nee* PLOO-*mahs,*
*noh poh-*DEH-*mohs ess-kree-*BEER.
If we have no pencils or pens, we cannot write.

Yo puedo tocar el reloj, subiendo (si subo) a la silla.
Yoh PWEH-*doh ton-*KAHR *ell* reh-LOH, *soob-*YEHN-*doh (see* soo-*bah)*
ah lah SEEI.-*yah.*
I can touch the clock by climbing (if I climb) on the chair.

Sin subir a la silla (si no subo) no puedo tocar el reloj.
*Seen soo-*BEER *ah lah* SEEL-*yah (see noh* soo-*boh) noh* PWEH-*doh toh-*KAHR
ell reh-LOH.
Without climbing (If I don't climb) on the chair, I cannot touch the clock.

Abriendo la puerta podemos salir del cuarto.
*Ahbr-*YEHN-*doh lah* PWEHR-*tah poh-*DEH-*mohs sah-*LEER *dehl* KWAHR-*toh.*
By opening the door we can go out of the room.

Sin abrirla, no podemos salir.
*Seen ah-*BREER-*lah, noh poh-*DEH-*mohs sah-*LEER.
Without opening it, we cannot go out.

Viniendo a la escuela puede Ud. hablar español.
*Veen-*YEHN-*doh ah lah ess-*KWEH-*lah* PWEH-*deh oos-*TEHD *ah-*BLAHR
*ess-pahn-*YOHL.
By coming to school you can speak Spanish.

Tomando lecciones de español, puede Ud. hablarlo.
*Toh-*MAHN-*doh lehkth-*YOH-*nehs deh ess-pahn-*YOHL, PWEH-*deh oos-*TEHD
*ah-*BLAHR-*loh.*
By taking Spanish lessons, you can speak it.

Sin estudiar, no puede Ud. hablar la lengua.
*Seen ess-tood-*YAHR, *noh* PWEH-*deh oos-*TEHD *ah-*BLAHR *lah* LEHN-*gwah.*
Without studying, you cannot speak the language.

NOTE: *Tomando* is the present participle of *tomar*. It is formed by adding *ando* to the root of the verb. *Tomando* means "taking," "by taking," "in taking," etc., but if used after *sin* (without), the verb must be put in the infinitive. The 2nd and 3rd conjugations form their present participles by adding *iendo* or *yendo* to the root. Ex: *leyendo, viendo, oyendo,* etc. Usually the present tense of a verb corresponds to both the English present *and* present progressive. Ex: *Leo:* "I read" *also* "I am reading." But you can also use the verb *estar* with the present participle to give the exact meaning of "I am reading" (at this moment). *Estar* can be used with the present participle of all verbs. Ex: *Estoy caminando:* "I am walking." *Estamos llegando:* "We are arriving." *Están hablando:* "They are talking."

La puerta está cerrada.
Lah PWEHR-*tah ess*-TAH *theh*-RRAH-*dah.*
The door is closed.

Ud. quiere salir;
Oos-TEHD *k'*YEH-*reh sah*-LEER;
You want to go out;

Ud. no puede salir, sin abrir la puerta;
oos-TEHD *noh* PWEH-*deh sah*-LEER, *seen ah*-BREER *lah* PWEHR-*tah;*
you cannot go out, without opening the door;

Ud. debe abrir la puerta.
oos-TEHD DEH-*beh ah*-BREER *lah* PWEHR-*tah.*
you must open the door.

No podemos ver, si no abrimos los ojos;
Noh poh-DEH-*mohs vehr, see noh ah*-BREE-*mohs loh* OH-*hohs;*
We cannot see, if we do not open our eyes;

debemos abrir los ojos para ver.
deh-BEH-*mohs ah*-BREER *lohs* OH-*hohs* PAH-*rah vehr.*
we must open our eyes to see.

Para escribir en la pizarra, debo tomar la tiza.
PAH-*rah ess-kree*-BEER *enn lah pee*-THAH-*rrah,* DEH-*boh toh*-MAHR *lah* TEE-*thah.*
To write on the blackboard, I must take the chalk.

Para tomar la sopa, debo tener una cuchara.
PAH-*rah toh*-MAHR *lah* SOH-*pah,* DEH-*boh teh*-NEHR *oo*-*nah koo*-CHAH-*rah.*
To eat soup, I must have a spoon.

Para comer la carne debo tener un cuchillo y un tenedor.
PAH-*rah koh*-MEHR *lah* KAHR-*neh* DEH-*boh teh*-NEHR *oon koo*-CHEEL-*yoh ee oon teh-neh*-DOHR.
To eat meat I must have a knife and a fork.

¿Qué debemos hacer para salir?
Keh deh-BEH-*mohs ah*-THEHR PAH-*rah sah*-LEER?
What do we have to do to go out?

Debemos abrir la puerta.
*Deh-*BEH-*mohs ah-*BREER *lah* PWEHR-*tah.*
We must open the door.

¿Qué debemos hacer para ver?
*Keh deh-*BEH-*mohs ah-*THEHR PAH-*rah vehr?*
What do we have to do to see?

Debemos abrir los ojos.
*Deh-*BEH-*mohs ah-*BREER *lohs* OH-*hohs.*
We must open our eyes.

¿Qué debo tener para escribir en la pizarra?
Keh DEH-*boh teh-*NEHR PAH-*rah ess-kree-*BEER *enn lah pee-*THAH-*rrah?*
What do I have to have to write on the blackboard?

Ud. debe tener una tiza.
*Oos-*TEHD DEH-*beh teh-*NEHR OO-*nah* TEE-*thah.*
You must have a (piece of) chalk.

¿Qué debemos tener para cortar la carne?
*Keh deh-*BEH-*mohs teh-*NEHR PAH-*rah kohr-*TAHR *lah* KAHR-*neh?*
What must we have to cut meat?

Debemos tener un cuchillo.
*Deh-*BEH-*mohs teh-*NEHR *oon koo-*CHEEL-*yoh.*
We must have a knife.

¿Qué debe Ud. hacer para hablar?
Keh DEH-*beh oos-*TEHD *ah-*THEHR PAH-*rah ah-*BLAHR?
What must you do to speak?

Debo abrir la boca.
DEH-*boh ah-*BREER *lah* BOH-*kah.*
I must open my mouth.

El libro de este señor está cerrado.
Ell LEE-*broh deh* ESS-*teh sehn-*YOHR *ess-*TAH *theh-*RRAH-*doh.*
This gentleman's book is closed.

¿Puede leer el señor?
PWEH-*deh leh-*EHR *ell sehn-*YOHR?
Can the gentleman read?

No, no puede leer.
Noh, noh PWEH-*deh leh-*EHR.
No, he cannot read.

Si quiere leer, ¿qué debe hacer?
*See k'*YEH-*reh leh-*EHR, *keh* DEH-*beh ah-*THEHR?
If he wants to read, what must he do?

Debe abrir su libro.
DEH-*beh ah-*BREER *soo* LEE-*broh.*
He must open his book.

Los alumnos no tienen papel ni lápices.
*Lohs ah-*LOOM*-nohs noh t'*YEH*-nehn pah-*PEHL *nee* LAH*-pee-thehs.*
The pupils have no paper or pencils.

¿Pueden escribir?	**No, no pueden escribir.**
PWEH*-dehn ess-kree-*BEER*?*	*Noh, noh* PWEH*-dehn ess-kree-*BEER.
Can they write?	No, they cannot write.

¿Por qué no?	Porque no tienen papel ni lápiz;
Pohr KEH *noh?*	POHR*-keh noh t'*YEH*-nehn pah-*PEHL *nee* LAH*-peeth;*
Why not?	Because they have no paper or pencil;

no pueden escribir sin papel ni lápices.
noh PWEH*-dehn ess-kree-*BEER *seen pah-*PEHL *nee* LAH*-pee-thehs.*
they cannot write without paper or pencils.

¿Qué deben tener si quieren escribir?
Keh DEH*-behn teh-*NEHR *see k'-*YEH*-rehn ess-kree-*BEER*?*
What must they have if they want to write?

Deben tener papel y lápices.
*D*EH*-behn teh-*NEHR *pah-*PEHL *ee* LAH*-pee-thehs.*
They must have paper and pencils.

NOTE: *Deber* meaning "must" or "should" takes an infinitive in the same fashion as *poder* and *querer.* Ex: "I must go to see my mother.": *Debo ir a ver a mi madre.* However, *deber* also means "to owe". Ex: "He owes me 500 pesos". *Él me debe quinientos pesos.*

THINKING IN SPANISH
(Answers on page 259)

1. ¿Qué quiere Chiquita?   2. ¿Puede ella comer la manzana?

3. ¿Por qué no puede comerla?   4. ¿Quiere el profesor darle la manzana?

5. ¿Puede Ud. comprar una manzana si no tiene dinero?

6. ¿Qué debemos tener para comprar comida?

7. ¿Podemos ir al teatro si no tenemos billetes?

8. ¿Podemos salir de la clase sin abrir la puerta?

9. ¿Podemos abrir la puerta de la casa si no tenemos llave?

10. ¿Que debemos tener para escribir en la pizarra?

11. ¿Qué debemos tener para escribir en el papel?

12. ¿Pueden los alumnos escribir si no tienen papel ni lápiz?

13. ¿Quiere Ud. hablar español?   14. ¿Quiere Ud. ir a México?

15. ¿Puede Ud. hablar español bien?

LECCIÓN 22

En el restaurante
Enn ell rehs-tah-oo-RAHN-teh
In the restaurant

JORGE: **Hola, Ana María, ¿quiere Ud. venir conmigo al**
OH-*lah,* AH-*nah Mah*-REE-*ah, k'*YEH-*reh oos*-TEHD *veh*-NEER
kohn-MEE-*goh ahl*
Hello, Ana Maria, do you want to come with me to the

restaurante "Buenos Aires"?
rehs-tah-oo-RAHN-*teh* "BWEH-*nohs* AH-*ee-rehs*"?
"Buenos Aires" restaurant?

Sirven unas comidas exquisitas.
SEER-*vehn* OON-*ahs koh*-MEE-*dahs ehks-kee*-SEE-*tahs.*
They serve exquisite food.

ANA MARÍA: **Con mucho gusto; tengo muchos deseos de**
Kohn MOO-*choh* GOOS-*toh;* TEHN-*goh* MOO-*chohs deh*-SEH-*ohs* **deh**
comer una comida española.
koh-MEHR OO-*nah koh*-MEE-*dah ess-pahn*-YOHL-*ah.*
With pleasure; I would like very much to have a Spanish **meal.**

¿Qué clase de restaurante es?
Keh KLAH-*seh deh rehs-tah-oo*-RAHN-*teh ess?*
What kind of restaurant is it?

JORGE: No es muy grande, pero tiene buena comida y además,
Noh ess mwee GRAHN-*deh,* PEH-*roh t'*YEH-*neh* BWEH-*nah koh-*MEE-*dal;*
*ee ah-deh-*MAHS,
It is not very large, but it has good food and in addition,

una pequeña orquesta que toca rumbas y tangos,
OO-*nah peh-*KEHN-*yah ohr-*KEHS-*tah keh* TOH-*kah* ROOM-*bahs*
ee TAHN-*gohs,*
a small orchestra that plays rumbas and tangos,

pero no se permite bailar.
PEH-*roh noh seh pehr-*MEE-*teh bah-ee-*LAHR.
but dancing is not allowed.

ANA MARÍA: ¡Qué lástima! Pero ¿qué importa? En este momento
Keh LAHS-*tee-mah!* PEH-*roh keh eem-*POHR-*tah?* Enn ESS-*teh*
*moh-*MEHN-*toh*
What a pity! But who cares? At this moment

prefiero comer que bailar.
*prehf-*YEH-*roh koh-*MEHR *keh bah-ee-*LAHR.
I prefer eating to dancing.

JORGE: Aquí estamos; tomemos una mesa hacia el centro.
*Ah-*KEE *ess-*TAH-*mohs; toh-*MEH-*mohs* OO-*nah* MEH-*sah* AHTH-*yah*
ell THEHN-*troh.*
Here we are; let us take a table towards the center.

MOZO (camarero): Buenas tardes, señores.
MOH-*thoh (kah-mah-*REH-*roh):* BWEH-*nahs* TAHR-*dehs, sehn-*YOH-*rehs.*
WAITER: Good evening, gentlemen.

Aquí tienen Uds. el menú.
*Ah-*KEE *t'*YEH-*nehn oos-*TEH-*dehs ell meh-*NOO.
Here you have the menu.

NOTE: Use *señores,* masc. plur., in addressing a man and
woman together.

JORGE: ¿Qué nos recomienda Ud. para hoy?
*Keh nohs reh-kohm-*YEHN-*dah oos-*TEHD PAH-*rah oy?*
What do you recommend to us for today?

MOZO: Como Ud. sabe, el arroz con pollo es la especialidad
KOH-*moh oos-*TEHD SAH-*beh, ell ah* RROHTH *koh* POHL-*yoh ess lah*
*ess-pehth-yah-lee-*DAHD
As you know, chicken with rice is the specialty

de la casa; pero también tenemos buenas carnes y pescado.
deh lah KAH-*sah;* PEH-*roh tahmb-*YEHN *teh-*NEH-*mohs* BWEH-*nahs*
KAHR-*nehs ee pehs-*KAH-*doh.*
of the house; but we have good meat and fish also.

ANA MARÍA: Yo prefiero el arroz con pollo.
*Yoh prehf-*YEH-*roh ell ah-*RROHTH *koh* POHL-*yoh.*
I prefer chicken with rice.

JORGE: Yo voy a pedir un filete con papas fritas.
*Yoh voy ah peh-*DEER *oon fee-*LEH-*teh kohn* PAH-*pahs* FREE-*tahs.*
I am going to order a steak with French fried potatoes.

Mozo: ¿Desean Uds. también sopa y ensalada?
*Deh-*SEH-*ahn oos-*TEHD-*ehs tahmb-*YEHN SOH-*pah ee enn-sah-*LAH-*dah!*
Do you also wish soup and salad?

ANA MARÍA: Sí, yo quiero sopa de esparragos, ensalada de
*See, yoh k'*YEHR-*oh* SOH-*pah deh ess-*PAH-*rrah-gohs, enn-sah-*LAH-*dah deu*
Yes, I want some asparagus soup, lettuce

lechuga y tomates y también quiero zanahorias y espinacas.
*leh-*CHOO-*gah ee toh-*MAH-*tehs ee tahmb-*YEHN *k'*YEH-*roh*
*thah-nah-*OHR-*yahs ee ess-pee-*NAH-*kahs.*
and tomato salad and I also want carrots and spinach.

JORGE: Mozo, puede traer lo mismo para mí.
MOH-*thoh,* PWEH-*deh trah-*EHR *loh* MEES-*moh* PAH-*rah mee.*
Waiter, you can bring the same for me.

ANA MARÍA: Este arroz con pollo está perfecto;
Ess-*teh ah-*RROHTH *kohn* POHL-*yoh ess-*TAH *pehr-*FEHK-*toh;*
This chicken with rice is perfect;

veo porque le gusta este restaurante.
VEH-*oh pohr-*KEH *leh* GOOS-*tah* ESS-*teh rehs-tah-oo-*RAHN-*teh.*
I see why you like this restaurant.

JORGE: También mi filete está muy bueno.
*Tahmb-*YEHN *mee fee-*LEH-*teh ess-*TAH *mwee* BWEH-*noh.*
My steak is also very good.

Mozo: ¿Qué quieren tomar de postre, señores?
*Keh k'*YEH-*rehn toh-*MAHR *deh* POHS-*treh, sehn-*YOH-*rehs!*
What do you wish for dessert, gentlemen?

ANA MARÍA: Yo quiero piña fría y una taza de café puro.
*Yoh k'*YEH-*roh* PEEN-*yah* FREE-*ah ee* OO-*nah* TAH-*thah deh kah-*FEH
POO-*roh.*
I want cold pineapple and a cup of black coffee.

JORGE: A mí me trae queso con guayaba y café puro,
Ah mee meh TRAH-*eh* KEH-*soh kohn gwah-*YAH-*bah ee kah-*FEH POO-*roh,*
Bring me some cheese with guava and black coffee,

y haga el favor de traernos la cuenta.
ee AH-*gah ell fah-*VOHR *deh trah-*EHR-*nohs lah* KWEHN-*tah.*
and please bring us the check.

(El mozo trae la cuenta).
(*Ell* MOH-*thoh* TRAH-*eh lah* KWEHN-*tah*).
(The waiter brings the check).

MOZO: La cuenta es cinco pesos cincuenta centavos.
Lah KWEHN-*tah ess* THEEN-*koh* PEH-*sohs theen-*KWEHN-*tah*
*thehn-*TAH-*vohs.*
The check is five pesos and fifty cents.

JORGE: Tenga—Guarde 50 centavos de propina.
TEHN-*gah—*GWAHR-*deh theen-*KWEHN-*tah thehn-*TAH-*vohs deh*
*proh-*PEE-*nah.*
Here—Keep fifty cents tip.

Ya estamos listos.
*Yah ess-*TAH-*mohs* LEES-*tohs.*
We are ready.

¿Quiere Ud. ir al teatro?
*K'*YEH-*reh oos-*TEHD *eer ahl teh-*AH-*troh?*
Do you want to go to the theater?

ANA MARÍA: Muy bien. Vamos.
*Mwee b'*YEHN. VAH-*mohs.*
Very well. Let us go.

MOZO: Muchas gracias y hasta la vista, señores.
MOO-*chahs* GRAHTH-*yahs ee* AHS-*tah lah* VEES-*tah, sehn-*YOH-*rehs.*
Thank you very much until next time, gentlemen.

EXPRESSIONS to Remember: *No se permite bailar:*
"Dancing is not permitted."
papas: "potatoes." In Spain, *patatas* is used. In Latin
America, however, *papas* is preferred.
de postre: "for dessert." This is an idiomatic use of *de* for
"for."
de propina: "for a tip." Use same as above.
a mi me trae: "bring me." Sr. Gómez should logically say *tráigame,* as that
is the imperative form. However, he prefers to use the regular indicative
form, which is often done in this case.
vamos: "Let's go." This is a word you will hear constantly. It has even
been adopted into American slang but is used incorrectly as "go away."
It really means "we are going" or "let's go."

THINKING IN SPANISH
(Answers on page 260)

1. ¿Con quién se encuentra Jorge?
2. ¿A dónde le invita a ir?
3. ¿A qué le invita?
4. ¿Cómo se llama el restaurante?
5. ¿Acepta Ana María la invitación?
6. ¿Por qué la acepta?
7. ¿Qué clase de comidas sirven en ese restaurante?
8. ¿Es muy grande el restaurante?
9. ¿Qué ofrece además de la comida?
10. ¿Qué clase de música toca la orquesta?
11. ¿Se permite bailar?
12. ¿Es muy caro el restaurante?
13. ¿En qué parte del restaurante se sientan?
14. ¿Quién les recibe?
15. ¿Qué les da el mozo?
16. ¿Qué se ve en un menú?
17. ¿Qué le pregunta Jorge al mozo?

18. ¿Qué les recomienda éste?
19. ¿Qué piden los señores?
20. ¿Qué dice Ana María del arroz con pollo?
21. ¿Cómo está el filete de Jorge?
22. ¿Qué postre piden los señores?
23. ¿Qué toman después del postre?
24. ¿Qué les da el mozo después de terminar la comida?
25. ¿Cuál es el valor de la cuenta?
26. ¿Cuánto le dan al mozo de propina?
27. ¿A dónde van después de comer?
28. ¿Qué les dice el mozo al recibir la propina?
29. ¿Cómo se despide el mozo de los señores?
30. ¿Cómo se despide Ud. de un amigo?

LECCIÓN 23

¿Qué hora es?

Keh OH-*rah ess?*

What time is it?

Éste es un reloj de bolsillo;
Ess-*teh ess oon* reh-LOH *deh bohl*-SEEL-*yoh;*
This is a pocket watch;

éste es un reloj de péndola, y ése un reloj de pared.
ESS-*teh ess oon* reh-LOH *deh* PEHN-*doh-lah, ee* EH-*seh* **oon**
reh-LOH *deh pah*-REHD.
this is a pendulum clock, and that is a wall clock.

El primero lo llevamos en nuestro bolsillo.
Ell pree-MEH-*roh loh l'yeh-*VΛH-*mohs enn* NWEHS-*troh bohl*-SEEL-**yoh.**
The first we carry in our pocket.

Los otros, están en la pared, o se ponen sobre una mesa.
Lohs OH-*trohs,* ess-TAHN *enn lah pah*-REHD, *oh seh* POH-*nehn* SOH-*breh*
oo-*nah* MEH-*sah.*
The others are on the wall, or are placed on a table.

Un reloj de péndola o de pared es de madera, mármol o bronce.
Oon reh-LOH deh PEHN-doh-lah oh deh pah-REHD ess deh mah-DEH-rah,
deh MAHR-mohl oh BROHN-theh.
A pendulum clock or a wall clock is of wood, marble or bronze.

Un reloj de bolsillo es de oro, plata u otro metal.
Oon reh-LOH deh bohl-SEEL-yoh ess deh OH-roh, PLAH-tah oo OH-troh
meh-TAHL.
A pocket watch is of gold, silver or other metal.

Un reloj despertador es de acero
Oon reh-LOH dehs-pehr-tah-DOHR ess deh ah-THEH-roh
An alarm clock is of steel

y se usa para despertarnos.
ee seh OO-sah PAH-rah dehs-pehr-TAHR-nohs.
and is used to wake us up.

En mi reloj hay tres manecillas:
Enn mee reh-LOH I trehs mah-neh-THEEL-yahs:
On my watch there are three hands:

una larga que señala los minutos,
oo-nah LAHR-gah keh sehn-YAH-lah lohs mee-NOO-tohs,
a long one which indicates the minutes,

y otra más corta que señala las horas;
ee OH-trah mahs KOHR-tah keh sehn-YAH-lah lahs OH-rahs;
and a shorter one which indicates the hours;

la tercera manecilla aún más corta que las dos anteriores,
lah tehr-THEH-rah mah-neh-THEEL-yah ah-OON mahs KOHR-tah keh lahs
dohs ahn-tehr-YOH-rehs,
the third hand, even shorter than the two others,

señala los segundos.
sehn-YAH-lah lohs seh-GOON-dohs.
points to the seconds.

NOTE on the Comparative: The comparison of adjectives
is extremely easy in Spanish. Suppose the adjective is *largo*.
If the noun modified is masculine, simply use *largo, más*
largo, el más largo, for "long, longer, and the longest." For
feminine forms, *larga, más larga,* and *la más larga.* Ex: "She
is the most beautiful in Havana." *Ella es la más hermosa de la Habana.*

EXCEPTION: Good, better, best—*bueno, mejor, el mejor.*
Bad. worse. worst—*malo, peor, el peor.*

Una hora tiene sesenta minutos
Oo-nah OH-*rah t'*YEH-*neh seh-*SEHN-*tah mee-*NOO-*tohs*
An hour has sixty minutes

y en cada minuto hay sesenta segundos.
ee enn KAH-*dah mee-*NOO-*toh I seh-*SEHN-*tah seh-*GOON-*dohs.*
and in each minute there are sixty seconds.

Veinticuatro horas hacen un día.
*Vain-tee-*KWAH-*troh* OH-*rahs* AH-*thehn oon* DEE-*ah.*
Twenty-four hours make a day.

En este cuarto hay un reloj que no anda, está parado;
Enn ESS-*teh* KWAHR-*toh I oon reh-*LOH *keh noh* AHN-*dah, ess-*TAH
*pah-*RAH-*doh;*
In this room there is a clock which does not go, it is stopped;

es preciso darle cuerda.
*ess pre-*THEE-*soh* DAHR-*leh* KWEHR-*dah.*
it is necessary to wind it up.

Yo pongo el reloj en hora; son las once y veinte minutos.
Yoh POHN-*goh ell reh-*LOH *enn* OH-*rah; sohn lahs* OHN-*theh ee*
VAIN-*teh mee-*NOO-*tohs.*
I set the clock on time; it is eleven twenty.

Si pongo el reloj a las once en punto, lo atraso;
See POHN-*goh ell reh-*LOH *ah lahs* OHN-*theh enn* POON-*toh, loh ah-*TRAH-*soh;*
If I set the watch at eleven o'clock, I set it back;

si lo pongo a las once y media lo adelanto.
see loh POHN-*goh ah lahs* OHN-*theh ee* MEHD-*yah loh ah-deh-*LAHN-*toh.*
if I set it at eleven thirty, I set it ahead.

Mi reloj anda muy bien;
*Mee reh-*LOH AHN-*dah mwee b'*YEHN;
My watch works very well;

ni se adelanta ni se atrasa: es exacto.
*nee seh ah-deh-*LAHN-*tah nee seh ah-*TRAH-*sah: ess ehk-*SAHK-*toh.*
it is not fast nor slow: it is exact.

¿Qué hora es, Srta. Rambaldo?
Keh OH-*rah ess, sehn-yoh-*REE-*tah Rahm-*BAHL-*doh?*
What time is it, Miss Rambaldo?

Son las doce menos cuarto.
Sohn lahs DOH-*theh* MEH-*nohs* KWAHR-*toh.*
It is a quarter to twelve.

La lección de la Sra. Quevedo
*Lah lehkth-*YOHN *deh lah sehn-*YOH-*rah Keh-*VEH-*doh*
empieza a las once y acaba a las doce;
*ehmp-*YEH-*thah ah lahs* OHN-*theh ee ah-*KAH-*bah ah lahs* DOH-*theh:*
Mrs. Quevedo's lesson begins at eleven and ends at twelve;

dura una hora.
DOO-*rah* OO-*nah* OH-*rah.*
it lasts an hour.

¿A qué hora empieza su lección?
Ah keh OH-*rah ehmp-*YEH-*thah soo lehkth-*YOHN?
At what time does your lesson begin?

Mi lección empieza a las once.
*Mee lehkth-*YOHN *ehmp-*YEH-*thah ah lahs* OHN-*theh.*
My lesson begins at eleven.

¿A qué hora acaba?
Ah keh OH-*rah ah-*KAH-*bah?*
At what time does it end?

Mi lección acaba a las doce.
*Mee lehkth-*YOHN *ah-*KAH-*bah ah lahs* DOH-*theh.*
My lesson ends at twelve.

¿Cuánto tiempo dura su lección?
KWAHN-*toh t'*YEHM-*poh* DOO-*rah soo lehkth-*YOHN?
How long does your lesson last?

Mi lección dura una hora.
*Mee lehkth-*YOHN DOO-*rah* OO-*nah* OH-*rah.*
My lesson lasts an hour.

¿A qué hora viene Ud. a la escuela?
Ah keh OH-*rah v'*YEH-*neh oos-*TEHD *ah lah ess-*KWEH-*lah?*
At what time do you come to school?

Yo vengo a la escuela a las once.
Yoh VEHN-*goh ah lah ess-*KWEH-*lah ah lahs* OHN-*theh.*
I come to school at eleven.

¿A qué hora almuerza Ud.?
Ah keh OH-*rah ahl-*MWEHR-*thah oos-*TEHD?
At what time do you have lunch?

REMEMBER: When you tell of what material something is made, use *de*. Ex: *Mi camisa es de seda.*
When you ask the time say: *¿Qué hora es?* But you only use *es* in the reply only if it is one o'clock. Otherwise you say, *son las doce, son las siete y media,* etc.

THINKING IN SPANISH
(Answers on page 260)

1. ¿Hay un reloj en este cuarto?
2. ¿Dónde está?
3. ¿Tiene Ud. reloj?
4. ¿Dónde está?
5. ¿De qué es la mesa?
6. ¿Señala su reloj los segundos?
7. ¿Qué hora es?
8. ¿A qué hora empieza su lección?
9. ¿A qué hora acaba?
10. ¿Cuántos minutos tiene una hora?
11. ¿De cuántas horas se compone un día?

12. ¿Cuántos segundos tiene un minuto?
13. ¿Está parado su reloj?
14. ¿Anda su reloj si Ud. no le da cuerda?
15. ¿Está adelantado su reloj de Ud.?
16. ¿Cuánto está adelantado?
17. ¿Está atrasado o adelantado el reloj del profesor?
18. ¿Cuánto?
19. ¿Es un reloj de pared más grande que un reloj de bolsillo?
20. ¿Es la mesa más grande que la silla?
21. ¿Es la pared más larga que la pizarra?
22. ¿Es la ventana tan ancha como la puerta?
23. ¿Tienen las señoras el cabello más largo que los señores?
24. ¿Son los sombreros de las señoras más bonitos que los sombreros de los señores?
25. ¿Es el agua mejor para beber que el té?
26. ¿Huele la violeta mejor que el tulipán?
27. ¿Huele el gas peor que la tinta?
28. ¿Es su pronunciación francesa mejor que su pronunciación española?
29. ¿Pronuncia Ud. bien el español?
30. ¿Pronuncia el profesor mejor que Ud.?
31. ¿Escribe Ud. tan bien como yo?
32. ¿Tiene Ud. buena vista?
33. ¿Ve Ud. bien?
34. ¿Ve el Sr. Berlitz bien sin gafas?
35. ¿Ve mejor con gafas?

¿En qué estación estamos?

*Enn keh ess-tahth-*YOHN *ess-*TAH*-mohs?*

In what season are we?

Aquí hay un calendario con los trescientos sesenta
*Ah-*KEE *I oon kah-lehn-*DAHR*-yoh kohn lohs trehs th'*YEHN*-tohs seh-*SEHN*-tah*
y cinco días que tiene un año.
ee THEEN*-koh* DEE*-ahs keh t'*YEH*-neh oon* AHN*-yoh.*
Here is a calendar with the three hundred and sixty-five days that a year contains.

El año se divide en doce meses y en cincuenta y dos semanas.
Ell AHN*-yoh seh dee-*VEE*-deh enn* DOH*-theh* MEH*-sehs*
*ee enn theen-*KWEHN*-tah ee dohs seh-*MAH*-nahs.*
The year is divided into twelve months and fifty-two weeks.

Una semana se compone de 7 días, que se llaman:
*Oo-nah seh-*MAH*-nah seh kohn-*POH*-neh deh s'*YEH*-teh* DEE*-ahs,*
*keh seh l'*YAH*-mahn:*
A week is formed of seven days, which are called:

150

lunes, martes, miércoles, jueves, viernes, sabado y domingo.
`LOO-*nehs,* MAHR-*tehs, m'*YEHR-*koh-lehs,* HWEH-*vehs, v'*YEHR-*nehs,*
SAH-*bah-doh ee doh-*MEEN-*goh.*
Monday, Tuesday, Wednesday, Thursday, Friday, Saturday and Sunday.

Trabajamos durante seis días de la semana,
*Trah-bah-*HAH-*mohs doo-*RAHN-*teh* SEH-*ees* DEE-*ahs deh lah seh-*MAH-*nah,*
We work during six days of the week,

y el séptimo día, domingo, no hacemos nada:
ee ell SEHP-*tee-moh* DEE-*ah, doh-*MEEN-*goh, noh ah-*THEH-*mohs* NAH-*dah:*
and the seventh day, Sunday, we do not do anything:

es día de fiesta.
ess DEE-*ah deh f'*YEHS-*tah.*
it is a holiday.

NOTE on the Passive: The construction *se forma* and *se compone* can be translated as "is formed" and "is composed". Ex: "The week is composed of 7 days": *La semana se compone de 7 días.*

Los meses son: enero, febrero, marzo, abril,
Los MEH-*sehs sohn: eh-*NEH-*roh, feh-*BREH-*roh,* MAHR-*thoh, ah-*BREEL,
The months are: January, February, March, April,

mayo, junio, julio, agosto, septiembre, octubre,
MAH-*yoh,* HOON-*yoh,* HOOL-*yoh, ah-*GOHS-*toh, sehpt-*YEHM-*breh, ohk-*TOO-*breh,*
May, June, July, August, September, October,

noviembre y diciembre.
*nohv-*YEHM-*breh ee deeth-*YEHM-*breh.*
November and December.

De estos meses, unos tienen 31, otros 30,
Deh ESS-*tohs* MEH-*sehs,* OO-*nohs t'*YEH-*nehn* TRAIN-*tah ee* OO-*noh,*
OH-*trohs* TRAIN-*tah*
Of these months, some have 31, others 30,

y febrero tiene sólo 28 días.
*ee feh-*BREH-*roh t'*YEH-*neh* SOH-*loh vain-tee-*OH-*choh* DEE-*ahs.*
and February has only 28 days.

Cada cuatro años, febrero tiene 29
KAH-*dah kwAH-troh* AHN-*yohs, feb-*BREH-*roh t'*YEH-*neh vain-tee-n*WEH-*veh*
días; y entonces, el año se llama año bisiesto.
DEE-*ahs; ee ehn-*TOH-*thehs, ell* AHN-*yoh seh l'*YAH-*mah* AHN-*yoh*
*beess-*YEHS-*toh.*
Every four years, February has 29 days; and then the year is called leap year.

En el año hay cuatro estaciones que son:
Enn ell AHN-*yoh I* KWAH-*troh ess-tahth-*YOH-*nehs keh sohn:*
In the year, there are four seasons which are:

invierno, primavera, verano y otoño.
*eenv-*YEHR-*noh, pree-mah-*VEH-*rah, veh-*RAH-*noh ee oh-*TOHN-*yoh.*
winter, spring, summer and autumn.

A WORD to Remember: *Entonces* usually means "then". It
can also mean "thereupon", "therefore" or even "well". It
is useful to bridge over pauses in conversation.

Marzo, abril y mayo son los meses
MAHR-*thoh, ah-*BREEL *ee* MAH-*yoh sohn lohs* MEH-*sehs*
de la primavera;
*deh lah pree-mah-*VEH-*rah;*
March, April and May are the months of spring;

junio, julio y agosto, los del verano,
HOON-*yoh,* HOOL-*yoh ee ah-*GOHS-*toh, lohs dehl veh-*RAH-*noh,*
June, July and August, those of summer,

septiembre, octubre y noviembre, los del otoño,
*sehpt-*YEHM-*breh, ohk-*TOO-*breh ee nohv-*YEHM-*breh, lohs dehl oh-*TOHN-*yoh;*
September, October and November, those of fall;

diciembre, enero y febrero, los del invierno.
*deeth-*YEHM-*breh, eh-*NEH-*roh ee feh-*BREH-*roh, lohs dehl eenv-*YEHR-*noh.*
December, January and February, those of winter.

Sírvase Ud. decirme en qué estación estamos.
SEER-*vah-seh oos-*TEHD *deh-*THEER-*meh enn keh ess-tahth-*YOHN *ess-*TAH-*mohs.*
Would you please tell me in what season we are?

Estamos en invierno.
*Ess-*TAH-*mohs enn eenv-*YEHR-*noh.*
We are in winter.

Esta estación dura hasta el 21 de marzo,
*Ess-tah es-tahth-*YOHN *DOO-rah* AHS-*tah ell* VAIN-*tee-*OO-*noh deh* MAHR-*thoh,*
This season lasts until the 21st of March,

el día en que comienza la primavera.
ell DEE-*ah enn keh kohm-*YEHN-*thah lah pree-mah-*VEH-*rah.*
the day on which spring begins.

Hoy es el 15 de enero, ayer fué el 14, mañana será el 16.
Oy ess ell KEEN-*theh deh eh-*NEH-*roh, ah-*YEHR *ſ*WEH *ell kah-*TOHR-*theh,*
*mahn-*YAH-*nah seh-*RAH *ell d'yehht-ee-*SEH-*ees.*
Today is January 15th, yesterday was the 14th, tomorrow will be the 16th.

Si Ud. quiere saber en qué día del mes o de la
*See oos-*TEHD *k'*YEH-*reh sah-*BEHR *enn keh* DEE-*ah dehl mehs oh deh lah*
If you want to know what day of the month or of the

semana estamos, lo ve en el calendario.
*seh-*MAH-*nah ess-*TAH-*mohs, loh veh enn ell kah-lehn-*DAHR-*yoh.*
week it is, you see it on the calendar.

Mire Ud., el año pasado,
MEE-*reh oos-*TEHD, *ell* AHN-*yoh pah-*SAH-*doh,*
1948, el primero
*meel noh-vehth-*YEHN-*tohs kwah-*REHN-*tah ee* OH-*choh, ell pree-*MEH-*roh*
de enero fué un jueves.
*deh eh-*NEH-*roh* FWEH *oon* HWEH-*vehs.*
Look, last year, 1948, January 1st was a Thursday.

Este año, 1949,
ESS-*teh* AHN-*yoh, meel noh-vehth-*YEHN-*tohs kwah-*REHN-*tah ee* NWEH-*veh,*
This year, 1949,

el primero de enero fué un sábado, y el año
*ell pree-*MEH-*roh deh eh-*NEH-*roh* FWEH *oon* SAH-*bah-doh, ee ell* AHN-*yoh*
January 1st was a Saturday, and next

próximo, 1950, será un domingo.
PROHK-*see-moh, meel noh-vehth-*YEHN-*tohs theen-*KWEHN-*tah,*
*seh-*RAH *oon doh-*MEEN-*goh.*
year, 1950, it will be a Sunday.

 IMPORTANT NOTE: You have seen that in this lesson we have used *fué* (was) and *será* (will be). These are past and future forms respectively of the verb *ser.* Do not worry about the other past and future forms of the other verbs yet, as we are reserving them for another lesson.

Ya son las doce, vamos a almorzar.
Yah sohn lahs DOH-*theh,* VAH-*mohs ah ahl-mohr-*THAHR.
It is already twelve o'clock, let's have lunch.

¿Oye Ud.? El reloj da la hora. Son las doce.
OH-*yeh oos-*TEHD? *Ell reh-*LOH *dah lah* OH-*rah. Sohn lahs* DOH-*theh.*
Do you hear? The clock strikes the hour. It is twelve o'clock.

THINKING IN SPANISH
(Answers on page 261)

1. ¿Cuántos días tiene un año?
2. ¿Cómo se llama el año que tiene trescientos sesenta y seis días?
3. ¿Cuándo comienza el año?
4. ¿Cuándo acaba?
5. ¿Cuál es el primero, segundo, tercero, cuarto, quinto, etc. mes del año?
6. ¿Cómo se llama el último mes del año?
7. ¿Cuáles son los siete días de la semana?
8. ¿Cuál es el ultimo día de la semana?
9. ¿En qué día de la semana estamos?
10. ¿Fué ayer domingo?
11. ¿Qué días estudia Ud.?
12. ¿Será sábado el quince?
13. ¿Qué fecha será el sábado?
14. ¿Cuándo será su cumpleaños?
15. ¿Qué día del mes será el lunes próximo?

16. ¿Qué día del mes fué el jueves pasado?
17. ¿Será mañana el último del mes?
18. ¿En qué estación estamos ahora?
19. ¿Cuántos meses dura una estación?
20. ¿Cuáles son los meses del verano?
21. ¿Qué estación sigue al invierno?
22. ¿Estamos en primavera?
23. ¿Qué día precede al domingo?
24. ¿Qué hora es?
25. ¿En qué días trabajamos?
26. ¿Trabaja Ud. el domingo?

LECCIÓN 25

El día y la noche
Ell DEE-*ah ee lah* NOH-*cheh*
Day and night

Las veinticuatro horas se dividen en dos partes:
Lahs VAIN-*tee-*KWAH-*troh* OH-*rahs seh dee-*VEE-*dehn enn dohs* PAHR-*tehs:*
el día y la noche.
ell DEE-*ah ee lah* NOH-*cheh.*
The twenty-four hours are divided into two parts: day and night.

El día es claro y podemos ver;
Ell DEE-*ah ess* KLAH-*roh ee poh-*DEH-*mohs vehr;*
pero la noche es obscura,
PEH-*roh lah* NOH-*cheh ess ohbs-*KOO-*rah,*
The day is light and we can see; but the night is dark,

y si queremos ver, debemos encender una luz.
*ee see keh-*REH-*mohs vehr, deh-*BEH-*mohs enn-thehn-*DEHR OO-*nah* looth,
and if we want to see, we must turn on a light.

156

En este cuarto, no hay bastante claridad:
Enn ESS-*teh* KWAHR-*toh, noh I bahs*-TAHN-*teh klah-ree-*DAHD;
In this room, there is not enough light;

haga el favor de encender la luz.
AH-*gah ell fah-*VOHR *deh enn-thehn-*DEHR *lah looth.*
please turn on the light.

Ya la luz eléctrica alumbra el cuarto.
*Yah lah looth eh-*LEHK-*tree-kah ah-*LOOM-*brah ell* KWAHR-*toh.*
Now the electric light lights up the room.

No acerque Ud. la mano a la bombilla; porque,
*Noh ah-*THEHR-*keh oos-*TEHD *lah* MAH-*noh ah lah bohm-*BEEL-*yah;* POHR-*keh*
Do not put your hand near the light, because,

aunque no tiene llama, como el gas, puede quemar.
*ah-*OON-*keh noh t'*YEH-*neh l'*YAH-*mah,* KOH-*moh ell gahs,* PWEH-*deh keh-*MAHR
although it has no flame, like gas, it can burn.

Encendemos el cigarrillo con un fósforo.
*Enn-thehn-*DEH-*mohs ell thee-gah-*RREEL-*yoh kohn oon* FOHS-*foh-roh.*
We light the cigarette with a match.

No necesitamos fósforo para encender la luz.
*Noh neh-theh-see-*TAH-*mohs* FOHS-*foh-roh* PAH-*rah enn-thehn-*DEHR *lah looth.*
We do not need a match to turn on the light.

¿Hay bastante luz en este cuarto ahora?
*I bahs-*TAHN-*teh looth enn* ESS-*teh* KWAHR-*toh ah-*OH-*rah?*
Is there enough light in this room now?

Sí, señor, hay bastante luz ahora.
*See, sehn-*YOHR, *i bahs-*TAHN-*teh looth ah-*OH-*rah.*
Yes, sir, there is enough light now.

¿Puede Ud. ver bien?
PWEH-*deh oos-*TEHD *vehr b'*YEHN?
Can you see well?

Sí, señor, yo puedo ver bien.
*See, sehn-*YOHR, *yoh* PWEH-*doh vehr b'*YEHN.
Yes, sir, I can see well.

Generalmente durante el día no usamos luz eléctrica.
*Heh-neh-rahl-*MEHN-*teh doo-*RAHN-*teh ell* DEE-*ah noh oo-*SAH-*mohs looth eh-*LEHK-*tree-kah.*
Generally during the day we do not use electric light.

Señor, sírvase apagar la luz.
*Sehn-*YOHR, SEER-*vah-seh ah-pah-*GAHR *lah looth.*
Sir, please turn the light off.

¿Qué hace Ud.?
Keh AH-*theh oos-*TEHD?
What do you do?

Yo apago la luz.
*Yoh ah-*PAH-*goh ιah* loetk.
I turn the light off.

¿Apago yo la luz?
*Ah-*PAH-*goh yoh lah looth?*
Do I turn the light off?

No, señor, Ud. no apaga la luz.
*Noh, sehn-*YOHR, *oos-*TEHD *noh ah-*PAH-*gah lah looth.*
No, sir, you do not turn the light off.

¿Está encendida o apagada la luz ahora?
*Ess-*TAH *enn-thehn-*DEE-*dah oh ah-pah-*GAH-*dah lah looth ah-*OH-*reh?*
Is the light on or off now?

La luz está apagada ahora.
*Lah looth ess-*TAH *ah-pah-*GAH-*dah ah-*OH-*rah.*
The light is off now.

¿Cuándo enciende Ud. la luz?
KWAHN-*doh ennth-*YEHN-*deh oos-*TEHD *lah looth?*
When do you turn the light on?

Yo enciendo la luz cuando está obscuro.
*Yoh ennth-*YEHN-*doh lah looth* kWAHN-*doh ess-*TAH *ohbs-*Kο····
I turn on the light when it is dark.

El profesor enciende un fósforo.
*Ell proh-feh-*SOHR *ennth-*YEHN-*deh oon* FOHS-*foh-roh.*
The teacher lights a match.

El profesor se quema.
*Ell proh-feh-*SOHR *seh* KEH-*mah.*
The teacher burns himself.

La luz del día viene del sol, que está en el cielo.
Lah looth dehl DEE-*ah v'*YEH-*neh dehl sohl, keh ess-*TAH *enn* εl·· ·ω ▼ατ-λοω.
The light of the day comes from the sun which is in the sky

Mire Ud. por la ventana.
MEE-*reh oos-*TEHD *pohr lah vehn-*TAH-*nah.*
Look out of the window.

¿Ve Ud. arriba el cielo azul?
*Veh oos-*TEHD *ah-*RREE-*bah ell th'*YEH-*loh ah-*THOOL?
Do you see the blue sky above?

De noche el sol no está visible,
Deh NOH-*cheh ell sohl noh ess*-TAH *vee*-SEE-*bleh,*
no podemos verlo;
noh poh-DEH-*mohs* VEHR-*loh;*
At night the sun is not visible, we can not see it;

pero vemos la luna y las estrellas.
PEH-*roh* VEH-*mohs lah* LOO-*nah ee lahs ess*-TREHL-*yahs.*
but we see the moon and the stars.

Las estrellas son innumerables,
Lahs ess-TREHL-*yahs sohn een-noo-meh*-RAH-*blehs,*
no se pueden contar.
noh seh PWEH-*dehn kohn*-TAHR.
The stars are innumerable, they can not be counted.

NOTE: *No se pueden contar* (they cannot be counted) is another striking use of the *se* used passively. It literally means "they cannot count themselves".

El principio del día se llama la mañana, y el fin la tarde.
Ell preen-THEEP-*yoh dehl* DEE-*ah seh l'*YAH-*mah lah mahn*-YAH-*nah,*
ee ell feen lah TAHR-*deh.*
The beginning of the day is called the morning, and the end, the evening.

Por la mañana sale el sol, y por la tarde se pone.
Pohr lah mahn-YAH-*nah* SAH-*leh ell sohl, ee pohr lah* TAHR-*deh seh* POH-*neh.*
In the morning the sun rises and in the evening it sets.

El este es el sitio por donde sale el sol,
Ell ESS-*teh ess ell* SEET-*yoh pohr* DOHN-*deh* SAH-*leh ell sohl,*
The east is the place where the sun rises,

y el oeste, por donde se pone.
ee ell oh-EHS-*teh, pohr* DOHN-*deh seh* POH-*neh.*
and the west, where it sets.

NOTE on *por: Por* means "by" and sometimes "through", "to", or "at". This is an excellent example of words in Spanish not having any single equivalent in English. Do not let this discourage you in Spanish, but note how the word is used in different contexts. Thus you will get a *feel* for it.

Los cuatro puntos cardinales son:
Lohs KWAH-*troh* POON-*tohs kahr-dee*-NAH-*lehs sohn:*
The four cardinal points are:

este, oeste, sur y norte.
ESS-*teh, oh*-EHS-*teh, soor ee* NOHR-*teh.*
East, West, South and North.

En verano el sol sale muy temprano, a las 4
Enn veh-RAH-*noh ell sohl* SAH-*leh mwee tehm*-PRAH-*noh, ah lahs* KWAH-*troh*
In summer the sun rises early, at 4

o 5 de la mañana, y los días son largos;
oh THEEN-*koh deh lah mahn*-YAH-*nah, ee lohs* DEE-*ahs sohn* LAHR-*gohs;*
or 5 in the morning, and the days are long;

pero en invierno sale tarde, a las 7,
PEH-*roh enn eenv*-YEHR-*noh* SAH-*leh* TAHR-*deh, ah lahs s'*YEH-*teh,*
but in winter it rises late, at 7,

y los días son cortos.
ee lohs DEE-*ahs sohn* KOHR-*tohs.*
and the days are short.

De noche, cuando tenemos sueño,
Deh NOH-*cheh, k*WAHN-*doh teh*-NEH-*mohs* SWEHN-*yoh,*
At night, when we are sleepy,

nos acostamos en la cama.
nohs ah-kohs-TAH-*mohs enn lah* KAH-*mah.*
we go to bed.

Por la mañana nos levantamos, nos bañamos,
Pohr lah mahn-YAH-*nah nohs leh-vahn*-TAH-*mohs, nohs bahn*-YAH-*mohs,*
In the morning we get up, we bathe,

nos afeitamos, nos peinamos, nos vestimos
nohs ah-fay-TAH-*mohs, nohs peh-ee*-NAH-*mohs, nohs vehs*-TEE-*mohs*
y nos desayunamos.
ee nos dehs-ah-yoo-NAH-*mohs.*
we shave, we comb our hair, we dress, and have breakfast.

NOTE on reflexive verbs: Most verbs having to do with care of one's person, such as to wash oneself, to dress oneself, etc., are reflexive. Ex. *vestirse* (to dress), *afeitarse* (to shave), *lavarse* (to wash), *bañarse* (to bathe), *cepillarse* (to brush one's hair), *acostarse* (to lie down), *levantarse* (to get up) and many others which you will encounter.

THINKING IN SPANISH
(Answers on page 262)

1. ¿Cómo se dividen las 24 horas del día?
2. ¿Cuándo hay claridad?
3. ¿Está oscuro ahora?
4. ¿De dónde viene la luz del día?
5. ¿Dónde está el sol?
6. ¿Alumbra el sol de noche?
7. ¿Con qué se alumbra este cuarto por la noche?
8. ¿Qué hacemos para ver cuando esta oscuro?
9. ¿Qué se ve en el cielo de noche?
10. ¿Cuáles son los cuatro puntos cardinales?
11. ¿Por qué punto sale el sol?
12. ¿Por dónde se pone?
13. ¿Dónde está el sol a mediodía?
14. ¿A qué hora sale el sol en marzo?
15. ¿Se pone temprano en verano?
16. ¿A qué hora se pone?

17. ¿En qué estación son largos los días?

18. ¿Son ahora las noches más largas que los días?

19. ¿Puede Ud. ver sin luz?

20. ¿Cuándo enciende Ud. la luz?

21. ¿Con qué se enciende el gas?

22. ¿Cuándo se acuesta Ud. generalmente?

23. ¿En qué se acuesta Ud.?

24. ¿Qué hace Ud. por la mañana?

25. ¿A qué hora se desayuna Ud.?

26. ¿Hasta qué hora trabaja Ud.?

27. ¿Le gusta a Ud. trabajar?

28. ¿Es la luz de la luna tan fuerte como la luz del sol?

29. ¿Cuándo alumbra la luna?

30. ¿Se pueden contar las estrellas?

31. ¿Tiene Ud. sueño de noche?

LECCIÓN 26

¿Qué tiempo hace?
*Keh t'*YEHM-*poh* AH-*theh?*
How is the weather?

El cielo está muy obscuro;
*Ell th'*YEH-*loh ess-*TAH *mwee ohbs-*KOO-*roh;*
está cubierto de nubes.
*ess-*TAH *koob-*YEHR-*toh deh* NOO-*behs.*
The sky is very dark; it is covered with clouds.

Empieza a llover, caen gotas.
*Ehmp-*YEH-*thah ah l'yoh-*VER, KAH-*ehn* GOH-*tahs.*
It is beginning to rain; drops are falling.

Abra Ud. su paraguas.
AH-*brah oos-*TEHD *soo pah-*RAH-*gwahs.*
Open your umbrella.

Ahora estamos preservados del agua del cielo;
*Ah-*OH-*rah ess-*TAH-*mohs preh-sehr-*VAH-*dohs dehl* AH-*gwah dehl* th'YEH-*Joh;*
Now we are protected from the water of the sky;

pero el piso está muy malo;
рЕН-roh ell PEE-*soh ess*-TAH *mwee* MAH-*loh;*
but the ground is very bad;

la calle está llena de charcos;
lah KAHL-*yeh ess*-TAH *l'*YEH-*nah deh* CHAHR-*kohs;*
the street is full of puddles;

y a cada paso que damos, nos ensuciamos.
ee ah KAH-*dah* PAH-*soh keh* DAH-*mohs, nohs enn-sooth-*YAH-*mohs.*
and with each step we take, we get dirty.

Volvamos a casa;
*Vohi-*VAH-*mohs ah* KAH-*sah;*
el tiempo está demasiado malo
*ell t'*YEHM-*poh ess*-TAH *deh-mahs-*YAH-*doh* MAH-*loh*
Let us go back home; the weather is too bad

para estar afuera.
PAH-*rah ess*-TAHR *ah*-FWEH-*rah.*
to remain outside.

Este cuarto está muy agradable.
Ess-*teh* KWAHR-*toh ess*-TAH *mwee ah-grah-*DAH-*bleh.*
This room is very pleasant.

Quitémonos la ropa mojada
Kee-TEH-*moh-nohs lah* ROH-*pah moh-*HAH-*dah*
y pongámonos otra seca.
*ee pohn-*GAH-*moh-nohs* OH-*trah* SEH-*kah.*
Let us take off our wet clothes and let us put on some dry ones.

¡Qué día tan desagradable!
Keh DEE-*ah tahn* DEHS-*ah-grah-*DAH-*bleh!*
What an unpleasant day!

Mire Ud., ya comienza a nevar.
MEE-*reh oos-*TEHD, *yah kohm-*YEHN-*thah ah neh-*VAHR.
Look, it is starting to snow.

Copos de nieve mezclados con gotas de lluvia,
KOH-*pohs deh n'*YEH-*veh mehth-*KLAH-*dohs kohn* GOH-*tahs deh l'*YOOV-*yah,*
Snow flakes, mixed with rain drops,

dan contra los cristales de las ventanas.
dahn KOHN-*trah lohs krees-*TAH-*lehs deh lahs vehn-*TAH-*nahs.*
fall against the window panes.

WORDS TO REMEMBER: *Ya:* "already", "no longer" (when used with "no"), *todavía:* "still". *Ya* has several other uses, one of which is simply to give emphasis to something said. Ex: *Lo creo:* "I think so". *Ya lo creo:* "I certainly think so".

La estación está muy avanzada para nevar;
*Lah ess-tahth-*YOHN *ess-*TAH *mwee ah-vahn-*THAH-*dah* PAH-*rah neh-*VAHR;
The season is quite advanced for snow; (it is very late in the season for snow);

estamos en abril, pero el tiempo es de diciembre:
*ess-*TAH-*mohs enn ah-*BREEL, PEH-*roh ell t'*YEHM-*poh ess deh deeth-*YEHM-*breh:*
we are in April, but the weather is (that) of December:

hace mucho frío.
AH-*theh* MOO-*choh* FREE-*oh.*
it is very cold.

Siéntese Ud. junto al fuego; caliéntese Ud.
S'YEHN-*teh-seh oos-*TEHD HOON-*toh ahl* FWEH-*goh; kahl-*YEHN-*teh-seh oos-*TEHD.
Sit down by the fire; warm yourself.

El fuego está casi apagado.
Ell FWEH-*goh ess-*TAH KAH-*see ah-pah-*GAH-*doh.*
The fire is almost out.

Juan, atice Ud. el fuego;
HWAHN, *ah-*TEE-*theh oos-*TEHD *ell* FWEH-*goh;*
John, poke the fire;

eche Ud. un poco de carbón.
EH-*cheh oos-*TEHD *oon* POH-*koh deh kahr-*BOHN.
throw on a little coal.

USEFUL EXPRESSIONS: Several constructions which are expressed in English by "I am" change to "I have" in Spanish:

"I am cold": *Tengo frío.*
"I am hot": *Tengo calor.*
"I am sleepy": *Tengo sueño.*
"I am hungry": *Tengo hambre.*
"I am thirsty": *Tengo sed.*

¿Todavía tiene Ud. frío?
*Toh-dah-*VEE-*ah t'*YEH-*neh oos-*TEHD FREE-*oh?*
Are you still cold?

Ya no gracias.
Yah noh GRAHTH-*yahs.*
Not any more, thank you.

Quítese Ud. los zapatos; es malo tener
KEE-*teh-seh* oos-TEHD *lohs thah-*PAH-*tohs; ess* MAH-*loh teh-*NEHR
los pies mojados.
*lohs pee-*EHS *moh-*HAH-*dohs.*
Take your shoes off; it is bad to have wet feet.

Puede coger un catarro.
PWEH-*deh koh-*HEHR *oon kah-*TAH-*rroh.*
You can catch a cold.

En Centroamérica hace mucho calor.
Enn THEHN-*troh-ah-*MEH-*ree-kah* AH-*theh* MOO-*choh kah-*LOHR.
In Central America it is very hot.

Nunca nieva, excepto en las montañas altas.
NOON-*kah n'*YEH-*vah, ehk-*THEHP-*toh enn lahs mohn-*TAHN-*yahs* AHL-*tahs.*
It never snows, except in the high mountains.

Hay solamente dos estaciones,
*I soh-lah-*MEHN-*teh dohs ess-tahth-*YOH-*nehs,*
There are only two seasons,

la estación seca y la estación de las lluvias.
*lah ess-tahth-*YOHN SEH-*kah ee lah ess-tahth-*YOHN *deh lahs l'*YOOV-*yahs.*
the dry season and the rainy season.

En la estación de las lluvias llueve casi todos
*Enn lah ess-tahth-*YOHN *deh lahs l'*YOOV-*yahs l'*YWEH-*veh* KAH-*see* TOH-*doh*
los días.
lohs DEE-*ahs.*
In the rainy season it rains almost every day.

REMEMBER these idioms: Many expressions about the
weather are formed with *hace*. Note the following:

> *Hace frío:* "It is cold".
> *Hace calor:* "It is hot".
> *Hace sol:* "The sun is shining".

NOTE: *Nunca*, like *nada* and *nadie*, must be used with *no*
with negative verb forms. Ex: "It never snows in Panama";
No nieva nunca en Panamá.

THINKING IN SPANISH
(Answers on page 262)

1. ¿Cómo está el cielo cuando hace mal tiempo?
2. ¿De qué está cubierto el cielo cuando llueve?
3. ¿Está lloviendo ahora?
4. ¿Qué cae del cielo en invierno?
5. ¿Está bueno el piso cuando llueve?
6. ¿Qué lleva Ud. para preservarse de la lluvia?
7. ¿Qué tiempo hace ahora?
8. ¿Sale Ud. cuando está lloviendo?
9. ¿Hace mucho calor en este cuarto?
10. ¿Hace frío afuera?
11. ¿En qué meses nieva?
12. ¿Nieva mucho en febrero?
13. ¿Nieva a menudo en abril?
14. Y ¿nieva alguna vez en agosto?
15. ¿Tiene Ud. frío?
16. ¿Con que se calienta la sala en invierno?

17. ¿Con que nos preservamos del frío?
18. ¿De dónde viene el calor?
19. ¿Calienta tanto el sol en invierno como en verano?
20. ¿Está siempre malo el piso cuando llueve?
21. ¿Junto a qué se sienta Ud. para calentarse?
22. ¿Le agrada a Ud. salir cuando hace mucho viento?
23. ¿En qué mes hace mucho viento?
24. ¿En qué meses se pone Ud. vestidos gruesos?

LECCIÓN 27

La clase de historia
Lah KLAH-*seh deh* ee-STOH-*ree-ah*
The history class

ALFREDO: Buenos días, Carlos. ¿Cómo está?
*Ahl-*FREH-*doh:* BWEH-*nohs* DEE-*ahs,* KAHR-*lohs.* KOH-*moh ess-*TAH?
ALFRED: Good morning, Charles. How are you?

CARLOS: Muy bien, gracias. ¿Y Ud.?
KAHR-*lohs: Mwee b'*YEHN, GRAHTH-*yahs. Ee oos-*TEHD?
CHARLES: Very well, thank you. And you?

ALFREDO: Cansado. Me acosté tarde anoche.
*Kahn-*SAH-*doh. Meh ah-kohs-*TEH TAHR-*deh ah-*NOH-*cheh.*
Tired. I went to bed late last night.

CARLOS: ¿Por qué? ¿Estudió mucho su lección?
Pohr KEH? *Ess-tood-*YOH MOO-*choh soo lehkth-*YOHN?
Why? Did you study your lesson much?

169

ALFREDO: No tuve tiempo para estudiar. Fuí a casa de
Noh TOO-*veh* t'YEHM-*poh* PAH-*rah* ess-tood-YAHR. FWEE *ah* KAH-*sah deh*
I did not have time to study. I went to Manuel's

Manuel, y desde allí fuímos juntos al cine.
Mah-NWEHL, *ee* DEHS-*deh ahl*-YEE FWEE-*mohs* HOON-*tohs ahl* THEE-*neh.*
house, and from there we went to the movies together.

CARLOS: ¿Vieron una película buena?
*V'*YEH-*rohn* OO-*nah peh*-LEE-*koo-lah* BWEH-*nah?*
Did you see a good picture?

ALFREDO: Vimos una nueva película de Jorge
VEE-*mohs* OO-*nah* NWEH-*vah peh*-LEE-*koo-lah deh* HOHR-*heh*
We saw a new picture of Jorge

Negrete. Fué muy divertida y con buena música también.
Neh-GREH-*teh.* FWEH *mwee dee-vehr-*TEE-*dah ee kohn* BWEH-*nah*
MOO-*see-kah tahmb*-YEHN.
Negrete. It was very amusing and had good music too.

CARLOS: ¿Qué hicieron después?
Keh eeth-YEH-*rohn dehs*-PWEHS?
What did you do afterwards?

ALFREDO: Después del cine fuimos a una fiesta
Dehs-PWEHS *dehl* THEE-*neh* FWEE-*mohs ah* OO-*nah f'*YEHS-*tah*
en casa de Anita.
enn KAH-*sah deh Ah*-NEE-*tah.*
After the movies we went to a party at Anita's house.

CARLOS: ¿Quiénes estuvieron allí?
*K'*YEH-*nehs ess-toov-*YEH-*rohn ahl*-YEE?
Who were there?

ALFREDO: Estuvieron Elena, Roberto, Vicente
*Ess-toov-*YEH-*rohn Eh*-LEH-*nah,* *Roh*-BEHR-*toh,* *Vee*-THEHN-*teh*
Helen, Robert, Vincent,

y muchos otros amigos, todos de la escuela.
ee MOO-*chohs* OH-*trohs ah*-MEE-*gohs,* TOH-*dohs deh lah ess*-KWEH-*lah.*
and many other friends were there, all from the school.

Tocamos unos discos nuevos en el fonógrafo y bailamos.
Toh-KAH-*mohs* OO-*nohs* DEES-*kohs* NWEH-*vohs enn ell foh*-NOH-*grah-foh*
*ee bah-ee-*LAH-*mohs.*
We played some new records on the phonograph, and we danced.

A medianoche Anita preparó una cena que
*Ah mehd-yah-*NOH-*cheh Ah-*NEE-*tah preh-pah-*ROH OO-*nah* THEH-*nah keh*
comimos con mucho gusto.
*koh-*MEE-*mohs kohn* MOO-*choh* GOOS-*toh.*
At midnight Anita prepared a supper which we enjoyed very much.

CARLOS: ¿Se divirtieron Uds. mucho?
*Seh dee-veert-*YEH-*rohn oos-*TEHD-*ehs* MOO-*choh?*
Did you enjoy yourselves very much?

ALFREDO: Llamamos a su casa por teléfono pero nadie contestó.
*L'yah-*MAH-*mohs ah soo* KAH-*sah pohr teh-*LEH-*foh-noh* PEH-*roh* NAHD-*yeh*
*kohn-tehs-*TOH.
We called your house on the phone, but nobody answered.

CARLOS: Aquí viene el profesor.
*Ah-*KEE *v'*YEH-*neh ell proh-feh-*SOHR.
Here comes the teacher.

Vamos a entrar en la clase......
VAH-*mohs ah enn-*TRAHR *enn lah* KLAH-*seh......*
Let's go into the class......

(en la clase)
(enn lah KLAH-*seh)*
(in the class)

PROFESOR: Hoy vamos a tener un repaso sobre
*Proh-feh-*SOHR: *Oy* VAH-*mohs ah teh-*NEHR *oon reh-*PAH-*soh* SOH-*breh*
algunas fechas históricas.
*ahl-*GOO-*nahs* FEH-*chahs ees-*TOH-*ree-kahs.*
PROFESSOR: Today we shall have a review of some historical dates.

Sr. Campana, ¿en qué año llegaron los españoles a México?
*Sehn-*YOHR *kahm-*PAH-*nah, enn keh* AHN-*yoh l'yeh-*GAH-*rohn lohs*
*ess-pahn-*YOH-*lehs ah* MEH-*hee-koh?*
Mr. Campana, in what year did the Spaniards arrive in Mexico?

ALFREDO: Pues......Colón llegó a las islas del Caribe
PWEHS......*Koh-*LOHN *l'yeh-*GOH *ah lahs* EES-*lahs dehl Kah-*REE-*bek*
en 1492......
enn meel KWAH-*troh th-*YEHN-*tohs noh-*VEHN-*tah ee dohs......*
Well......Columbus arrived at the Caribbean isles in 1492......

PROFESOR: Yo no le pregunté nada de Colón.
*Yoh noh leh preh-goon-*TEH NAH-*dah deh Koh-*LOHN.
I did not ask you anything about Columbus.

Conteste a mi pregunta.
*Kohn-*TEHS-*teh ah mee preh-*GOON-*tah.*
Answer my question.

ALFREDO: ......(Silencio)
......(*See-*LEHNTH-*yoh*)
......(Silence)

PROFESOR: Sr. Bertín, ¿sabe Ud.?
*Sehn-*YOHR BEHR-TEEN, SAH-*beh oos-*TEHD?
Mr. Bertin, do you know?

CARLOS: Cortez y su pequeño ejército llegaron a México en 1519.
*Kohr-*TEHTH *ee soo peh-*KEHN-*yoh eh-*HEHR-*thee-toh l'yeh-*GAH-*rohn ah*
MEH-*hce-koh enn meel keen-*YEHN-*tohs d'*YEHTH *ee* NWEH-*veh.*
Cortez and his small army arrived in Mexico in 1519.

PROFESOR: Correcto. Ahora, Alfredo, díganos algo de Simón Bolívar.
*Koh-*RREHK-*toh. Ah-*OH-*rah, Ahl-*FREH-*doh,* DEE-*gah-nohs* AHL-*goh aeh*
*See-*MOHN *Boh-*LEE-*vahr.*
Right. Now, Alfred, tell us something about Simon Bolivar.

ALFREDO: Simón Bolívar libertó varios países de Sur América.
*See-*MOHN *Boh-*LEE-*vahr lee-behr-*TOH VAHR-*yohs pah-*EE-*sehs deh Soor*
*Ah-*MEH-*ree-kah.*
Simon Bolivar liberated several countries of South America.

Nació en Caracas, estudió en Europa,
*Nahth-*YOH *enn Kah-*RAH-*kahs, ess-tood-*YOH *enn Eh-oo-*ROH-*pah,*
He was born in Caracas, studied in Europe,

y ganó muchas batallas contra los españoles.
*ee gah-*NOH MOO-*chahs bah-*TAHL-*yahs* KOHN-*trah lohs ess-pahn-*YOH-*lehs.*
and won many battles against the Spaniards.

PROFESOR: ¿No sabe Ud. cuando nació o cuando murió?
Noh SAH-*beh oos-*TEHD KWAHN-*doh nahth-*YOH *oh* KWAHN-*doh moor-*YOH?
Don't you know when he was born, or when he died?

ALFREDO: No, señor. No sé el año exacto.
*Noh, sehn-*YOHR. *Noh seh ell* AHN-*yoh ehk-*SAHK-*toh.*
No, sir, I do not know the exact year.

PROFESOR: Sr. Bertín, ¿sabe Ud.?
*Sehn-*YOHR *Behr-*TEEN, SAH-*beh oos-*TEHD?
Mr. Bertin, do you know?

CARLOS: Sí, nació en 1783
    *See, nahth-*YOH *enn meei seh-tehth-*YEHN-*tohs oh-*CHEHN-*tah ee trehs*
    y murió en 1830. Ganó la
    *ee moor-*YOH *enn meel oh-chohth-*YEHN-*tohs* TRAIN-*tah.* Gah-NOH *lah*
    gran batalla de Boyacá
    *grahn bah-*TAHL-*yah deh Boh-yah-*KAH
    en 1819.
    enn meel OH-*choh th'*YEHN-*tohs d'*YEHTH *ee* NWEH-*veh.*
    Yes, he was born in 1783 and he died in 1830. He won the great battle
    of Boyacá in 1819.

(después de la clase)
(*dehs-*PWEHS *deh lah* KLAH-*seh*)
(after class)

ALFREDO: ¡Qué desgracia! No supe la contestación
    *Keh dehs-*GRAHTH-*yah! Noh* SOO-*peh lah kohn-tehs-tahth-*YOHN
    What a shame! I did not know the answer

de ninguna pregunta que hizo el profesor.
    *deh neen-*GOO-*nah preh-*GOON-*tah keh* EE-*thoh ell proh-feh-*SOHR.
    of any of the questions the teacher asked.

¿Por qué fuí al cine anoche?
    Pohr KEH FWEE *ahl* THEE-*neh ah-*NOH-*cheh?*
    Why did I go to the movies last night?

NOTE ON THE PAST TENSE: The Past Tense is really
quite easy.
    You will remember that all verbs are divided into three
conjugations which we can recognize by their infinitive
endings—*ar, er,* and *ir.* Notice the difference in the past and
present forms in the following table:

—tomar—		—aprender—		—vivir—	
Present	*Past*	*Present*	*Past*	*Present*	*Past*
Yo tomo	tomé	aprendo	aprendí	vivo	viví
Ud. toma	tomó	aprende	aprendió	vive	vivió
él (ella) toma	"	"	"	"	"
nosotros tomamos	tomamos	aprendemos	aprendimos	vivimos	vivimos
Uds. (ellos) (ellas)					
toman	tomaron	aprenden	aprendieron	viven	vivieron

Actually you have only 2 regular endings to learn:
1. For —*AR*— verbs—*é, ó, amos* and *aron.*
2. For all others—*í, ió, imos, ieron.*

However the Spanish are not different from ourselves when it comes to verbs. Those you use most frequently are irregular, of course.

Take careful note of the following:

Infinitive—Past form.

to be—*ser*   —*fui, fué, fuimos, fueron.* } This is no misprint,
to go—*ir*   —*fui, fué, fuimos, fueron.* } they really are the same.
to give—*dar*   —*di, dió, dimos, dieron.*
to come—*venir*   —*vine, vino, vinimos, vinieron.*
to say—*decir*   —*dije, dijo, dijimos, dijeron.*

to walk—*andar*   —*anduve, anduvo, anduvimos, auduvieron.*
to know—*saber*   —*supe, supo, supimos, supieron.*
to have—*tener*   —*tuve, tuvo, tuvimos, tuvieron.*
to put—*poner*   —*puse, puso, pusimos, pusieron.*
to do—*hacer*   —*hice, hizo, hicimos, hicieron.*
to be able—*poder*   —*pude, pudo, pudimos, pudieron.*

to produce—*producir*   —*produje, produjo, produjimos, produjeron.*
to want—*querer*   —*quise, quiso, quisimos, quisieron.*
to bring—*traer*   —*traje, trajo, trajimos, trajeron.*
to be—*estar*   —*estuve, estuvo, estuvimos, estuvieron.*
(auxiliary)—*haber*   —*hube, hubo, hubimos, hubieron.*

Verbs in the last group are similar in their irregularity.—1st conjugation endings in the singular and 2nd conjugation endings in the plural.

CHECK YOUR ACCENTS! We have already told you to stress an accented syllable. Now that you are working with the past tense, watch your accents even more carefully, both in pronouncing and in writing. One accent may change the whole meaning of a sentence. Look at this:

Mato a mi suegra: "I kill my mother-in-law."
Mató a mi suegra: "He killed my mother-in-law."

THINKING IN SPANISH

(Answers on page 263)

1. ¿Cuándo llegaron los españoles a México?
2. ¿Quién fué Hernán Cortés?
3. ¿Quién fué Simón Bolívar?
4. ¿En qué ciudad nació?
5. ¿Estudió Alfredo su lección de historia?
6. ¿Por qué no la estudió?
7. ¿Qué hicieron Alfredo y Manuel después del cine?
8. ¿Fueron a una fiesta?
9. ¿Qué personas estuvieron en la fiesta?
10. ¿Qué pregunta le hizo el profesor a Alfredo?
11. ¿Quién contestó bien a las preguntas del profesor?
12. ¿A qué hora se despierta Ud.?
13. ¿A que hora se despertó ayer?
14. ¿Cuándo se levantó?

15. ¿Qué hizo Ud. antes de desayunarse?
16. ¿Qué traje se puso?
17. ¿Se lavó Ud. con agua fría?
18. ¿Se vistió muy de prisa?
19. ¿Se desayunó temprano?
20. ¿Tomó Ud. café con leche?
21. ¿Bebió leche?
22. ¿Fué a dar un paseo?
23. ¿Recibió algunas cartas?
24. ¿Las contestó Ud.?
25. ¿Dió Ud. un paseo ayer?
26. ¿Adónde fué?
27. ¿A qué hora almorzó Ud.?
28. ¿Tuvo Ud. buen apetito?
29. ¿Tuvo mucho que hacer ayer?
30. ¿Estuvo muy ocupado?
31. ¿Oyó Ud. muchos conciertos el invierno pasado?
32. ¿Dónde nació Ud.?
33. ¿Estuve yo en su casa el domingo?
34. ¿Comimos anoche juntos?
35. ¿Fuimos anoche al teatro?
36. ¿Estuvo Ud. en la ciudad el invierno pasado?
37. ¿Rió Ud. mucho en el cine ayer?

LECCIÓN 28

Los animales
*Lohs ah-nee-*MAII-*lehs*
The animals

El hombre y los animales pueden moverse porque viven.
Ell OHM-*breh ee lohs ah-nee-*MAH-*lehs* PWEH-*dehn moh-*VEHR-*seh* POR-*keh*
VEE-*vehn.*
Man and the animals can move because they live.

Para vivir deben respirar, comer y beber; sin
PAH-*rah vee-*VEER DEH-*behn rehs-pee-*RAHR, *koh-*MEHR *ee beh-*BEHR; *seen*
To live they must breathe, eat, and drink; without

aire ni alimento no pueden vivir, mueren.
AH-*ee-reh nee ah-lee-*MEHN-*toh noh* PWEH-*dehn vee-*VEER, MWEH-*rehn.*
air or food they cannot live, they die.

El hombre y la mayor parte de los animales
Ell OHM-*breh ee lah mah-*YOHR PAHR-*teh deh lohs ah-nee-*MAH-*lehs*
Man and most animals

177

tienen cinco sentidos, que son: la vista, el oído,
t'YEH-nehn THEEN-*koh sehn*-TEE-*dohs, keh sohn: lah* VEES-*tah, ell oh*-EE-*doh,*
have five senses, which are: sight, hearing,

el olfato, el gusto y el tacto.
ell ohl-FAH-*toh, ell* GOOS-*toh ee ell* TAHK-*toh.*
smell, taste and touch.

Los órganos de la vista son los ojos;
Lohs OHR-*gah-nohs deh lah* VEES-*tah sohn lohs* OH-*hohs;*
The organs of sight are the eyes;

los del oído son los oídos, que están dentro de las
lohs dehl oh-EE-*doh sohn lohs oh*-EE-*dohs, keh ess*-TAHN DEHN-*troh deh lahs*
those of hearing are the ear-drums, which are inside the

orejas; el olfato está en la nariz; el sitio del
oh-REH-*hahs; ell ohl*-FAH-*toh ess*-TAH *enn lah nah*-REETH; *ell* SEET-*yoh dehl*
ears; smell is in the nose; the location of

gusto está en la lengua, y el tacto se extiende por todo el cuerpo.
GOOS-*toh ess*-TAH *enn lah* LEHN-*gwah, ee ell* TAHK-*toh seh ehkst*-YEHN-*deh*
pohr TOH-*doh ell* KWEHR-*poh.*
taste is in the tongue and touch is spread over the whole body.

La vista nos indica el color, la forma, la
Lah VEES-*tah nohs een*-DEE-*kah ell koh*-LOHR, *lah* FOHR-*mah, lah*
Sight tells us the color, shape,

dimensión, el lugar y la posición de los
dee-mehnth-YOHN, *ell loo*-GAHR *ee lah poh-seeth*-YOHN *deh lohs*
dimension, place and position of

objetos; por el oído, percibimos los sonidos;
ohb-HEH-*tohs; pohr ell oh*-EE-*do, pehr-thee*-BEE-*mohs lohs sohn*-EE-*dohs;*
objects; through hearing, we perceive sounds;

por el tacto sentimos el frío del hielo, el calor
pohr ell TAHK-*toh sehn*-TEE-*mohs ell* FREE-*oh dehl* YEH-*loh, ell kah*-LOHR,
through touch we feel the cold of ice, the heat

del radiador, dolor cuando nos quemamos, y la
dehl rahd-yah-DOHR, *doh*-LOHR KWAHN-*doh nohs keh*-MAH-*mohs, ee lah*
of the radiator, pain when we burn ourselves, and the

blandura o dureza de los cuerpos.
blahn-DOO-*rah oh doo*-REH-*thah deh lohs* KWEHR-*pohs.*
softness or hardness of objects.

Los animales pueden clasificarse
*Lohs ah-nee-*MAH-*lehs* PWEH-*dehn klah-see-fee-*KAHR-*seh*
en cuadrúpedos, aves, peces, reptiles e insectos.
*enn kwah-*DROO-*peh-dohs,* AH-*vehs,* PEH-*says rehp-*TEE-*lehs eh een-*SEHK-*tohs.*
Animals can be classified into quadrupeds, birds, fish, reptiles and insects.

NOTE: *Y* means "and." However, when the next word begins with an *i*, replace *y* with *e.* Ex: *americanos e ingleses:* "Americans and Englishmen."

Similarly, *o* means "or," but changes to *u* when the next word begins with an *o.* Ex: "Seven or eight": *Siete u ocho.*

Los cuadrúpedos viven en la tierra; tienen cuatro patas para andar,
*Lohs kwah-*DROO-*peh-dohs* VEE-*vehn enn lah t'*YEH-*rrah;*
*t'*YEH-*nehn* KWAH-*troh* PAH-*tahs* PAH-*rah ahn-*DAHR,
The quadrupeds live on the ground; they have four legs to walk,

correr y saltar, y su cuerpo está cubierto de pelos.
*koh-*RREHR *ee sahl-*TAHR, *ee soo* KWEHR-*poh ess-*TAH *koob-*YEHR-*toh deh*
PEH-*lohs.*
run and jump, and their bodies are covered with hair.

Cuadrúpedos son: el caballo, el buey,
*Kwah-*DROO-*peh-dohs sohn: ell kah-*BAHL-*yoh, ell* BWEH-*ee,*
(Some) quadrupeds are: the horse, the ox,

la vaca, el asno, el carnero, el perro, el gato,
lah VAH-*kah, ell* AHS-*noh, ell kahr-*NEH-*roh, ell* PEH-*rroh, ell* GAH-*toh,*
the cow, the donkey, the sheep, the dog, the cat,

los cuales son animales domésticos; el león, el
lohs KWAH-*lehs sohn ah-nee-*MAH-*lehs doh-*MEHS-*tee-kohs; ell leh-*OHN, *ell*
which are domestic animals; the lion, the

tigre, el oso, la hiena, el lobo, la zorra, que son animales salvajes (fieras).
TEE-*greh, ell* OH-*soh, lah* YEH-*nah, ell* LOH-*boh, lah* THOH-*rrah,*
*keh sohn ah-nee-*MAH-*lehs sahl-*VAH-*hehs (f'*YEH-*rahs).*
tiger, the bear, the hyena, the wolf, the fox, which are wild animals.

La llama es un animal doméstico de Sur América que vive en los Andes.
*Lah l'*YAH-*mah ess oon ah-nee-*MAHL *doh-*MEHS-*tee-koh deh Soor*
*Ah-*MEH-*ree-kah keh* VEE-*veh enn lohs* AHN-*dehs.*
The llama is a domestic animal of South America which lives in the Andes.

Las aves viven en la tierra y en el aire;
Lahs AH-*vehs* VEE-*vehn enn lah t'*YEH-*rrah ee enn ell* AH-*ee-reh;*
Birds live on the ground and in the air;

tienen dos patas, y además dos alas con las
*t'*YEH-*nehn dohs* PAH-*tahs, ee ah-deh-*MAHS *dohs* AH-*lahs kohn lahs*
they have two legs and also two wings with

cuales vuelan; tienen pico para comer.
ᴋᴡᴀʜ-*lehs* ᴠᴡᴇʜ-*lahn;* *t'*ʏᴇʜ-*nehn* ᴘᴇᴇ-*koh* ᴘᴀʜ-*rah* koh-ᴍᴇʜʀ.
which they fly; they have a beak for eating.

Su cuerpo está cubierto de plumas. Son aves: la gallina, el pato, el pavo,
Soo ᴋᴡᴇʜʀ-*poh* ess-ᴛᴀʜ *koob*-ʏᴇʜʀ-*toh* deh ᴘʟᴏᴏ-*mahs.*
Sohn ᴀʜ-*vehs:* lah gahl-ʏᴇᴇ-*nah,* ell ᴘᴀʜ-*toh,* ell ᴘᴀʜ-*voh,*
Their bodies are covered with feathers. (Some) birds are: the hen, the duck,
the turkey,

el pavo real, el ganso, el loro, el águila,
ell ᴘᴀʜ-*voh* reh-ᴀʜʟ, *ell* ɢᴀʜɴ-*soh,* *ell* ʟᴏʜ-*roh,* *ell* ᴀʜ-*gee-lah,*
el avestruz, el buho, la golondrina, el gorrión.
ell ah-vehs-ᴛʀᴏᴏᴛʜ, *ell* ʙᴏᴏ-*oh,* lah *goh-lohn*-ᴅʀᴇᴇɴ-*nah,* *ell* gohrr-ʏᴏʜɴ.
the peacock, the goose, the parrot, the eagle, the ostrich, the owl,
the swallow, the sparrow.

El hombre y estas dos clases de animales tienen
Ell ᴏʜᴍ-*breh* ee ᴇss-*tahs* dohs ᴋʟᴀʜ-*sehs* deh ah-nee-ᴍᴀʜ-*lehs* *t'*ʏᴇʜ-*nehn*
Man and these two kinds of animals have

sangre roja y caliente, y un corazón que la hace
ꜱᴀʜɴ-*greh* ʀᴏʜ-*hah* ee kahl-ʏᴇʜɴ-*teh,* ee oon koh-rah-ᴛʜᴏʜɴ keh lah ᴀʜ-*theh*
red, warm blood, and a heart which makes it

circular; tienen pulmones para respirar,
theer-koo-ʟᴀʜʀ; *t'*ʏᴇʜ-*nehn* *pool*-ᴍᴏʜ-*nehs* ᴘᴀʜ-*rah* rehs-pee-ʀᴀʜʀ,
circulate; they have lungs for breathing,

y un estómago para digerir el alimento.
ee oon ess-ᴛᴏʜ-*mah-goh* ᴘᴀʜ-*rah* dee-heh-ʀᴇᴇʀ ell ah-lee-ᴍᴇʜɴ-*toh.*
and a stomach to digest food.

Si alguno de esos órganos ᴌᴠ funciona bien,
See ahl-ɢᴏᴏ-*noh* deh ᴇss-*ohs* ᴏʜʀ-*gah-nohs* noh foonth-ʏᴏʜ-*nah* b'ʏᴇʜɴ,
If one of these organs does not work well,

estamos enfermos y debemos ir al médico.
ess-ᴛᴀʜ-*mohs* enn-ꜰᴇʜʀ-*mohs* ee deh-ʙᴇʜ-*mohs* eer ahl ᴍᴇʜ-*dee-koh.*
we are sick and we must go to a doctor.

Los peces viven en el agua. No tienen patas ni alas,
Lohs ᴘᴇʜ-*thehs* ᴠᴇᴇ-*vehn* enn ell ᴀʜ-*gwah.*
Noh *t'*ʏᴇʜ-*nehn* ᴘᴀʜ-*tahs* nee ᴀʜ-*lahs,*
Fish live in the water. They have no legs or wings,

pero están provistos de aletas, con las cuales
ᴘᴇʜ-*roh* ess-ᴛᴀʜɴ *proh*-ᴠᴇᴇꜱ-*tohs* deh ah-ʟᴇʜ-*tahs,* kohn lahs ᴋᴡᴀʜ-*lehs*
but they are provided with fins, with which

se mueven al nadar; y algunos pueden volar.
seh ᴍᴡᴇʜ-*vehn* ahl nah-ᴅᴀʜʀ, ee ahl-ɢᴏᴏ-*nohs* ᴘᴡᴇʜ-*dehn* voh-ʟᴀʜʀ.
they can move by swimming; and some can fly.

El tiburón es el pez más feroz.
*Ell tee-boo-*ROHN *ess ell pehth mahs feh-*ROHTH.
The shark is the most ferocious fish.

Hay mucho tiburones en el mar Caribe, y son
I MOO-*chohs tee-boo-*ROH-*nehs enn ell mahr Kah-*REE-*beh, ee sohn*
There are many sharks in the Caribbean Sea, and they

peligrosos. Si Ud. ve un tiburón donde hay gente
*peh-lee-*GROH-*sohs. See oos-*TEHD *veh oon tee-boo-*ROHN DOHN-*deh I* HEHN-*teh,*
are dangerous. If you see a shark where there are people

nadando, Ud. grita,— ¡Cuidado! ¡Hay tiburones!
*nah-*DAHN-*doh, oos-*TEHD GREE-*tah, —Kwee-*DAH-*doh! I tee-boo-*ROH-*nehs!*
swimming, you shout,—"Look out! There are sharks!"

USEFUL PHRASES: The following interjections and commands are commended to use, with the hope that you will
not need some of them.

Help!— *¡Socorro!*	Go away!— *¡Váyase!*
Look out!— *¡Cuidado!*	Police!— *¡Policía!*
Stop!— *¡Alto!*	Hurrah!— *¡Viva!*

El reptil principal es la serpiente;
*Ell rehp-*TEEL *preen-thee-*PAHL *ess lah sehrp-*YEHN-*teh;*
The most important reptile is the snake;

no tiene patas y se arrastra por tierra.
*noh t'*YEH-*neh* PAH-*tahs ee seh ah-*RRAHS-*trah pohr t'*YEH-*rrah.*
it has no legs and crawls on the ground.

Los cocodrilos viven en los grandes ríos
*Lohs koh-koh-*DREE-*lohs* VEE-*vehn enn lohs* GRAHN-*dehs* REE-*ohs*
tales como el Orinoco y el Amazonas.
TAH-*lehs* KOH-*moh ell Oh-ree-*NOH-*koh ee ell Ah-mah-*THOH-*nahs.*
Crocodiles live in large rivers such as the Orinoco and the Amazon.

La rana vive en la tierra y en el agua.
Lah RAH-*nah* VEE-*veh enn lah t'*YEH-*rrah ee enn ell* AH-*gwah.*
The frog lives on the ground and in the water.

La abeja produce miel, y el gusano de seda produce seda;
*Lah ah-*BEH-*hah proh-*DOO-*theh m'*YEHL,
*ee ell goo-*SAH-*noh deh* SEH-*dah proh-*DOO-*theh* SEH-*dah;*
The bee produces honey, and the silk worm produces silk;

estos insectos son útiles.
ESS-*tohs een-*SEHK-*tohs sohn* OO-*tee-lehs.*
these insects are useful.

La mosca y el mosquito son, por el contrario, insectos nocivos.
Lah MOHS-*kah ee ell mohs-*KEE-*toh sohn,*
*pohr ell kohn-*TRAHR-*yoh, een-*SEHK-*tohs noh-*THEE-*vohs.*
The fly and the mosquito are, on the contrary, harmful insects.

THINKING IN SPANISH
(Answers on page 264)

1. ¿Pueden las plantas moverse?
2. ¿Qué deben hacer los animales para vivir?
3. ¿Podemos vivir si no comemos?
4. ¿Tienen las plantas necesidad de agua?
5. ¿De qué tenemos necesidad para vivir?
6. ¿Cuáles son los 5 sentidos?
7. ¿Cuáles son los órganos de estos sentidos?
8. ¿Cómo se dividen los animales?
9. ¿Cómo se llaman los principales animales domésticos?
10. ¿Qué diferencia hay entre las aves y los cuadrúpedos?
11. ¿Cuál es el ave más grande? 12. ¿Es útil?
13. ¿Qué ave tiene el plumaje más hermoso?
14. ¿Cuáles son los órganos de la digestión y de la respiración?
15. ¿Está Ud. bien de salud? 16. ¿Qué es un pez?
17. ¿Cómo se mueve la serpiente? 18. ¿Anda la rana?
19. ¿Cuál es la utilidad de la abeja y del gusano de seda?
20. ¿Es nocivo el mosquito?

LECCIÓN 29

Los choferes están enojados. Doña Felicidad tiene miedo. Chiquita se ríe del accidente. El Profesor está fastidiado porque el tiempo pasa.

El hombre y sus emociones
Ell OHM-breh ee soos eh-mohth-YOH-nehs
Man and his emotions

¿Es el hombre superior a los animales?
Ess ell OHM-breh soo-pehr-YOHR ah lohs ah-nee-MAH-lehs?
Is man superior to the animals?

Los animales pueden hacer muchas cosas mejor que el hombre.
Lohs ah-nee-MAH-lehs PWEH-dehn ah-THEHR MOO-chahs KOH-sahs meh-HOHR keh ell OHM-breh.
The animals can do many things better than man.

Por ejemplo: el águila tiene una vista mejor,
Pohr eh-HEHM-ploh: ell AH-gee-lah t'YEH-neh OO-nah VEES-tah meh-HOHR,
For instance: the eagle has better sight,

el pez nada mejor, el caballo puede correr más ligero,
ell pehth NAH-dah meh-HOHR, ell kah-BAHL-yoh PWEH-deh koh-RREHR mahs
the fish swims better, the horse can run faster

que el hombre, y el elefante es más
lee-HEH-roh, ee ell OHM-breh, ee ell ehl-leh-FAHN-teh ess mahs
than man, and the elephant is more

183

poderoso que muchos hombres juntos.
*poh-deh-*ROH*-soh keh* MOO*-chohs* OHM*-brehs* HOON*-tohs.*
powerful than many men together.

Sin embargo el hombre es superior a los animales por su cerebro.
*Seen ehm-*BAHR*-goh ell* OHM*-breh ess soo-pehr-*YOHR *ah lohs ah-nee-*MAH*-lehs*
*pohr soo theh-*REH*-broh.*
Nevertheless, man is superior to animals because of his brain.

Se dice que el león es el rey de los animales, pero no es verdad;
Seh DEE*-theh keh ell leh-*OHN *ess ell* REH*-ee deh lohs ah-nee-*MAH*-lehs,*
PEH*-roh noh ess vehr-*DAHD*;*
They say that the lion is the king of beasts but it is not true;

el hombre es el rey por su cerebro más desarrollado.
ell OHM*-breh ess ell* REH*-ee pohr soo theh-*REH*-broh mahs*
*deh-sah-rrohl-*YAH*-doh.*
man is the king because of his more highly developed brain.

Con el cerebro, que se halla en la cabeza, pensamos.
*Kohn ell theh-*REH*-broh, keh seh* AHL*-yah enn lah kah-*BEH*-thah,*
*pehn-*SAH*-mohs.*
With the brain, which is in the head, we think.

Sin pensar no podemos hablar.
*Seen pehn-*SAHR *noh poh-*DEH*-mohs ah-*BLAHR.
Without thinking we cannot speak.

Tenemos en el cerebro imágenes llamadas ideas.
*Teh-*NEH*-mohs enn ell theh-*REH*-broh ee-*MAH*-heh-nehs l'yah-*MAH*-dahs*
*ee-*DEH*-ahs.*
We have in our brain images called ideas.

Hablamos para comunicar nuestras ideas a otras personas.
*Ah-*BLAH*-mohs* PAH*-rah koh-moo-nee-*KAHR NWEHS*-trahs ee-*DEH*-ahs*
ah OH*-trahs pehr-*SOH*-nahs.*
We speak to communicate our ideas to other persons.

Pensamos en personas y cosas presentes o ausentes.
*Pehn-*SAH*-mohs enn pehr-*SOH*-nahs ee* KOH*-sahs preh-*SEHN*-tehs oh*
*ah-oo-*SEHN*-tehs.*
We think of persons and things which are present or absent.

Ud. piensa ahora en su lección.
*Oos-*TEHD *p'*YEHN*-sah ah-*OH*-rah enn soo lehkth-*YOHN.
You are thinking of your lesson now.

Si Ud. piensa en otra cosa, no puede comprenderme bien.
*See oos-*TEHD *p'*YEHN*-sah enn* OH*-trah* KOH*-sah,*
noh PWEH*-deh kohm-prehn-*DEHR*-meh b'*YEHN.
If you are thinking of something else, you cannot understand me well.

Muy a menudo Ud. piensa en sus lecciones cuando está en su casa.
*Mwee ah meh-*NOO-*doh oos-*TEHD *p'*YEHN-*sah enn soos lehkth-*YOH-*nehs*
KWAHN-*doh ess-*TAH *enn soo* KAH-*sah.*
Very often you think of your lessons when you are at home.

¿En qué piensa Ud. a las doce cuando la mesa está puesta?
*Enn keh p'*YEHN-*sah oos-*TEHD *ah lahs* DOH-*theh*
KWAHN-*doh lah* MEH-*sah ess-*TAH PWEHS-*tah?*
Of what do you think at twelve o'clock when the table is set?

Si una persona piensa mucho y bien, se dice que es inteligente.
See OO-*nah pehr-*SOH-*nah p'*YEHN-*sah* MOO-*choh ee b'*YEHN,
seh DEE-*theh keh ess een-teh-lee-*HEHN-*teh.*
If a person thinks much and well, we say that he is intelligent.

Las personas inteligentes aprenden fácilmente.
*Lahs pehr-*SOH-*nahs een-teh-lee-*HEHN-*tehs ah-*PREHN-*dehn*
FAH-*theel-*MEHN-*teh.*
Intelligent persons learn easily.

¿Es el burro inteligente? No; el burro es estúpido.
Ess ell BOO-*rroh een-teh-lee-*HEHN-*teh? Noh; ell* BOO-*rroh ess ess-*TOO-*pee-doh*
Is the donkey intelligent? No, the donkey is stupid.

Sabemos una cosa, cuando la aprendemos bien.
*Sah-*BEH-*mohs* OO-*nah* KOH-*sah,* KWAHN-*doh lah ah-prehn-*DEH-*mohs b'*YEHN.
We know something, when we learn it well.

Ud. sabe contar en español; pero, ¿sabe Ud. contar en ruso?
*Oos-*TEHD SAH-*beh kohn-*TAHR *een ess-pahn-*YOHL;
PEH-*roh,* SAH-*beh oos-*TEHD *kohn-*TAHR *enn* ROO-*soh?*
You know how to count in Spanish, but do you know how to count in
Russian?

¿Sabe Ud. hablar chino?
SAH-*beh oos-*TEHD *ah-*BLAHR CHEE-*noh?*
Do you know how to speak Chinese?

Yo sé su nombre.   ¿Sabe Ud. también el mio?
Yoh seh soo NOHM-*breh.* SAH-*beh oos-*TEHD *tahmb-*YEHN *ell* MEE-*oh?*
I know your name.   Do you also know mine?

Ud. sabe lo que tengo en mi mano, porque lo ve;
*Oos-*TEHD SAH-*beh loh keh* TEHN-*goh enn mee* MAH-*noh, pohr-keh loh veh;*
You know what I have in my hand because you see it;

pero no sabe lo que tengo en mi bolsillo.
PEH-*roh noh* SAH-*beh loh keh* TEHN-*goh enn mee bohl-*SEEL-*yoh.*
but you do not know what I have in my pocket.

No retenemos todo lo que aprendemos;
*Noh reh-teh-*NEH*-mohs* TOH*-doh loh keh ah-prehn-*DEH*-mohs;*
We do not retain all we learn;

algunas cosas se nos van de la cabeza; las olvidamos.
*ahl-*GOO*-nahs* KOH*-sahs seh nohs vahn deh lah kah-*BEH*-thah;*
*lahs ohl-vee-*DAH*-mohs.*
some things slip out of our heads; we forget them.

¿Retiene Ud. todas las frases que aprende en la clase?
*Reht-*YEH*-neh oos-*TEHD TOH*-dahs lahs* FRAH*-sehs keh ah-*PREHN*-deh enn lah*
KLAH*-seh?*
Do you remember all the phrases you learn in class?

¿Es fácil olvidar apellidos?
Ess FAH*-theel ohl-vee-*DAHR *ah-pehl-*YEE*-dohs?*
Is it easy to forget names?

 NOTE: *Querer* means "to wish" or "to want" and also "to love" and "to like." *Amar* also means "to love" but it i . not in popular use. When whispering sweet nothings to your beloved, use the verb *querer (a).*

En el hombre las sensaciones y los sentimientos
Enn ell OHM*-breh lahs sehn-sahth-*YOH*-nehs ee lohs sehn-teem-*YEHN*-tohs*
son más vivos que en los animales.
sohn mahs VEE*-vohs keh enn lohs ah-nee-*MAH*-lehs.*
In man, sensations and feelings are stronger than in the animals.

Los animales quieren a sus hijos; pero el amor de
*Lohs ah-nee-*MAH*-lehs k'*YEH*-rehn ah soos* EE*-hohs;* PEH*-roh ell ah-*MOHR *deh*
Animals love their young; but the love of

nuestra madre es mucho más fuerte.
NWEHS*-trah* MAH*-dreh ess* MOO*-choh mahs* FWEHR*-teh.*
our mother is much stronger.

Queremos a nuestra familia, amamos a nuestro país.
*Keh-*REH*-mohs ah* NWEHS*-trah fah-*MEEL*-yah, ah-*MAH*-mohs ah* NWEHS*-troh*
*pah-*EES.
We love our family, we love our country.

Si nos sucede algo agradable, nos alegramos.
*See nohs soo-*THEH*-deh* AHL*-goh ah-grah-*DAH*-bleh, nohs ah-leh-*GRAH*-mohs.*
If something pleasant happens to us, we are glad.

Si nos sucede algo desagradable, lo sentimos.
*See nohs soo-*THEH*-deh* AHL*-goh deh-sah-grah-*DAH*-bleh, loh sehn-*TEE*-mohs.*
If something unpleasant happens to us, we are sorry.

Si su profesor le dice que Ud. es muy buen alumno, se alegra.
*See soo proh-feh-*SOHR *leh* DEE-*theh keh oos-*TEHD *ess mwee* BWEHN
*ah-*LOOM-*noh, seh ah-*LEH-*grah.*
If your teacher tells you that you are a very good pupil, you are glad.

Si está lloviendo mucho y no puede salir, Ud. lo siente.
*See ess-*TAH *l'yohv-*YEHN-*doh* MOO-*choh ee noh* PWEH-*deh
sah-*LEER, *oos-*TEHD *loh s'*YEHN-*teh.*
If it is raining hard and you cannot go out, you are sorry.

Cuando su amigo le dice que no puede ir a casa
KWAHN-*doh soo ah-*MEE-*goh leh* DEE-*theh keh noh* PWEH-*deh eer ah* KAH-*sah*
When your friend tells you that he cannot go to your house

porque está enfermo, Ud. le dice:
POHR-*keh ess-*TAH *enn-*FEHR-*moh, oos-*TEHD *leh* DEE-*theh:*
because he is ill, you say to him:

Lo siento mucho, espero que mañana esté mejor.
*Loh s'*YEHN-*toh* MOO-*choh, ess-*PEH-*roh keh mahn-*YAH-*nah
ess-*TEH *meh-*HOHR.
I am very sorry, I hope that tomorrow you will be better.

NOTE: *Esté* is the form you have learned for the imperative.
This form is really the imperative-subjunctive. If you say
you wish or want something done, you use the same form as
if you were giving a direct order. Ex:—"Bring me the
newspaper." *Tráigame el periódico.* "I hope you bring me
the newspaper." *Espero que Ud. me traiga el periódico.*

Otra sensación es el miedo.
OH-*trah sehn-sahth-*YOHN *ess ell m'*YEH-*doh.*
Another sensation is fear.

Los animales pequeños tienen miedo de los más grandes y fuertes.
*Lohs ah-nee-*MAH-*lehs peh-*KEHN-*yohs t'*YEH-*nehn m'*YEH-*doh
deh lohs mahs* GRAHN-*dehs ee* FWEHR-*tehs.*
The small animals are afraid of the larger and stronger ones.

Los niños tienen miedo de la oscuridad.
Lohs NEEN-*yohs t'*YEH-*nehn m'*YEH-*doh deh lah ohs-koo-ree-*DAHD.
Children are afraid of darkness.

Algunas muchachas tienen miedo de las arañas, ratones y culebras.
*Ahl-*GOO-*nahs moo-*CHAH-*chahs t'*YEH-*nehn m'*YEH-*doh deh lahs ah-*RAHN-*yahs,
rah-*TOH-*nehs ee koo-*LEH-*brahs.*
Some girls are afraid of spiders, mice and snakes.

Si un hombre no tiene miedo de nada, es valiente.
See oon OHM-*breh noh t'*YEH-*neh m'*YEH-*doh deh* NAH-*dah, ess* vahl-YEHN-*teh*
If a man is not afraid of anything, he is brave.

¿Fué Simón Bolívar valiente?
FWEH *See-*MOHN *Boh-*LEE-*vahr* vahl-YEHN-*teh?*
Was Simon Bolivar brave?

Las cosas desagradables nos disgustan.
Lahs KOH-*sahs dehs-ah-grah-*DAH-*blehs nohs dees-*GOOS-*tahn.*
We dislike unpleasant things.

Nos disgusta mucho el ruido cuando queremos dormir.
*Nohs dees-*GOOS-*tah* MOO-*choh ell* RWEE-*doh* KWAHN-*doh keh-*REH-*mohs*
*dohr-*MEER.
We dislike noise when we want to sleep.

Nos disgustan las picaduras de los mosquitos.
*Nohs dees-*GOOS-*tahn lahs pee-kah-*DOO-*rahs deh lohs mohs-*KEE-*tohs.*
We dislike mosquito bites.

Cuando una persona está muy disgustada se dice que está enojada.
KWAHN-*doh* OO-*nah pehr-*SOH-*nah ess-*TAH *mwee dees-goos-*TAH-*dah*
seh DEE-*theh keh ess-*TAH *eh-noh-*HAH-*dah.*
When a person is very much annoyed, we say that he is angry.

Cuando chocan dos automóviles, los choferes se enojan.
KWAHN-*doh* CHOH-*kahn dohs ah-oo-toh-*MOH-*vee-lehs,*
*lohs choh-*FEH-*rehs seh en-*NOH-*hahn.*
When two automobiles collide, the chauffeurs become angry.

Las cosas graciosas nos hacen reir.
Lahs KOH-*sahs grahth-*YOH-*sahs nohs* AH-*thehn reh-*EER.
Funny things make us laugh.

Al ver un actor cómico en el cine, ¿se ríe Ud.?
*Ahl vehr oon ahk-*TOHR KOH-*mee-koh enn ell* THEE-*neh, seh* REE-*eh* oos-TEHD.
When you see a comedian in the movies, do you laugh?

Algunas veces lloramos cuando estamos tristes.
*Ahl-*GOO-*nahs* VEH-*thehs l'yoh-*RAH-*mohs* KWAHN-*doh ess-*TAH-*mohs* TREES-*tehs*
Sometimes we cry when we are sad.

¿Lloran mucho los niños?
L'YOH-*rahn* MOO-*choh lohs* NEEN-*yohs?*
Do children cry much?

¿Qué es más agradable,
*Keh ess mahs ah-grah-*DAH-*bleh,*
un niño que llora o uno que no llora?
oon NEEN-*yoh keh l'*YOH-*rah oh* OO-*noh keh noh l'*YOH-*rah?*
Which is more pleasant, a child who cries or one who does not cry?

IDIOMS TO REMEMBER: *se dice:* "it is said" or "they say"

sin embargo: "however," "nevertheless"
pensar en: "to think about"
muy a menudo: "very often"
saber hablar: "to know how to speak."

Saber by itself means "to know." But with an infinitive it means "to know how to"

tener miedo: "to be afraid"
tener verguenza: "to be ashamed"
tener gana de: "to wish to"
sentir: "to be sorry" (It really means "to feel.")
al ver: "upon seeing"

(This is a special construction of *al* with the infinitive, and can be used with practically any verb.)

AN OLD SPANISH CUSTOM: *apellido:* "last name"
nombre: "first name"

In Latin America you add your mother's maiden name to your father's name. This gives everyone two last names and helps to avoid confusion. Suppose your name is Arturo Ortiz-Córdoba and your wife's name is Zoraida Toro-Parra. If you have a daughter named Elisa, then *her* name will be Elisa Ortiz-Toro.

El Profesor está contento porque tiene mucho dinero. Chiquita llora porque su muñeca está rota. Doña Felicidad llora porque nadie la quiere.

THINKING IN SPANISH
(Answers on page 264)

1. ¿Está triste o contento el profesor?
2. ¿Por qué está contento?   3. ¿Por qué llora Chiquita?
4. ¿Se ríe Doña Felicidad?   5. ¿Por qué está triste?
6. ¿Es el hombre superior a los animales en todo?
7. ¿Piensa Ud. en su lección cuando no está en clase?
8. ¿Se puede hablar correctamente sin pensar?
9. ¿Qué es necesario para saber una cosa?
10. ¿Qué aprende Ud. en este momento?
11. ¿Dónde aprenden los niños a leer y a escribir?   12. ¿Sabe Ud. nadar?
13. ¿Se puede leer sin aprender?   14. ¿Puede Ud. leer sin ver?
15. ¿Sabe Ud. cuánto dinero tengo en el bolsillo?
16. ¿Sabemos cuántas estrellas hay en el cielo?
17. ¿Olvida Ud. fácilmente?   18. ¿Quiere Ud. a su madre?
19. ¿Ama Ud. a su país?   20. ¿Admira Ud. la música española?
21. ¿Se alegra Ud. de saber que toda su familia está en buena salud?
22. Si un amigo suyo está enfermo, ¿lo siente Ud.?
23. Al ver un ratón, ¿tienen las señoritas miedo?
24 ¿Cuántos apellidos tiene un señor español?

LECCIÓN 30

¿Dónde ha estado Ud.?

DOHN-*deh ah* ess-TAH-*doh* oos-TEHD?

Where have you been?

AJA: ¡Mi amigo Rodríguez! ¿Dónde ha estado Ud.?
AH-*hah: Mee ah*-MEE-*goh Roh*-DREE-*gehth!* DOHN-*deh ah* ess-TAH-*doh*
oos-TEHD?
AJA: My friend Rodríguez! Where have you been?

Desde hace un mes no lo he visto.
DEHS-*deh* AH-*theh oon mehs noh loh* ch VEES-*tɔh.*
I have not seen you for a month.

191

RODRÍGUEZ: He estado en la Habana. ¿No ha
*Roh-*DREE-*gehth: Eh ess-*TAH-*doh enn lah Ah-*BAH-*nah. Noh ah*
recibido Ud. las tarjetas postales que le he enviado?
*reh-thee-*BEE-*doh oos-*TEHD *lahs tahr-*HEH-*tahs pohs-*TAH-*lehs keh leh eh*
*ehnv-*YAH-*doh?*
RODRÍGUEZ: I have been in Havana. Have you not received the post cards
that I sent you?

AJA: No he recibido nada.
*Noh eh reh-thee-*BEE-*doh* NAH-*dah.*
I have not received anything.

RODRÍGUEZ: Le he escrito dos. Pienso que todavía no han llegado.
*Leh eh ess-*KREE-*toh dohs. P'*YEHN-*soh keh toh-dah-*VEE-*ah noh ahn*
*l'yeh-*GAH-*doh.*
I wrote two. I think they have not yet arrived.

AJA: ¿Ha tenido buen viaje?
*Ah teh-*NEE-*doh* BWEHN *v'*YAH-*heh?*
Have you had a good trip?

RODRÍGUEZ: No muy bueno. He viajado en barco y el mar
Noh mwee BWEH-*noh. Eh v'yah-*HAH-*doh enn* BAHR-*koh ee ell mahr*
Not very good. I traveled by ship and the sea

ha estado malo todo el tiempo.
*ah ess-*TAH-*doh* MAH-*loh* TOH-*doh ell t'*YEHM-*poh.*
was rough the whole time.

AJA: ¿Y qué me dice Ud. de la Habana? ¿Se ha divertido Ud.?
Ee keh meh DEE-*theh oos-*TEHD *deh lah Ah-*BAH-*nah? Seh ah*
*dee-vehr-*TEE-*doh oos-*TEHD?*
And what do you say about Havana? Have you enjoyed yourself?

RODRÍGUEZ: No he tenido tiempo para divertirme.
*Noh eh teh-*NEE-*doh t'*YEHM-*poh* PAH-*rah dee-vehr-*TEER-*meh.*
I have not had time to enjoy myself.

He estado ocupado todo el tiempo en negocios.
*Eh ess-*TAH-*doh oh-koo-*PAH-*doh* TOH-*doh ell t'*YEHM-*pok enn*
*neh-*GOHTH-*yohs.*
I have been busy the whole time with business.

AJA: ¿Qué negocios tiene Ud. allí?
*Keh neh-*GOHTH-*yohs t'*YEH-*neh oos-*TEHD *ahl-*YEE?*
What business have you there?

RodrÍguez: **Tengo unas casas en la Habana que quiero vender.**
Tehn-*goh* oo-*nahs* KAH-*sahs* enn lah Ah-BAH-*nah keh* k'YEH-*roh*
*vehn-*DEHR.
I have some houses in Havana which I want to sell.

Aja: **Y ¿las ha vendido?**
Ee *lahs* ah vehn-DEE-*doh?*
And have you sold them?

RodrÍguez: **No he podido venderlas. No me han**
*Noh eh poh-*DEE-*doh vehn-*DEHR-*lahs. Noh meh ahn*
ofrecido un precio suficiente.
oh-*freh-*THEE-*doh oon* PREHTH-*yoh soo-feeth-*YEHN-*teh.*
I could not sell them. They have not offered me enough money.

He hablado con un corredor de casas y me ha
*Eh ah-*BLAH-*doh kohn oon koh-rreh-*DOHR *deh* KAH-*sahs ee meh ah*
I spoke with a real estate broker and he told

dicho que ahora no es el momento para venderlas.
DEE-*choh keh ah-*OH-*rah noh ess ell moh-*MEHN-*toh* PAH-*rah*
*vehn-*DEHR-*lahs.*
me that this is not the time to sell them.

Aja: **Sí, es mejor esperar.**
*See, ess meh-*HOHR *ess-peh-*RAHR.
Yes, it is better to wait.

NOTE ON THE PERFECT TENSE: You have seen that it is formed simply by combining *he, ha, hemos,* and *han* with the past participle of the verb.

The past participle ends in *ado* for the first conjugation and usually in *ido* for the other two.

Note how it is used below.

> "I have received"—*Yo he recibido.*
> "He has taken"—*El ha tomado.*
> "We have given"—*Nosotros hemos dado.*
> "They have heard"—*Ellos han oído.*

HOWEVER, in English usage we often use the simple past where Spanish uses the perfect.

WATCH OUT! A very few verbs do not form their past participle in this easy way. Some of these exceptions, with their past participles in parenthesis, are:

> volver (*vuelto*), hacer (*hecho*), poner (*puesto*), ver (*visto*), escribir (*escrito*), romper (*roto*), decir (*dicho*), abrir (*abierto*).

RODRÍGUEZ: ¿Ha visto Ud. a Salgado y a su señora?
Ah VEES-*toh* oos-TEHD *ah Sahl-*GAH-*doh ee ah soo sehn-*YOH-*rah?*
Have you seen Salgado and his wife?

Ellos me han pedido unas cosas de la Habana
EHL-*yohs meh ahn peh-*DEE-*doh* OH-*nahs* KOH-*sahs deh lah Ah-*BAH-*nah*
They asked me for some things from Havana

y me han dado el dinero para comprarlas.
ee meh ahn DAH-*doh ell dee-*NEH-*roh* PAH-*rah kohm-*PRAHR-*lahs.*
and they gave me the money to buy them.

AJA: No les he visto. Ellos salieron de la ciudad
Noh lehs eh VEES-*toh.* EHL-*yohs sahl-*YEH-*rohn deh lah th'yoo-*DAHD
I have not seen them. They left the city

hace dos semanas y no han vuelto todavía.
AH-*theh dohs seh-*MAH-*nahs ee noh ahn* VWEHL-*toh toh-dah-*VEE-*ah.*
two weeks ago and they have not returned yet.

¿Qué les ha traído Ud.?
*Keh lehs ah trah-*EE-*doh* oos-TEHD?
What have you brought them?

IDIOMS TO REMEMBER: *pasar:* "to pass", also "to happen"

¿*qué pasa?:* "what is happening?"
divertirse: "to have a good time", "to enjoy oneself."

RODRÍGUEZ: Les he traído unos cigarros de la Habana
*Lehs eh trah-*EE-*doh* oo-*nohs thee-*GAH-*rrohs deh lah Ah-*BAH-*nah*
I brought them some cigars from Havana

y un frasco de perfume;
ee oon FRAHS-*koh deh pehr-*FOO-*meh;*
and a flask of perfume;

pero durante el viaje, el frasco se ha roto.
PEH-*roh doo-*RAHN-*teh ell v'*YAH-*heh, ell* FRAHS-*koh seh ah* ROH-*toh.*
but during the trip, the flask broke.

AJA: ¿Cómo ha pasado eso?
KOH-*moh ah pah-*SAH-*doh* EH-*soh?*
How did that happen?

RODRÍGUEZ: No sé como ha pasado. Creo que uno de los
Noh seh KOH-*moh ah pah-*SAH-*doh.* KREH-*oh keh* oo-*noh deh lohs*
I do not know how it has happened. I think that one of the

porteros ha dejado caer la maleta en el muelle.
*pohr-*TEH-*rohs ah deh-*HAH-*doh kah-*EHR *lah mah-*LEH-*tah enn ell*
MWEHL-*yeh.*
porters dropped the bag on the pier.

THINKING IN SPANISH
(Answers on page 265)

1. ¿Dónde se ha acostado el profesor?   2. ¿Se ha quitado el saco?

3. ¿Ha leído el periódico?   4. ¿Ha bebido el vaso de limonada?

5. ¿Ha leído Ud. el periódico hoy?   6. ¿Dónde ha estado el Sr. Rodríguez?

7. ¿Vió el Sr. Aja al Sr. Rodríguez hace un mes?

8. ¿Ha escrito el Sr. Rodríguez tarjetas postales?   9. ¿Han llegado?

10. ¿Cómo ha estado el mar durante el viaje?

11. ¿Le ha gustado al Sr. Rodríguez el viaje?

12. ¿Se ha divertido el Sr. Rodríguez en la Habana?

13. ¿Por qué no se ha divertido?   14. ¿Ha estado Ud. en la Habana?

15. ¿En qué países latinos ha estado Ud.?

16. ¿Ha vendido el Sr. Rodríguez sus casas en la Habana?

17. ¿Por qué no las ha vendido?

18. ¿Qué ha traído Rodríguez para el Sr. Salgado?

19. ¿Qué ha pasado con el perfume?   20. ¿Ha viajado Ud. a España?

21. ¿Por dónde ha viajado Ud.?   22. ¿Ha leído muchos libros en español?

LECCIÓN 31

¿Qué pasará mañana?

*Keh pah-sah-*RAH *mahn-*YAH-*nah?*

What will happen tomorrow?

SEÑOR ARANGO: ¿Está Ud. muy ocupado hoy?
*Sehn-*YOHR *Ah-*RAHN-*goh: Ess-*TAH *oos-*TEHD *mwee oh-koo-*PAH-*doh oy?*
MR. ARANGO: Are you very busy today?

SEÑOR SARMIENTO: Hoy no; pero mañana tendré
*ſehn-*YOHR *Sahrm-*YEHN-*toh: Oy noh;* PEH-*roh mahn-*YAH-*nah tehn-*DREH
    mucho que hacer;
    MOO-*choh keh ah-*THEHR;
    estaré muy ocupado todo el día.
    *ess-tah-*REH *mwee oh-koo-*PAH-*doh* TOH-*doh ell* DEE-*ah.*
MR. SARMIENTO: Not today; but tomorrow I shall have
    a lot to do; I shall be very busy all day long.

ARANGO: ¿Qué tendrá usted que hacer?
    *Keh tehn-*DRAH *oos-*TEHD *keh ah-*THEHR?
    What will you have to do?

SARMIENTO: Me levantaré temprano, a las ocho de la mañana,
*Meh leh-vahn-tah-*REH *tehm-*PRAH*-noh, ah lahs* OH*-choh
*de lah mahn-*YAH*-nah,*
I shall get up early, at eight o'clock in the morning,

tomaré una lección, luego escribiré unos ejercicios,
*toh-mah-*REH OO*-nah lehkth-*YOHN,
LWEH*-goh ess-kree-bee-*REH OO*-nohs eh-hehr-*THEETH*-yohs,*
I shall take a lesson, then I shall write some exercises,

y leeré unas páginas del libro
*ee leh-eh-*REH OO*-nahs* PAH*-hee-nahs dehl* LEE*-broh*
and read a few pages of the book

que mi profesor me dió el otro día.
*key mee proh-feh-*SOHR *meh dee-*OH *ell* OH*-troh* DEE*-ah.*
that my teacher gave me the other day.

ARANGO: ¿Y qué hará Ud. a hacer después?
*Ee keh ah-*RAH *oos-*TEHD *dehs-*PWEHS?
And what will you do later?

¿Se quedará Ud. en casa o comerá con nosotros?
*Seh keh-dah-*RAH *oos-*TEHD *enn* KAH*-sah oh koh-meh-*RAH *kohn
noh-*SOH*-trohs?*
Will you stay at home or will you eat with us?

SARMIENTO: A las doce saldré y comeré con Uds.
Ah lahs DOH*-theh sahl-*DREH *ee koh-meh-*REH *kohn oos-*TEH*-dehs.*
At twelve I shall go out and eat with you,

y enseguida iré a casa del pintor.
*ee ehn-seh-*GEE*-dah ee-*REH *ah* KAH*-sah dehl peen-*TOHR.
and then I shall go to the painter's (house).

Si Ud. viene conmigo, verá mi retrato
*See oos-*TEHD *v'*YEH*-neh kohn-*MEE*-goh veh-*RAH *mee reh-*TRAH*-toh*
If you come with me, you will see my portrait

comenzado; podrá esperarme allí,
*koh-mehn-*THAH*-doh; poh-*DRAH *ess-peh-*RAHR*-meh ahl-*YEE,
begun; you can wait for me there,

o ir al teatro por la tarde.
*oh eer ahl teh-*AH*-troh pohr lah* TAHR*-deh.*
or go to the theater in the afternoon.

ARANGO: Si usted gusta, iremos al teatro mañana;
*See oos-*TEHD GOOS*-tah, ee-*REH*-mohs ahl teh-*AH*-troh mahn-*YAH*-nah;*
If you like, we shall go to the theater tomorrow;

sacaremos los billetes con anticipación
*sah-kah-*REH*-mohs lohs beel-*YEH*-tehs kohn ahn-tee-thee-pahth-*YOHN
we shall buy the tickets in advance,

y en los entreactos, saldremos a tomar aire.
*ee enn lohs enn-treh-*AHK*-tohs, sahl-*DREH*-mohs ah toh-*MAHR AH-*ee-reh.*
and during the intermission we shall go out for some air.

Si la función termina temprano, volveremos
*See lah foonth-*YOHN *tehr-*MEE*-nah tehm-*PRAH*-noh, vohl-veh-*REH*-moht*
If the performance is over early, we shall go back

a casa y cenaremos ligeramente.
ah KAH*-sah ee theh-nah-*REH*-mohs lee-heh-rah-*MEHN*-teh.*
home and have a light supper.

De esta manera pasaremos una noche muy agradable.
Deh ESS*-tah mah-*NEH*-rah pah-sah-*REH*-mohs*
OO*-nah* NOH*-cheh mwee ah-grah-*DAH*-bleh.*
This way we shall spend a very pleasant evening.

SARMIENTO: Sí, pero no es posible, porque mañana espero
See, PEH*-roh noh ess poh-*SEE*-bleh,* POHR*-keh mahn-*YAH*-nah ess-*PEH*-roh*
Yes, but that is not possible, because tomorrow I expect

al Sr. Santos. El pasará la noche con nosotros.
*ahl sehn-*YOHR SAHN*-tohs. Ell pah-sah-*RAH *lah* NOH*-cheh*
*kohn noh-*SOH*-trohs.*
Mr. Santos. He will spend the night with us.

ARANGO: Escriba Ud. al Sr. Santos diciéndole
*Ess-*KREE*-bah oos-*TEHD *ahl sehn-*YOHR SAHN*-tohs deeth-*YEHN*-doh-leh*
Write to Mr. Santos telling him

que Ud. no podrá estar en casa mañana.
*keh oos-*TEHD *noh poh-*DRAH *ess-*TAHR *enn* KAH*-sah mahn-*YAH*-nah.*
that you will not be able to be at home tomorrow.

El recibirá la carta antes del mediodía
*Ell reh-thee-bee-*RAH *lah* KAHR*-tah* AHN*-tehs dehl mehd-yoh-*DEE*-ah*
He will receive the letter before noon

y tendrá tiempo para hacer otros planes.
*ee tehn-*DRAH *t'*YEHM*-poh* PAH*-rah ah-*THEHR OH*-trohs* PLAH*-nehs*
and will have time to make other plans.

Creo que así será mejor.
KREH*-oh keh ah-*SEE *seh-*RAH *meh-*HOHR.
I think that will be better.

SARMIENTO: No; porque no vendrá solo, traerá a su
Noh; POHR-keh noh vehn-DRAH SOH-loh, trah-eh-RAH ah soo
No, because he will not come alone, he will bring his

señora; ellos no querrán posponer su visita para otro día.
sehn-YOH-rah; EHL-yohs noh keh-RRAHN pohs-poh-NEHR soo vee-SEE-tah
PAH-rah OH-troh DEE-ah.
wife, they won't wish to postpone their visit to another day.

Prefiero ir al teatro en otra ocasión.
Prehf-YEH-roh eer ahl teh-AH-troh enn OH-trah oh-kahs-YOHN.
I prefer to go to the theater some other time.

ARANGO: **Bueno, como Ud. quiera, iremos pasado mañana.**
BWEH-noh, KOH-moh oos-TEHD k'YEH-rah, ee-REH-mohs pah-SAH-doh
mahn-YAH-nah.
Well, as you wish; we will go the day after tomorrow.

Y los Sres. Santos, ¿permanecerán en la ciudad todo el verano?
Ee lohs Sehn-YOH-rehs SAHN-tohs, pehr-mah-neh-theh-RAHN enn lah
th'yoo-DAHD TOH-doh ell veh-RAH-noh?
And Mr. and Mrs. Santos, will they remain in town all summer?

SARMIENTO: No, irán al campo por un mes,
Noh, ee-RAHN ahl KAHM-poh pohr oon mehs,
No, they will go to the country for a month,

y reanudarán su curso de inglés en otoño.
ee reh-ah-noo-dah-RAHN soo KOOR-soh deh een-GLEHS enn oh-TOHN-yoh.
and will continue their English course in the fall.

En esa estación frecuentará la Escuela Berlitz mucha gente;
Enn ESS-sah ess-tahth-YOHN freh-kwehn-tah-RAH lah Ess-KWEH-lah
BEHR-leets MOO-chah HEHN-teh;
During that season many people will attend the Berlitz School:

unos tomarán lecciones de español,
OO-nohs toh-mah-RAHN lehkth-YOHN-nehs deh ess-pahn-YOHL,
some will take Spanish lessons,

y otros de francés o de alemán.
ee OH-trohs deh frahn-THEHS oh deh ah-leh-MAHN.
and others French or German.

Ya me voy, ¿no viene Ud. conmigo?
Yah meh voy, noh v'YEH-neh oos-TEHD kohn-MEE-goh?
I shall leave now, are you coming with me?

ARANGO: Bueno, le acompañaré a Ud.
BWEH-*noh, leh ah-kohm-pahn-yah-*REH *ah oos-*TEHD.
Good, I shall accompany you.

NOTE to Student: The future is an extremely easy tense to form. Simply take the endings *é, á, emos,* and *án* and add them to the infinitive. Thus "I will be" is *yo seré* and "he will go" is *él irá.* Certain verbs however, such as *saber, venir, poner, poder, salir,* etc. are somewhat irregular in the future. Note the first person: *sabré, vendré, pondré, podré, saldré.*

¿Seré yo un día
estrella de Holly-
wood?
¿Con quién me
casaré?
¿Me llevarán al
teatro
esta noche?

¿Qué comeré en
casa de
Doña Felicidad
esta noche?
¿Adónde iré para
mis vacaciones
este verano?

¿A que hora iré a la
iglesia mañana?
¿Llegará el profesor
a tiempo para la co-
mida esta noche?

THINKING IN SPANISH
(Answers on page 265)

1. ¿En qué está pensando Chiquita?
2. ¿En qué está pensando Doña Felicidad?
3. ¿Adónde irá el profesor esta noche?
4. ¿A qué invita el Sr. Arango al Sr. Sarmiento?
5. ¿Acepta el Sr. Sarmiento?
6. ¿Dónde almorzarán?
7. ¿Adónde irá el Sr. Sarmiento después?
8. Si van al teatro, ¿cuándo sacarán los billetes?
9. ¿Qué harán durante los entreactos?
10. ¿Quién vendrá a visitar al Sr. Sarmiento?
11. ¿Podrá el Sr. Sarmiento ir al teatro?
12. ¿Cuándo irán al teatro?
13. ¿Se quedará la familia de Santos en la ciudad todo el verano?
14. Y Ud., ¿adónde irá este verano?
15. ¿Visitarán México muchos norteamericanos este año?
16. ¿Vendrán muchos suramericanos a Nueva York?

LECCIÓN 32

La invitación al viaje
Lah een-vee-tahth-YOHN ahl v'YAH-heh
The invitation to the trip

FERNÁNDEZ: Hola, amigo Nelson. ¿Qué tal está? Mucho gusto en verle.
Fehr-NAHN-dehth: OH-lah, ah-MEE-goh NEHL-sohn. Keh tahl ess-TAH?
Moo-choh GOOS-toh enn VEHR-leh.
FERNÁNDEZ: Hello, my friend Nelson. How are you? Glad to see you.

 An Old Spanish Custom: When you meet a friend you may say: *Mucho gusto en verle.* ("Pleased to see you"). When you meet someone for the first time: *Mucho gusto en conocerle.* ("Pleased to know you") and when you leave a new acquaintance, *Mucho gusto en haberle conocido.* ("Pleased to have met you"). If the friend is a lady you may use *la* instead of *le*.

NELSON: El gusto es mio. ¿Cómo está?
NEHL-sohn: Ell GOOS-toh ess MEE-oh. KOH-moh ess-TAH?
NELSON: The pleasure is mine. How are you?

FERNÁNDEZ: Muy bien, gracias. ¿Desde cuándo está aquí en la Habana?
Mwee b'YEHN, GRAHTH-*yahs.* DEHS-*deh* KWAHN-*doh* ess-TAH *ah-KEE enn lah Ah-*BAH-*nah?*
Very well, thank you. Since when have you been here in Havana?

202

NELSON: Hace una semana vine de Nueva York.
AH-*theh* OO-*nah* seh-MAH-*nah* VEE-*neh* d*eh* NWEH-*vah* Yohrk.
I came from New York a week ago.

Estoy aquí de visita y también en viaje de negocios.
Ess-TOY ah-KEE *deh* vee-SEE-*tah* ee tahmb-YEHN enn v'YAH-*heh* deh neh·
GOHTH-*yohs.*
I am here on a visit and also on business.

Pero, Ud. vive en México, ¿no es verdad?
PEH-*roh,* oos-TEHD VEE-*veh* enn MEH-*hee-koh,* noh ess vehr-DAHD?
But, you live in Mexico, don't you?

FERNÁNDEZ: Sí. También estoy aquí de visita.
See. Tahmb-YEHN ess-TOY ah-KEE deh vee-SEE-*tah.*
Yes. I am also here on a visit.

Me voy pronto para México.
Meh voy PROHN-*toh* PAH-*rah* MEH-*hee-koh.*
I am going to Mexico soon.

¿Se quedará Ud. aquí algunos días?
Seh keh-dah-RAH oos-TEHD ah-KEE ahl-GOO-*nohs* DEE-*ahs?*
Will you stay here a few days?

NELSON: No. En estos momentos voy a sacar mi billete para ir a México.
Noh. Enn ESS-*tohs* moh-MEHN-*tohs* voy ah sah-KAHR mee beel-YEH-*teh*
PAH-*rah* eer ah MEH-*hee-koh.*
No. Just now I am going to buy my ticket to go to Mexico.

FERNÁNDEZ: ¡Qué bien! Mire, yo también iré a México la próxima semana.
Keh b'YEHN! MEE-*reh,* yoh tahmb-YEHN ee-REH ah MEH-*hee-koh*
lah PROHK-*see-mah* seh-MAH-*nah.*
That is fine! Look, I am also going to Mexico next week.

¿Por qué no vamos juntos?
Pohr KEH noh VAH-*mohs* HOON-*tohs?*
Why do we not go together?

Vamos a ver si podemos conseguir pasaje para el mismo día.
VAH-*mohs* ah vehr see poh-DEH-*mohs* kohn-seh-GEER pah-SAH-*heh*
PAH-*rah* ell MEES-*moh* DEE-*ah.*
Let us see if we can obtain passage for the same day.

NELSON: La idea me gusta mucho.
Lah ee-DEH-*ah* meh GOOS-*tah* MOO-*choh.*
The idea appeals to me very much.

Nunca he estado en la capital de México.
NOON-*kah* eh ess-TAH-*doh* enn lah kah-pee-TAHL deh MEH-*hee-koh.*
I have never been in the capital of México.

Vamos a entrar en esta oficina de aviación.
VAH-*mohs ah enn-*TRAHR *enn* ESS-*tah oh-fee-*THEE-*nah deh*
*ahv-yahth-*YOHN.
Let us go into this airline office.

EMPLEADO: **Buenos días, señores.**
*Ehm-pleh-*AH-*doh:* BWEH-*nohs* DEE-*ahs, sehn-*YOH-*rehs.*
EMPLOYEE: Good morning, gentlemen.

¿En qué puedo servirles?
Enn keh PWEH-*doh sehr-*VEER-*lehs?*
How may I serve you?

FERNÁNDEZ: **¿Puede Ud. darnos dos reservaciones para**
PWEH-*deh oos-*TEHD DAHR-*nohs dohs reh-sehr-vahth-*YOH-*nehs* PAH-*rah*
la Ciudad de México?
*lah Th'yoo-*DAHD *deh* MEH-*hee-koh?*
Can you give us two reservations for Mexico City?

EMPLEADO: **¿Para cuándo, señores?**
PAH-*rah* KWAHN-*doh, sehn-*YOH-*rehs?*
For when, gentlemen?

NELSON: **Para este lunes.**
PAH-*rah* ESS-*teh* LOO-*nehs.*
For this Monday.

EMPLEADO: **Muy bien, señores. Tenemos un avión**
*Mwee b'*YEHN, *sehn-*YOH-*rehs.* Teh-NEH-*mohs oon ahv-*YOHN
Very well, gentlemen. We have an airplane

que sale a las 9 y otro que sale a las 11.
keh SAH-*leh ah lahs* NWEH-*veh ee* OH-*troh keh* SAH-*leh ah lahs* OHN-*theh.*
that leaves at 9 and another that leaves at 11.

El que sale más temprano va directamente a la
Ell keh SAH-*leh mahs tehm-*PRAH-*noh vah dee-rehk-tah-*MEHN-*teh ah lah*
The one that leaves earlier goes straight to

Ciudad de México, pero el otro para en Veracruz.
*Th'yoo-*DAHD *deh* MEH-*hee-koh,* PEH-*roh ell* OH-*troh* PAH-*rah enn*
*Veh-rah-*CROOTH.
Mexico City, but the other one stops at Veracruz.

FERNÁNDEZ: **Me gusta más salir en el avión de las 9.**
Meh GOOS-*tah mahs sah-*LEER *enn ell ahv-*YOHN *deh lahs* NWEH-*veh.*
I prefer to leave on the nine o'clock plane.

No quiero parar en Veracruz—hace mucho calor.
*Noh k'*YEH-*roh pah-*RAHR *enn Veh-rah-*CROOTH—*ah-theh* MOO-*choh*
*kah-*LOHR.
I do not want to stop at Veracruz—it is very hot.

NELSON: ¿Cuánto vale el pasaje?
KWAHN-*toh* VAH-*leh ell pah*-SAH-*heh?*
How much is the fare?

EMPLEADO: 90 pesos ida y 160 ida y vuelta.
Noh-VEHN-*tah* PEH-*sohs* EE-*dah ee th'*YEHN-*toh-seh*-SEHN-*tah* EE-*dah ee*
VWEHL-*tah.*
90 pesos one way and 160 round trip.

FERNÁNDEZ: Deme un billete de ida solamente.
DEH-*meh oon beel*-YEH-*teh deh* EE-*dah soh-lah*-MEHN-*teh.*
Give me a one way ticket only.

Tengo mi casa en México y no sé cuando
TEHN-*goh mee* KAH-*sah enn* MEH-*hee-koh ee noh seh* KAHN-*doh*
My home is in Mexico and I do not know when

volveré a la Habana.
vohl-veh-REH *ah lah Ah*-BAH-*nah.*
I shall return to Havana.

EMPLEADO: ¿Y Ud., señor?
Ee oos-TEHD, *sehn*-YOHR?
And you, sir?

NELSON: Haga el favor de darme un billete de ida y vuelta.
AH-*gah ell fah*-VOHR *deh* DAHR-*meh oon beel*-YEH-*teh deh* EE-*dah ee*
VWEHL-*tah.*
Please, give me a round trip ticket.

EMPLEADO: Gracias. ¿Quieren darme sus direcciones
aquí en la Habana?
GRAH-*th'yahs. K'*YEH-*rehn* DAHR-*meh soos dee-rehkth*-YOH-*nehs*
ah-KEE *enn lah Ah*-BAH-*nah?*
Thank you. Will you give me your addresses here in Havana?

NELSON: Yo vivo en el Hotel Nacional.
Yoh VEE-*voh enn ell Oh*-TEHL *Nahth-yoh*-NAHL.
I live at the National Hotel.

FERNÁNDEZ: Estoy hospedado en el Sevilla Biltmore.
Ess-TOY *ohs-peh*-DAH-*doh enn ell Seh*-VEEL-*yah Beelt*-MOHR.
I am stopping at the Sevilla Biltmore.

EMPLEADO: Muy bien. Mandaremos el automóvil
*Mwee b'*YEHN. *Mahn-dah*-REH-*mohs ell ah-oo-toh*-MOH-*veel*
Very well. We shall send the automobile

por Uds. el lunes a las 6 de la mañana.
pohr oos-TEH-*dehs ell* LOO-*nehs ah lahs* SEH-*ees deh lah mahn*-YAH-*nah.*
to pick you up on Monday at 6 in the morning.

NELSON: ¿Por qué a las 6 si el avión no sale hasta las 9?
Pohr keh ah lahs SEH-*ees see ell ahv-*YOHN *noh* SAH-*leh* AHS-*tah lahs*
NWEH-*veh?*
Why at 6 o'clock if the plane does not leave until 9?

EMPLEADO: Es un viaje de media hora entre la Habana
*Ess oon v'*YAH-*heh deh* MEHD-*yah* OH-*rah* ENN-*treh lah Ah-*BAH-*nah*
y el aeropuerto.
*ee ell ah-*EH-*roh-*PWEHR-*toh.*
It is a half an hour trip between Havana and the airport.

También es necesario pesar el equipaje.
*Tahmb-*YEHN *ess neh-theh-*SAHR-*yoh peh-*SAHR *ell eh-kee-*PAH-*heh.*
It is also necessary to weigh the baggage.

FERNÁNDEZ: Además la compañía de aviación no quiere que los pasajeros
*Ah-deh-*MAHS *lah kohm-pahn-*YEE-*ah deh ahv-yah-th'*YOHN *noh k'*YEH-
*reh keh lohs pah-sah-*HEH-*rohs*
Besides the airline company does not want the passengers

lleguen tarde y los hace venir con bastante anticipación;
*l'*YEH-*gehn* TAHR-*deh ee lohs* AH-*theh veh-*NEER *kohn bahs-*TAHN-*teh*
*ahn-tee-thee-pahth-*YOHN;
to arrive late and makes them come well ahead of time;

así nos quitan el sueño.
*ah-*SEE *nohs* KEE-*tahn ell* SWEHN-*yoh.*
so they rob us of sleep.

IDIOMS TO REMEMBER: *¿Desde cuándo está aquí?*
"How long have you been here?" (Note the use of the
present tense.)
vamos a ver: "Let's see."
un billete de ida y vuelta: "a round trip ticket."
estoy hospedado en el Sevilla: "I am stopping at the Sevilla."
con anticipación: "Ahead of time."

THINKING IN SPANISH
(Answers on page 266)

1. ¿Dónde están los señores Fernández y Nelson?
2. ¿De dónde es el señor Nelson?
3. ¿Desde cuándo está en la Habana?
4. ¿Qué hace el señor Nelson en la Habana?
5. ¿Es el señor Fernández cubano?
6. ¿De dónde es el señor Fernández?
7. ¿Adónde irá el señor Nelson al salir de la Habana?
8. ¿Se quedará el señor Fernández en la Habana?
9. ¿A qué le invita el señor Fernández al señor Nelson?
10. ¿Ha estado en México antes el señor Nelson?
11. ¿Acepta el señor Nelson la invitación del Sr. Fernández?
12. ¿Podrá el Sr. Fernández servirle de guía?
13. ¿Necesita Ud. un guía en Nueva York?
14. ¿Adónde van los señores para sacar sus pasajes?
15. ¿Es fácil conseguir pasaje en avión para el mismo día?
16. ¿Qué dice Ud. al empleado de la compañía de aviación?

17. ¿Cómo pide Ud. un billete de ferrocarril?

18. ¿A qué hora sale el primer avión para México?

19. ¿Por qué se deciden a tomar el avión de las 9?

20. ¿Adónde para el otro avión?

21. ¿Es más agradable viajar en un tren expreso que en uno que para es todas las estaciones?

22. ¿Por qué no quiere el Sr. Fernández un billete de ida y vuelta?

23. ¿Por qué el empleado quiere saber las direcciones de los señores?

24. ¿Vive Ud. en una ciudad?

25. ¿Cuál es su dirección?

26. ¿A qué hora irá el automóvil por los señores?

27. ¿Le gusta a Ud. dormir la mañana?

28. ¿Por qué es necesario levantarse tan temprano?

29. Si Ud. se levanta muy temprano, ¿tiene Ud. sueño?

LECCIÓN 33

La salida del aeropuerto
Lah sah-LEE-dah dehl ah-EH-roh-PWEHR-toh
The departure from the airport

(El teléfono suena.)
(*Ehl teh-LEH-foh-noh SWEH-nah.*)
(The telephone rings.)

NELSON: (contesta)—Hola—¿Quién habla?
NEHL-sohn: (kohn-TEHS-tah)—OH-lah—K'YEHN AH-blah?
NELSON: (answers)—Hello—Who is speaking?

TELEFONISTA: Son las 6, Sr. Nelson.
Teh-leh-foh-NEES-tah: Sohn lahs SEH-ees, sehn-YOHR NEHL-sohn.
OPERATOR: It is 6 o'clock, Mr. Nelson.

Es la segunda vez que hemos llamado.
Ess lah seh-GOON-dah vehth keh EH-mohs l'yah-MAH-doh.
This is the second time we have called.

NELSON: ¡Caramba! No tengo mucho tiempo.
Kah-RAHM-bah! Noh TEHN-goh MOO-choh t'YEHM-poh.
Great Scott! I do not have much time.

Dígale al cajero que quiero arreglar mi cuenta.
DEE-*gah-leh ahl kah*-HEH-*roh keh k'*YEH-*roh ah-rreh*-GLAHR *mee* KWEHN-*tah.*
Tell the cashier that I want to settle my bill.

TELEFONISTA: **Bien, señor.—Mandaré un muchacho por su equipaje.**
B'YEHN, *sehn*-YOHR.—*Mahn-dah*-REH *oon moo*-CHAH-*choh pohr soo eh-kee*-PAH-*heh.*
All right, sir.—I shall send a boy to get your luggage.

(**En la oficina del hotel**)
(*Enn lah oh-fee*-THEE-*nah dehl oh*-TEHL)
(In the office of the hotel)

CAJERO: **Aquí está su cuenta, señor:**
Kah-HEH-*roh: Ah*-KEE *ess*-TAH *soo* KWEHN-*tah, sehn*-YOHR:
CASHIER: Here is your bill, sir:

125 pesos.
*th'*YEHN-*toh* VAIN-*tee*-THEEN-*koh* PEH-*sohs.*
125 pesos.

NELSON: **¿Está todo incluído?**
Ess-TAH TOH-*doh een-kloo*-EE-*doh?*
Is everything included?

CAJERO: **Sí, señor.**
See, sehn-YOHR.
Yes, sir.

Incluye sus gastos de restaurante
Een-KLOO-*yeh soos* GAHS-*tohs deh rehs-tah-oo*-RAHN-*teh*
It includes your restaurant charges

y llamadas de teléfono también.
ee l'yah-MAH-*dahs deh teh*-LEH-*foh-noh tahmb*-YEHN.
and phone calls too.

NELSON: **Aquí tiene Ud. el dinero,**
Ah-KEE *t'*YEH-*neh oos*-TEHD *ell dee*-NEH-*roh,*
Here is the money,

y la llave la dejé en el cuarto.
*ee lah l'*YAH-*veh lah deh*-HEH *enn ell* KWAHR-*toh.*
and I left the key in the room.

CAJERO: **Gracias, señor.**
GRAHTH-*yahs, sehn*-YOHR.
Thank you, sir.

Que tenga Ud. buen viaje. ¡Muchacho!
Keh TEHN-*gah oos*-TEHD *bwehn v'*YAH-*heh. Moo*-CHAH-*choh!*
Have a good trip. Boy!

Lleve el equipaje del Sr. Nelson al automóvil.
L'YEH-veh ell eh-kee-PAH-heh dehl sehn-YOHR NEHL-sohn ahl ah-oo-toh-MOH-veel.
Take Mr. Nelson's baggage to the automobile.

NELSON: Muchas gracias. (al muchacho)
MOO-chahs GRAHTH-yahs. (ahl moo-CHAH-choh)
Thank you very much. (to the boy)

No tome la maleta pequeña.
Noh TOH-meh lah mah-LEH-tah peh-KEHN-yah.
Do not take the small bag.

Tiene todos mis documentos.
T'YEH-neh TOH-dohs mees doh-koo-MEHN-tohs.
It has all my documents.

Yo mismo la llevaré.
Yoh MEES-moh lah l'yeh-vah-REH.
I shall carry it myself.

No quiero perderla.
Noh k'YEH-roh pehr-DEHR-lah.
I do not want to lose it.

(En el automóvil)
(Enn ell ah-oo-toh-MOH-veel)
(In the automobile)

FERNÁNDEZ: ¿Qué tal, amigo?
Fehr-NAHN-dehth: Keh tahl, ah-MEE-goh?
FERNÁNDEZ: How are you, my friend?

¿Por qué tardó tanto?
Pohr KEH tahr-DOH TAHN-toh?
Why were you so late?

NELSON: No me desperté a tiempo.
Noh meh dehs-pehr-TEH ah t'YEHM-poh.
I did not wake up in time.

En Nueva York nunca nos levantamos tan temprano.
Enn NWEH-vah Yohrk NOON-kah nohs leh-vahn-TAH-mohs tahn tehm-PRAH-noh.
In New York we never get up so early.

FERNÁNDEZ: En el trópico, nos levantamos temprano.
Enn ell TROH-pee-koh, nohs leh-vahn-TAH-mohs tehm-PRAH-noh.
In the tropics, we get up early.

Hace fresco y es la mejor parte del día.
AH-theh FREHS-koh ee ess lah meh-HOHR PAHR-teh dehl DEE-ah.
It is cool and it is the best part of the day.

NELSON: Sí, pero Uds. duermen la siesta al mediodía, y nosotros no.
See, PEH-roh oos-TEHD-ehs DWEHR-mehn lah s'YEHS-tah ahl mehd-yoh-DEE-ah, ee noh-SOH-trohs noh.
Yes, but you take a siesta at noon, and we do not.

(En el aeropuerto)
(*Enn ell ah-*EH-*roh-*PWEHR-*toh*)
(At the airport)

FERNÁNDEZ: Somos los Sres. Fernández y Nelson
SOH-*mohs lohs sehn-*YOH-*rehs Fehr-*NAHN-*dehth ee* NEHL-*sohn*
We are Messrs. Fernández and Nelson

y vamos a tomar el avión de las 9 para México.
ee VAH-*mohs ah toh-*MAHR *ell ahv-*YOHN *deh lahs* NWEH-*veh* PAH-*raa*
MEH-*hee-koh.*
and we are going to take the 9 o'clock plane for Mexico.

ENCARGADO: Muy bien, señores, sus nombres están en la lista.
*Enn-kahr-*GAH-*doh: Mwee b'*YEHN, *sehn-*YOH-*rehs, soos* NOHM-*brehs est-*TAHN
enn lah LEES-*tah.*
AGENT: Very well, gentlemen; your names are on the list.

¿Cuánto pesan Uds.?
KWAHN-*toh* PEH-*sahn oos-*TEH-*dehs?*
How much do you weigh?

FERNÁNDEZ: 75 kilos.
*Seh-*TEHN-*tah ee* THEEN-*koh* KEE-*lohs.*
75 kilos. (165 lbs.–1 kilo = 2.2 lbs.)

NELSON: Lo mismo.
Loh MEES-*moh.*
The same.

ENCARGADO: Me parece que pesa Ud. un poco más, señor.
*Meh pah·*REH-*theh keh* PEH-*sah oos-*TEHD *oon* POH-*koh mahs, sehn-*YOHR.
It seems to me that you weigh a little more, sir.

Vamos a poner 80.
VAH-*mohs ah poh-*NEHR *oh-*CHEHN-*tah.*
Let us put 80.

Ahora pasen Uds. a pesar el equipaje.
*Ah-*OH-*rah* PAH-*sehn oos-*TEHD-*ehs ah peh-*SAHR *ell eh-kee-*PAH-*heh.*
Now, step over to weigh your luggage.

NELSON: ¿Qué peso de equipaje se permite sin pagar extra?
Keh PEH-*soh deh eh-kee-*PAH-*heh seh pehr-*MEE-*teh seen pah-*GAHR
EHKS-*trah?*
What amount of luggage is allowed without paying extra?

ENCARGADO: 25 kilos, señor.
*Vain-tee-*THEEN-*koh* KEE-*lohs, sehn-*YOHR.
25 kilos. sir.

FERNÁNDEZ: Vamos al restaurante, me muero de hambre.
VAH-*mohs ahl rehs-tah-oo-*RAHN-*teh, meh* MWEH-*roh deh* AHM-*breh.*
Let us go to the restaurant, I am dying of hunger.

No he tenido tiempo para desayunarme.
*Noh eh teh-*NEE-*doh t'*YEHM-*poh* PAH-*rah dehs-ah-yoo-*NAHR-*meh.*
I have not had time to have breakfast.

FERNÁNDEZ: **Bueno. Arriba hay un restaurante.**
BWEH-*noh. Ah-*RREE-*bah I oon rehs-tah-oo-*RAHN-*teh.*
Good. There is a restaurant upstairs.

ANUNCIADOR: **Pasajeros para el vuelo número 505**
*Ah-noonth-yah-*DOHR: *Pah-sah-*HEH-*rohs* PAH-*rah ell* VWEH-*loh* NOO-*meh-roh
keen-*YEHN-*tohs* THEEN-*koh*
ANNOUNCER: Passengers for flight number 505

para México, sírvanse subir al avión.
PAH-*rah* MEH-*hee-koh,* SEER-*vahn-seh soo-*BEER *ahl ahv-*YOHN.
to Mexico, please board the plane.

NELSON: **¡Qué desgracia! Ahora no voy a poder comer nada.**
*¡Keh dehs-*GRAHTH-*yah! Ah-*OH-*rah noh voy ah poh-*DEHR *koh-*MEHR
NAH-*dah.*
How unfortunate! Now I won't be able to eat anything.

FERNÁNDEZ: **No se preocupe.**
*Noh seh pre-oh-*KOO-*peh.*
Do not worry.

Creo que sirven algo para comer a bordo.
KRE-*oh keh* SEER-*vehn* AHL-*goh* PAH-*rah koh-*MEHR *ah* BOHR-*doh.*
I think that they serve something to eat on board.

EXPRESSIONS TO REMEMBER: *¡Hola! ¿Quién habla?*
Either expression is used in answering the telephone.
¡Caramba! This famous interjection is perfectly respectable
and means anything from "Ye gods!" to "Goodness
gracious!"

Que tenga Ud. buen viaje: "May you have a good trip."
NOTE: Use the subjunctive-imperative when you are wish-
ing someone something.

La siesta—the siesta is an old Latin custom. It is a universally accepted nap
which shuts up everything from noon until about 2 P.M.

Me parece: "it seems to me".
Se permite: "is allowed" or "is permitted". Ex: *¿Se permite fumar?:* "Is
smoking allowed?"
Está bien: "All right".
¡Cómo no!: "Yes." This is an unusual way to say "yes". It literally means:
"In what way not?"
Sírvanse: "Please." To be used for the plural; *sírvase* for the singular.
Preocuparse: "to worry."

THINKING IN SPANISH

(Answers on page 266)

1. ¿Está durmiendo el Sr. Nelson al sonar el teléfono?
2. ¿Quién le llama?
3. ¿Le gusta al Sr. Nelson levantarse tan temprano?
4. ¿Quién llevará el equipaje del Sr. Nelson al auto?
5. ¿Qué hace el Sr. Nelson después de la llamada de teléfono?
6. ¿Con quién habla el Sr. Nelson en la oficina del hotel?
7. ¿Donde dejó la llave?
8. ¿Por qué no le permite al muchacho llevar el maletín?
9. ¿Dónde le espera el Sr. Fernández?
10. ¿Se despertó temprano el Sr. Nelson?
11. ¿Se duerme la siesta en Nueva York?
12. ¿Dónde es costumbre dormir la siesta?
13. ¿Tienen que decir su peso los pasajeros?
14. ¿Cuál es el límite de peso de equipaje que pueden llevar sin pagar?
15. ¿Por qué tiene hambre el Sr. Nelson?
16. ¿Comió algo antes de venir al aeropuerto?
17. ¿Por qué no pueden comer en el aeropuerto?
18. ¿Qué dice el Sr. Nelson al saber que no tiene tiempo para comer?
19. ¿Se sirven comidas a bordo de los aviones?
20. ¿Cuándo hizo Ud. un viaje por avión?

LECCIÓN 34

La llegada a México
*Lah l'yeh-*GAH-*dah ah* MEH-*hee-koh*
The arrival in Mexico

(En el avión)
(*Enn ell ahv-*YOHN)
(In the plane)

NELSON: ¿Llegaremos pronto?
*L'yeh-gah-*REH-*mohs* PROHN-*toh?*
Will we arrive soon?

¿Cuánto tiempo falta?
KWAHN-*toh t'*YEHM-*poh* FAHL-*tah?*
How much time is left?

FERNÁNDEZ: No falta mucho tiempo.
Noh FAHL-*tah* MOO-*choh t'*YEHM-*poh.*
Not much time.

Ya se ven algunas fincas y pueblos.
*Yah seh vehn ahl-*GOO-*nahs* FEEN-*kahs ee* PWEH-*blohs.*
Some farms and towns can already be seen.

La Ciudad de México está al otro lado de esas montañas.
*Lah Th'yoo-*DAHD *deh* MEH-*hee-koh ess-*TAH *ahl* OH-*troh* LAH-*doh
deh* ESS-*ahs mohn-*TAHN-*yahs.*
The City of Mexico is beyond those mountains.

NELSON: ¿Cuál es el Popocatépetl?
KWAHL ess ell Poh-poh-kah-TEHP-tel?
Which is Popocatepetl?

FERNÁNDEZ: Aquella montaña grande que tiene la cima
Ah-KEHL-yah mohn-TAHN-yah GRAHN-deh keh t'YEH-neh lah THEE-mah
That big mountain which has its summit

cubierta de nieve.
koob-YEHR-tah deh n'YEH-veh.
covered with snow.

NELSON: El avión está dando una vuelta.
Ell ahv-YOHN ess-TAH DAHN-doh OO-nah VWEHL-tah.
The plane is making a turn.

Creo que estamos llegando.
KREH-oh keh ess-TAH-mohs l'yeh-GAHN-doh.
I think that we are arriving.

FERNÁNDEZ: Mire, allí está la capital.
MEE-reh, ahl-YEE ess-TAH lah kah-pee-TAHL.
Look, there is the capital.

NELSON: ¡Qué ciudad tan grande y bonita!
Keh th'yoo-DAHD tahn GRAHN-deh ee boh-NEE-tah!
What a large and beautiful city!

(En el aeropuerto)
(Enn ell ah-EH-roh-PWEHR-toh)
(At the airport)

INSPECTOR DE INMIGRACIÓN:
Eens-pehk-TOHR deh Een-mee-grahth-YOHN:
IMMIGRATION INSPECTOR:

Hagan el favor de mostrarme sus pasaportes
AH-gahn ell fah-VOHR deh mohs-TRAHR-meh soos pah-sah-POHR-tehs
Please show me your passports

o tarjetas de turistas.
oh tahr-HEH-tahs deh too-REES-tahs.
or your tourist cards.

FERNÁNDEZ: Yo soy mexicano. Aquí están mis papeles.
Yoh soy meh-hee-KAH-noh. Ah-KEE ess-TAHN mees pah-PEHL-ehs.
I am Mexican. Here are my papers.

INSPECTOR: Bien. Pase Ud. a la aduana.
B'YEHN. PAH-seh oos-TEHD ah lah ah-DWAH-nah.
Good. Step over to the Customs House.

NELSON: Yo soy norteamericano.
*Yoh soy nohr-teh-ah-meh-ree-*KAH-*noh.*
I am North American.

Aquí tiene mi pasaporte y tarjeta.
*Ah-*KEE *t'*YEH-*neh mee pah-sah-*POHR-*teh ee tahr-*HEH-*tah.*
Here are my passport and card.

INSPECTOR: ¿Cuánto tiempo se quedará aquí?
KWAHN-*toh t'*YEHM-*poh se keh-dah-*RAH *ah-*KEE?
How long will you stay here?

NELSON: Dos semanas nada más.
*Dohs seh-*MAH-*nahs* NAH-*dah mahs.*
Not more than two weeks.

INSPECTOR: Bien. Pase, señor.
*B'*YEHN. PAH-*seh, sehn-*YOHR.
Good. Pass along, sir.

NELSON: Perdone, ¿dónde puedo cambiar dólares por pesos?
*Pehr-*DOH-*neh,* DOHN-*deh* PWEH-*doh kahmb-*YAHR DOH-*lah-rehs pohr*
PEH-*sohs?*
I beg your pardon, where can I change dollars for pesos?

INSPECTOR: Hay una oficina de cambios en el aeropuerto, señor.
I OO-*nah oh-fee-*THEE-*nah deh* KAHMB-*yohs enn ell ah-eh-roh-*PWEHR-*toh,*
*sehn-*YOHR.
There is an Exchange Counter at the airport, sir.

Ahora el cambio es de 5 pesos por dólar, más o menos.
*Ah-*OH-*rah ell* KAHMB-*yoh ess deh* THEEN-*koh* PEH-*sohs pohr* DOH-*lahr,*
mahs oh MEH-*nohs.*
The rate is now 5 pesos to the dollar, more or less.

NELSON: Gracias. Ahora voy a buscar mi equipaje.
GRAHTH-*yahs. Ah-*OH-*rah voy ah boos-*KAHR *mee eh-kee-*PAH-*heh.*
Thank you. Now I am going to look for my luggage.

(Afuera)
(*Ah-*FWEH-*rah*)
(Outside)

ENCARGADO DE EQUIPAJES: ¿Sus comprobantes, señor?
*Enn-kahr-*GAH-*doh deh Eh-kee-*PAH-*hehs: Soos kohm-pro-*BAHN-*tehs,*
*sehn-*YOHR?
BAGGAGE MASTER: Your checks, sir?

NELSON: Aquí están. Esas dos maletas pardas son mías.
*Ah-*KEE *ess-*TAHN. *Ess-ahs dohs mah-*LEH-*tahs* PAHR-*dahs sohn* MEE-*ahs.*
Here they are. Those two brown bags are mine.

ENCARGADO: Un momento, señor. El inspector tiene que revisarlas.
Oon moh-MEHN-*toh, sehn*-YOHR. *Ell eens-pehk*-TOHR *t'*YEH-*neh keh reh-vee*-SAHR-*lahs.*
One moment, sir. The inspector has to check them.

NELSON: ¡Qué molestia! Siempre tengo que abrir y cerrar las maletas.
Keh moh-LEHST-*yah!* S'YEHM-*preh* TEHN-*goh keh ah*-BREER *ee theh-*RRAHR *lahs mah*-LEH-*tahs.*
What a bother! I always have to open and close the bags.

(En la Aduana)
(*Enn lah Ah*-DWAH-*nah*)
(At the Customs)

INSPECTOR: Abra las maletas.
AH-*brah lahs mah*-LEH-*tahs.*
Open your bags.

¿Tiene tabaco, perfumes o licores para declarar?
*T'*YEH-*neh tah*-BAH-*koh, pehr*-FOO-*mehs oh lee*-KOH-*rehs* PAH-*rah deh-klah*-RAHR?
Have you tobacco, perfume or liquors, to declare?

NELSON: Sólo estos tabacos.
SOH-*loh* ESS-*tohs tah*-BAH-*kohs.*
Only these cigars.

INSPECTOR: Está bien.
Ess-TAH *b'*YEHN.
All right.

Se permite a los turistas
Seh pehr-MEE-*teh ah lohs too*-REES-*tahs*
The tourists are allowed

traer cien tabacos al país sin pagar impuestos.
trah-EHR *th'*YEHN *tah*-BAH-*kohs dehl pah*-EES *seen pah*-GAHR *eem*-PWEHS-*tohs.*
to bring in a hundred cigars without paying taxes.

FERNÁNDEZ: ¡Hola, Nelson!
OH-*lah,* NEHL-*sohn!*
Hello, Nelson!

Perdóneme por haberle dejado pero
Pehr-DOH-*neh-meh pohr ah*-BEHR-*leh deh*-HAH-*doh* PEH-*roh*
Pardon me for having left you but

tuve que telefonear a mi esposa.
TOO-*veh keh teh-leh-foh-neh*-AHR *ah mee ess*-POH-*sah.*
I had to call my wife.

Me voy para casa. ¿A qué hotel va?
Meh voy PAH-*rah* KAH-*sah. Ah keh oh-*TEHL *vah?*
I am going home. To what hotel are you going?

NELSON: **No sé. ¿Puede Ud. indicarme un buen hotel?**
Noh seh. PWEH-*deh oos-*TEHD *een-dee-*KAHR-*meh oon bwehn oh-*TEHL?
I don't know. Can you recommend me a good hotel?

FERNÁNDEZ: **Sí. El Hotel Reforma es muy bueno.**
*See. Ell Oh-*TEHL *Reh-*FOHR-*mah ess mwee* BWEH-*noh.*
Yes. The Hotel Reforma is very good.

Tiene todas las comodidades modernas y está céntrico.
*T'*YEH-*neh* TOH-*dahs lah koh-moh-dee-*DAH-*dehs moh-*DEHR-*nahs ee
ess-tah* THEHN-*tree-koh.*
It has all modern conveniences and is centrally located.

NELSON: **Excelente. Iré allí. ¿Cuándo nos veremos?**
*Ehk-theh-*LEHN-*teh. Eee-*REH *ahl-*YEE. KWAHN-*doh nohs veh-*REH-*mohs?*
Excellent. I shall go there. When shall we see each other?

FERNÁNDEZ: **Yo iré primero a mi casa y pasaré por Ud. esta tarde.**
*Yoh ee-*REH *pree-*MEH-*roh ah mee* KAH-*sah ee pah-sah-*REH *pohr oos-*TEHD
ESS-*tah* TAHR-*deh.*
I shall go first to my house and I shall pick you up this afternoon.

Le voy a mostrar algo de la capital.
*Leh voy ah mohs-*TRAHR AHL-*goh deh lah kah-pee-*TAHL.
I am going to show you some of the capital.

NELSON: **Magnífico. Taxi, al Hotel Reforma, por favor.**
*Mahg-*NEE-*fee-koh.* TAHK-*see, ahl Oh-*TEHL *Reh-*FOHR-*mah, pohr
fah-*VOHR.
Wonderful. Taxi, to the Reforma Hotel, please.

(En el hotel)
*(Enn ell oh-*TEHL)
(At the hotel)

NELSON: **Buenos días— Quiero un cuarto con baño.**
BWEH-*ohs* DEE-*ahs. K'*YEH-*roh oon* KWAHR-*toh kohn* BAHN-*yoh.*
Good morning I want a room with bath.

DEPENDIENTE DEL HOTEL: **¿Lo quiere por día, o por semana, señor?**
*Deh-pehnd-*YEHN-*teh dehl Oh-*TEHL: *Loh k'*YEH-*reh pohr* DEE-*ah, oh pohr
seh-*MAH-*nah, sehn-*YOHR?
HOTEL CLERK: Do you want it by the day or by the week, sir?

NELSON: **Voy a estar aquí dos semanas.**
*Voy ah ess-*TAHR *ah-*KEE *dohs seh-*MAH-*nahs.*
I shall be here two weeks.

DEPENDIENTE: **Muy bien. Le damos el número 1125.**
*Mwee b'*YEHN. *Leh* DAH-*mohs ell* NOO-*meh-roh meel th'*YEHN-*toh*
VAIN-*tee-*THEEN-*koh.*
Very well. We shall give you number 1125.

NELSON: **Un momento. ¿Cuál es el precio del cuarto?**
*Oon moh-*MEHN-*toh.* KWAHL *ess ell* PREHTH-*yoh dehl* KWAHR-*toh?*
One moment. What is the price of the room?

DEPENDIENTE: **20 pesos por día, señor.**
VAIN-*teh* PEH-*sohs pohr* DEE-*ah, sehn-*YOHR.
20 pesos a day, sir.

NELSON: **Está bien. Sírvase mandar un muchacho**
ESS-TAH *b'*YEHN. SEER-*vah-seh mahn-*DAHR *oon moo-*CHAH-*choh*
All right. Please send a boy

para buscar mi equipaje que está en el taxi.
PAH-*rah boos-*KAHR *mee eh-kee-*PAH-*heh keh ess-*TAH *enn ell* TAHK-*see,*
to get my luggage, which is in the taxi.

DEPENDIENTE: **En seguida, señor.**
*Enn seh-*GGEE-*dah, sehn-*YOHR.
At once, sir.

NELSON: **Y una cosa más. ¿Dónde está el comedor?**
Ee OO-*nah* KOH-*sah mahs.* DOHN-*deh ess-*TAH *ell koh-meh-*DOHR?
And another thing. Where is the dining room?

Desde esta mañana no he comido nada.
DEHS-*deh* ESS-*tah mahn-*YAH-*nah noh eh koh-*MEE-*doh* NAH-*dah.*
I have eaten nothing since this morning.

 IDIOMS TO REMEMBER: *faltar:* "to lack" or "to be lacking." *dar una vuelta:* "to turn" also "to take a walk." (Note that one expression sometimes has two different meanings.)

más o menos: "more or less."

perdóneme por haberle dejado: "pardon me for having left you."

tener que: "to have to."
para casa "(to my, your, his) home." Ex: "Go home!": *¡Vaya para casa!*
en seguida: "at once."

THINKING IN SPANISH

(Answers on page 267)

1. ¿Qué ve Ud. desde un avión?
2. ¿Qué montaña grande ven los señores desde el avión?
3. ¿Qué documentos desea ver el inspector de inmigración?
4. ¿Qué les dice el inspector de aduana?
5. ¿Es cortés el inspector de aduana?
6. ¿Son los inspectores de aduana siempre corteses?
7. ¿Necesitamos pasaporte para viajar de un país a otro?
8. ¿Cuánto tiempo se quedará en México el Sr. Nelson?
9. ¿Por qué busca el Sr. Nelson la oficina de cambios?

10. ¿Dónde se hospedará el Sr. Nelson durante su visita a México?
11. ¿Por qué el Sr. Fernández recomienda el Hotel Reforma a su amigo?
12. ¿Irá el Sr. Fernández también al hotel?
13. ¿Por qué no?
14. ¿Dónde vive el Sr. Fernández?
15. ¿Quién será el guía del Sr. Nelson en México?
16. ¿Con quién habla el Sr. Nelson en el hotel?
17. ¿Puede conseguir un cuarto?
18. ¿Cuánto vale?
19. ¿Es difícil algunas veces conseguir un cuarto en un hotel?
20. ¿Dónde dejó el Sr. Nelson su equipaje?
21. ¿Quién va a buscarlo?
22. Cuando Ud. viaja por ferrocarril, ¿lleva Ud. mismo su equipaje?
23. ¿Quién lo lleva?
24. ¿Qué le da Ud. al portero?
25. ¿Es fácil olvidar cosas cuando uno está viajando?

LECCIÓN 35

De compras en la capital
Deh KOHM-*prahs enn lah kah-pee-*TAHL
Shopping in the capital

FERNÁNDEZ: Buenas tardes, amigo. ¿Ya almorzó Ud.?
BWEH-*nahs* TAHR-*dehs, ah-*MEE-*goh. Yah ahl-mohr-*THOH *oos-*TEHD?
Good afternoon, my friend. Have you had lunch?

NELSON: Sí, gracias. Aquí sirven buena comida.
See, GRAHTH-*yahs. Ah-*KEE SEER-*vehn* BWEH-*nah koh-*MEE-*dah.*
Yes, thank you. They serve good food here.

FERNÁNDEZ: ¿Qué le parece dar una vuelta por la avenida?
*Keh leh pah-*REH-*theh dahr* OO-*nah* VWEHL-*tah pohr lah ah-veh-*NEE-*dah?*
How would you like to go for a walk along the avenue?

NELSON: Vamos.
VAH-*mohs.*
Let us go.

FERNÀNDEZ: Estamos en el Paseo de la Reforma.
*Ess-*TAH-*mohs enn ell Pah-*SEH-*oh deh lah Reh-*FOHR-*mah.*
We are in the *Paseo de la Reforma.*

Después de esa estatua está la avenida Juárez.
*Dehs-*PWEHS *deh* ESS-*ah ess-*TAH-*twah ess-*TAH *lah ah-veh-*NEE-*dah* HWAH-*rehth.*
Beyond that statue is Juarez Avenue.

NELSON: ¡Cuánto tráfico en las calles!
KWAHN-*toh* TRAH-*fee-koh enn lahs* KAHL-*yehs!*
What traffic in the streets!

Casi hay más que en Nueva York.
KAH-*see I mahs keh enn* NWEH-*vah Yohrk.*
There is almost more than in New York.

FERNÁNDEZ: Aquel parque que ve a la izquierda se llama "La Alameda".
*Ah-*KEHL PAHR-*keh keh veh ah lah eethk-*YEHR-*dah seh l'*YAH-*mah Lah Ah-lah-*MEH-*dah.*
That park which you see on your left is called "La Alameda".

Caminamos hacia el centro de la ciudad.
*Kah-mee-*NAH-*mohs* AHTH-*yah ell* THEHN-*troh deh lah th'yoo-*DAHD.
We are walking towards the center of the city.

NELSON: Quiero comprar un sombrero nuevo. El mío está muy usado.
*K'*YEH-*roh kohm-*PRAHR *oon sohm-*BREH-*roh* NWEH-*voh. Ell* MEE-*oh ess-*TAH *mwee oo-*SAH-*doh.*
I want to buy a new hat. Mine is very worn.

FERNÁNDEZ: Aquí hay una sombrerería. Entremos.
*Ah-*KEE *I* OO-*nah sohm-breh-reh-*REE-*ah. Enn-*TREH-*mohs.*
Here is a hat store. Let us go in.

(En la tienda)
(*Enn lah t'*YEHN-*dah*)
(In the store)

EMPLEADO: ¿Qué desean los señores?
*Keh deh-*SEH-*ahn lohs sehn-*YOH-*rehs?*
What do the gentlemen desire?

NELSON: Quiero un sombrero parecido a aquel
*K'*YEH-*roh oon sohm-*BREH-*roh pah-reh-*THEE-*doh ah ah-*KEHL
I want a hat like that

gris que está en el escaparate.
*greess keh ess-*TAH *enn ell es-kah-pah-*RAH-*teh.*
grey one which is in the show-window.

EMPLEADO: Bien, señor. ¿Su número?
*B'YEHN, sehn-*YOHR. *Soo* NOO-*meh-roh?*
Yes, sir. Your size?

NELSON: 40.—¿Cuánto vale?
*Kwah-*REHN-*tah.* KWAHN-*toh* VAH-*leh?*
7½. How much does it cost?

EMPLEADO: 55 pesos.
*Theen-*KWEHN-*tah ee* THEEN-*koh* PEH-*sohs.*
55 pesos.

NELSON: ¿No tiene Ud. alguno más barato?
*Noh t'*YEH-*neh oos-*TEHD *ahl-*GOO-*noh mahs bah-*RAH-*toh?*
Haven't you a cheaper one?

EMPLEADO: Éste vale 38, señor. También es muy elegante.
ESS-*teh* VAH-*leh* TRAIN-*tah ee* OH-*choh. Tahmb-*YEHN *ess mwee
eh-leh-*GAHN-*teh.*
This one costs 38, sir. It is also very elegant.

NELSON: Bien. Lo tomaré. Tenga. (Le da un billete de 50 pesos)
*B'*YEHN. *Loh toh-mah-*REH. TEHN-*gah. (Leh dah oon beel-*YEH-*teh deh
theen-*KWEHN-*tah* PEH-*sohs)*
Good. I shall take it. Here you are. (Gives him a 50 peso bill)

EMPLEADO: ¿Debemos mandarlo, señor, o se lo lleva consigo?
*Deh-*BEH-*mohs mahn-*DAHR-*loh, sehn-*YOHR, *oh seh loh l'*YEH-*vah
kohn-*SEE-*goh?*
Must we send it, sir, or will you take it with you?

NELSON: Me lo llevo. Manden este sombrero viejo al
*Meh loh l'*YEH-*voh.* MAHN-*dehn* ESS-*teh sohm-*BREH-*roh v'*YEH-*hoh ah*\
I'll wear it. Send this old hat to the

Hotel Reforma, cuarto 1125.
*Oh-*TEHL *Reh-*FOHR-*mah,* KWAHR-*toh meel th'*YEHN-*toh
vain-*tee-THEEN-*koh.*
Hotel Reforma, room 1125.

EMPLEADO: Gracias, caballero. Aquí tiene su cambio,
GRAHTH-*yahs, kah-bahl-*YEH-*roh. Ah-*KEE *t'*YEH-*neh soo* KAHMB-*yoh,*
Thank you, sir. Here is your change,

12 pesos. Vuelvan otra vez, señores.
DOH-*theh* PEH-*sohs.* VWEHL-*vahn* OH-*trah vehth, sehn-*YOH-*rehs.*
12 pesos. Come again, gentlemen.

(En la calle)
(*Enn lah* KAHL-*yeh*)
(In the street)

FERNÁNDEZ: Ahora estamos entrando en la calle Francisco I. Madero.
*Ah-*OH-*rah* ess-TAH-*mohs* enn-TRAHN-*doh* enn *lah* KAHL-*y*ɂh
*Frahn-*THEES-*koh* ee *Mah-*DEH-*roh.*
Now we are entering Francisco I. Madero Street.

Es el centro del comercio de la ciudad.
Ess ell THEHN-*troh dehl koh-*MEHRTH-*yoh deh lah th'yoo-*DAHD.
It is the commercial center of the city.

Aquí hay tiendas, bancos y muchas casas de negocios.
*Ah-*KEE *I t'*YEHN-*dahs,* BAHN-*kohs ee* MOO-*chahs* KAH-*sahs deh*
*neh-*GOHTH-*yohs.*
Here there are stores, banks and many commercial houses.

NELSON: ¿Dónde puedo comprar película para mi
DOHN-*deh* PWEH-*doh kohm-*PRAHR *peh-*LEE-*koo-lah* PAH-*rah mee*
Where can I buy film for my

cámara, tarjetas postales y estampillas?
KAH-*mah-rah, tahr-*HEH-*tahs pohs-*TAH-*lehs ee ess-tahm-*PEEL-*yahs?*
camera, post cards and stamps?

FERNÀNDEZ: Hay muchas tiendas en esta calle donde se pueden
I MOO-*chahs t'*YEHN-*dahs enn* ESS-*tah* KAHL-*yeh* DOHN-*deh seh* PWEH-*dehn*
There are many stores on this street where you can

comprar esas cosas. Aquí hay una. Entremos.
*kohm-*PRAHR ESS-*ahs* KOH-*sahs. Ah-*KEE *I* OO-*nah. Enn-*TREH-*mohs*
buy those things. Here is one. Let us go in.

(Después)
*(Dehs-*PWEHS)
(Later)

NELSON: Dígame, ¿qué es ese gran edificio blanco?
DEE-*gah-meh, keh ess* ESS-*eh grahn eh-dee-*FEETH-*yoh* BLAHN-*koh?*
Tell me, what is that big white building?

FERNÁNDEZ: Es el palacio de Bellas Artes.
*Ess ell pah-*LAHTH-*yoh deh* BEHL-*yahs* AHR-*tehs.*
It is the Palace of Fine Arts.

Se usa como teatro y también como museo.
Seh OO-*sah* KOH-*moh teh-*AH-*troh ee tahmb-*YEHN KOH-*moh moo-*SEH-*oh.*
It is used as a theater and also as a museum.

A propósito, ¿quiere ir al teatro esta noche?
*Ah proh-*POH-*see-toh, k'*YEH-*reh eer ahl teh-*AH-*troh* ESS-*tah* NOH-*cheh?*
By the way, do you wish to go to the theater tonight?

NELSON: Muchas gracias: pero Ud. acaba de volver
Moo-chahs GRAHTH-*yahs;* PEH-*roh* oos-TEHD *ah*-KAH-*bah deh vohl*-VEHR
Thank you very much; but you have just come back

a su casa y quiere estar con su familia.
ah soo KAH-*sah ee k'*YEH-*reh ess*-TAHR *kohn soo fah*-MEEL-*yah.*
home and wish to be with your family.

No se preocupe por mí.
*Noh seh preh-oh-*KOO-*peh pohr mee.*
Do not worry about me.

FERNÁNDEZ: Pero mi esposa quiere que Ud. venga a cenar con nosotros.
PEH-*roh mee ess*-POH-*sah k'*YEH-*reh keh oos*-TEHD VEHN-*gah
ah theh*-NAHR *kohn noh*-SOH-*trohs.*
But my wife wants you to come to have supper with us.

No diga más, iré a buscarlo a su hotel a las 8.
Noh DEE-*gah mahs, ee*-REH *ah boos*-KAHR-*loh ah soo oh*-TEHL
ah lahs OH-*choh.*
Say no more, I shall pick you up at your hotel at 8.

NELSON: Mil gracias. Ud. es muy amable conmigo.
Meel GRAHTH-*yahs. Oos*-TEHD *ess mwee ah*-MAH-*bleh kohn*-MEE-*goh.*
A thousand thanks. You are very kind to me.

FERNÁNDEZ: Ahora vamos a tomar un taxi y a dar una vuelta. ¡Taxi!
*Ah-*OH *ah* VAH-*mohs ah toh*-MAHR *oon* TAHK-*see ee ah dahr oo-nah*
VWEHL-*tah.* TAHK-*see!*
Now let us take a taxi and go for a drive. Taxi!

CHOFER: ¿Señor?
Choh-FEHR: *Sehn*-YOHR?
Driver: Sir?

FERNÁNDEZ: ¿Cuánto vale por hora?
KWAHN-*toh* VAH-*leh pohr* OH-*rah?*
How much will it cost us per hour?

CHOFER: ¿Adónde van?
Ah-DOHN-*deh vahn?*
Where are you going?

FERNÁNDEZ: Vamos al bosque de Chapultepec.
VAH-*mohs ahl* BOHS-*kek deh Chah-pool-teh*-PEHK.
Let us go to the *Chapultepec* woods.

CHOFER: Eso será doce pesos por hora, señor.
*Ess-oh seh-*RAH DOH-*theh* PEH-*sohs pohr* OH-*rah, sehn*-YOHR.
That will be twelve pesos an hour, sir.

FERNÁNDEZ: **Es muy caro.**
Ess mwee KAH-*roh.*
It is very expensive.

CHOFER: **Lo puedo hacer por 10.**
Loh PWEH-*doh ah-*THEHR *pohr d'*YEHTH.
I can do it for ten.

FERNÁNDEZ: **Bueno. Pase por el Zócalo primero y después**
BWEH-*noh.* PAH-*seh pohr ell* THOH-*kah-loh pree-*MEH-*roh ee dehs-*PWEHS
Good. Pass by the *Zocalo* first and then

siga por la Reforma y continúe hasta Chapultepec.
SEE-*gah pohr lah Reh-*FOHR-*mah ee kohn-tee-*NOO-*eh* AHS-*tah*
*Chah-pool-teh-*PEHK.
go on through *la Reforma* and on to *Chapultepec.*

EXPRESSIONS TO REMEMBER:
vuelva otra vez: "come back again"
a propósito: "by the way"
Ud. es muy amable: "You are very kind."
acaba de volver: "Has just returned"

This *acabar de* construction is extremely useful. Ex: "I have just read your article": *Acabo de leer su artículo.* (Literally: "I finish reading your article)

NOTE: The ending *ería* added to the name of an article or tradesman, generally indicates the store or place of business.

carnicería: "butcher shop"
joyería: "jeweler's"
sastrería: "tailor's"
cafetería: "coffee shop."

THINKING IN SPANISH
(Answers on page 267)

1. ¿Por dónde empiezan los señores su paseo?
2. ¿Hay mucho tráfico en las calles?
3. ¿Cómo se llama el parque que ven?
4. ¿Qué vemos en las calles de una ciudad grande?
5. ¿Cómo se llama una tienda que vende sombreros?
6. ¿Es el sombrero del Sr. Nelson nuevo o usado?
7. ¿Es mi sombrero nuevo?
8. ¿Qué dice el Sr. Nelson al empleado de la sombrerería?
9. ¿Le gusta el primer sombrero que ve?
10. ¿Por qué prefiere el segundo sombrero?
11. ¿Lo compra?
12. Cuándo salen de la tienda ¿adónde van?
13. ¿Por qué quiere comprar estampillas el Sr. Nelson?
14. Cuando Ud. está viajando, ¿manda Ud. tarjetas postales a sus amigos?
15. ¿Cómo se llama el gran edificio blanco que ven los señores?
16. ¿Invita el Sr. Fernández al Sr. Nelson a ir al teatro por la noche?
17. ¿Por qué no quiere aceptar el Sr. Nelson la invitación?

18. ¿A qué le invita entonces?
19. ¿Adónde deciden ir en taxi?
20. ¿Cuánto quiere cobrar el chofer?
21. ¿Cree el Sr. Fernández que eso es demasiado?
22. ¿Cobran mucho los choferes a los turistas?
23. ¿Cuánto pagará el Sr. Fernández?
24. ¿Conoce el Sr. Fernández bien la ciudad?

LECCIÓN 36

Turista y guía
Too-REES-*tah ee* GGEE-*ah*
Tourist and guide

FERNÁNDEZ: Esta plaza grande se llama el Zócalo.
Ess-*tah* PLAH-*thah* GRAHN-*deh seh* l'YAH-*mah ell* THOH-*kah-loh.*
This large square is called the Zocalo.

Era el centro de la ciudad de los indios
EH-*rah ell* THEHN-*troh deh lah* th'yoo-DAHD *deh lohs* EEND-*yohs*
It used to be the central part of the city of the

aztecas que vivían aquí antes de la llegada de los españoles.
*ahth-*TEH-*kahs keh* vee-VEE-*ahn ah-*KEE AHN-*tehs deh lah* l'yeh-GAH-*dah deh lohs ess-pahn-*YOH-*lehs.*
Aztec Indians, who lived here before the arrival of the Spaniards.

NELSON: Cuando yo estudiaba en la escuela
KWAHN-*doh yoh ess-tood-*YAH-*bah enn lah ess-*KWEH-*lah*
When I studied at school

231

leía algo sobre la historia de México.
*leh-*EE*-ah* AHL*-goh* SOH*-breh lah ees-*TOHR*-yah deh* MEH*-hee-koh.*
I used to read some Mexican History.

Los indios eran muy civilizados, ¿no?
Lohs EEND*-yohs* EH*-rahn mwee thee-vee-*THAH*-dohs, noh?*
The Indians were highly civilized, were they not?

FERNÁNDEZ: Sí, tenían una ciudad muy grande.
*See, teh-*NEE*-ahn* OO*-nah th'yoo-*DAHD *mwee* GRAHN*-deh.*
Yes, they had a very large city.

Allí, donde ve la catedral, había un templo azteca.
*Ahl-*YEE DOHN*-deh veh lah kah-teh-*DRAHL*, ah-*BEE*-ah oon* TEHM*-ploh*
*ahth-*TEH*-kah.*
Over there, where you see the cathedral, there used to be an Aztec
temple.

NELSON: ¡Qué interesante!
*Keh een-teh-reh-*SAHN*-teh!*
How interesting!

FERNÁNDEZ: Antes, Ciudad de México estaba en medio
AHN*-tehs, Th'yoo-*DAHD *deh* MEH*-hee-koh ess-*TAH*-bah enn* MEHD*-yoh*
Formerly, Mexico City was in the middle

de un lago, y donde hay calles ahora, antes
deh oon LAH*-goh ee* DOHN*-deh I* KAHL*-yehs ah-*OH*-rah,* AHN*-tehs*
of a lake, and where there are streets now, formerly

había canales. Los indios iban por los
canales en sus canoas.
*ah-*BEE*-ah kah-*NAH*-lehs. Lohs* EEND*-yohs* EE*-bahn pohr lohs*
*kah-*NAH*-lehs enn soos kah-*NOH*-ahs.*
there were canals. The Indians went through the canals in their canoes.

NOTE on the Imperfect Tense: The Imperfect tense is
used to denote something that *was happening* at a specific
moment in the past or an action that *used to happen re-
peatedly.* Except for this, Spanish has no form for "used to",
Ex: "When I was living in Madrid, I used to go to the bull
fights every Sunday".—*Cuando yo vivía en Madrid, iba a las
corridas de toros todos los domingos.*

To form the imperfect use the endings *aba, aba, ábamos, aban,* attached
to the base of first conjugation verbs; in the second and third conjugations
use the endings *ía, ía, íamos, ían.*

NOTE THESE EXAMPLES: "In 1938 we were in Mexico."—*En 1938 estábamos en México.* "Each day he used to come at 4 o'clock." *Cada día venía a las 4.* "When you were traveling in Europe, did you go to Granada?" *Cuando Ud. viajaba por Europa, ¿fué a Granada?*

NELSON: ¿Vamos ahora hacia Chapultepec?
VAH-mohs ah-OH-rah AHTH-yah Chah-pool-teh-PEHK?
Are we going now towards Chapultepec?

FERNÁNDEZ: Sí. Vamos por el Paseo de la Reforma,
See. VAH-mohs pohr ell Pah-SEH-oh deh lah Reh-FOHR-mah,
Yes. We are going along the Paseo de la Reforma,

y esa otra calle es la Avenida de Chapultepec.
ee EH-sah OH-trah KAHL-yeh ess lah Ah-veh-NEE-dah deh Chah-pool-teh-
PEHK.
and that other street is the Avenue of Chapultepec.

NELSON: ¡Qué bonitas casas hay por aquí!
Keh boh-NEE-tahs KAH-sahs I pohr ah-KEE!
What beautiful houses there are here!

FERNÁNDEZ: Es uno de los barrios más ricos de la ciudad.
Ess OO-noh deh lohs BAHRR-yohs mahs REE-kohs deh lah th'yoo-DAHD.
It is one of the richest sections of the city.

NELSON: Y ese palacio en la loma, ¿qué es?
Ee ESS-eh pahl-AHTH-yoh enn lah LOH-mah, keh ess?
And what is that palace on the hill?

FERNÁNDEZ: Es el castillo de Chapultepec.
Ess ell kahs-TEEL-yoh deh Chah-pool-teh-PEHK.
It is the castle of Chapultepec.

Allí vivía el Emperador Maximiliano hace 80 años.
Ahl-YEE vee-VEE-ah ell Ehm-peh-rah-DOHR Mahk-see-meel-YAH-noh
AH-theh oh-CHEHN-tah AHN-yohs.
There lived the Emperor Maximilian 80 years ago.

NELSON: Quiero sacar unas fotos. ¿Qué le parece?
K'YEH-roh sah-KAHR OO-nahs FOH-tohs. Keh leh pah-REH-theh?
I want to take some pictures. What do you think?

FERNÁNDEZ: Muy bien. Chofer. Pare aquí.
Mwee b'YEHN. Choh-FEHR. PAH-reh ah-KEE.
Very well. Driver. Stop here.

Queremos bajar un rato. Espérenos.
Keh-REH-mohs bah-HAHR oon RAH-toh. Ess-PEH-reh-nohs.
We want to get out for a while. Wait for us.

NELSON: ¡Qué interesante era eso!
*Keh een-teh-reh-*SAHN-*teh* EH-*rah* EH-*soh!*
Y la vista desde arriba era magnífica.
Ee lah VEES-*tah* DEHS-*deh ah-*RREE-*bah* EH-*rah mahg-*NEE-*fee-kah.*
How interesting that was! And the view from above was wonderful.

NOTE: There are only three exceptions in the imperfect tense:

Ser, forming the imperfect: *era—era—éramos—eran*
Ir, " " " : *iba—iba—íbamos—iban*
Ver, " " " : *veía—veía—veíamos—veían*

FERNÁNDEZ: **Usted no ha visto mucho todavía.**
*Oos-*TEHD *noh ah* VEES-*toh* MOO-*choh toh-dah-*VEE-*ah.*
You haven't seen much yet.

Mañana daremos una vuelta por los alrededores.
*Mahn-*YAH-*nah dah-*REH-*mohs* OO-*nah* VWEHL-*tah pohr lohs*
Tomorrow we shall take a drive around the outskirts.

Iremos a Xochimilco y al Desierto de los Leones.
*ahl-reh-deh-*DOH-*rehs. Ee-*REH-*mohs ah Zoh-chee-*MEEL-*koh ee ahl*
*Dehs-*YEHR-*toh deh lohs Leh-*OH-*nehs.*
We shall go to Xochimilco and to the Desert of the Lions.

NELSON: **Yo también deseaba ir a la Villa de Guadalupe.**
*Yoh tahmb-*YEHN *deh-seh-ah-bah eer ah lah* VEEL-*yah deh*
*Gwah-dah-*LOO-*peh.*
I also wished to go to the Villa of Guadalupe. (*a famous shrine.*)

¿Está lejos?
*Ess-*TAH *leh-hohs?*
Is it far away?

FERNÁNDEZ: **Está cerca. Podemos ir otro día.**
*Ess-*TAH THEHR-*kah. Poh-*DEH-*mohs eer* OH-*troh* DEE-*ah.*
It is nearby. We can go some other day.

NELSON: **Es Ud. muy amable en llevarme a todos estos sitios.**
*Ess oos-*TEHD *mwee ah-*MAH-*bleh enn l'yeh-*VAHR-*meh ah* TOH-*dohs*
ess-tohs SEET-*yohs.*
You are very kind to take me to all these places.

FERNÁNDEZ: **¡Hombre! Es un gusto para mí.**
OHM-*breh! Ess oon* GOOS-*toh* PAH-*rah mee.*
Why, it is a pleasure for me.

Y no se olvide que esta noche comerá en mi casa.

*Ee noh seh ohl-*VEE*-deh keh* ESS*-tah* NOH*-cheh koh-meh-*RAH *enn mee* KAH*-sah.*

And do not forget that tonight you will dine at my house.

IDIOMS TO REMEMBER: *Se llama:* "is called"—literally "calls itself". When you ask a person's name you say: *¿Cómo se llama Ud.?*

Sacar unas fotos:—"to take some photos"
un rato:—"a moment". Do not confuse with   *un ratón:*—"a mouse".

hace 80 años:—"80 years ago". Put *hace* before a Spanish word where you would use "ago" after an English word.

¡Hombre!:—An all-purpose interjection, used to express amazement, scorn, deprecation, joy, shock and practically any other emotion or sentiment you can imagine.

THINKING IN SPANISH
(Answers on page 268)

1. ¿En qué plaza están los señores?
2. ¿Quiénes vivían en México antes de los españoles?
3. ¿Cómo se llamaban esos indios?
4. ¿Tenían una ciudad grande?
5. ¿Estaba la ciudad de México en un lago?
6. ¿Qué había antes en lugar de calles?
7. ¿Dónde vivía el Emperador Maximiliano hace muchos años?
8. ¿Dónde vivía Ud. el año pasado?
9. ¿Dónde vivía Ud. hace 10 años?
10. ¿Tomaba Ud. lecciones durante el invierno pasado?
11. ¿Iba Ud. mucho a la playa?
12. ¿Tenía Ud. automóvil el año pasado?
13. ¿Por qué paran el automóvil en Chapultepec?
14. ¿Quién quiere sacar fotos?
15. ¿Qué harán los señores el próximo día?
16. ¿Está lejos o cerca de Ciudad de México la Villa de Guadalupe?

17. ¿Está Los Angeles lejos de México?
18. ¿Está Cuba cerca de los Estados Unidos?
19. ¿Adónde irá el Sr. Nelson por la noche?
20. ¿Está invitado a una comida?
21. Cuando un amigo le invita a una comida, ¿qué le dice Ud.?
22. ¿Se divierte el Sr. Nelson en su viaje?

LECCIÓN 37

Mi casa es suya
Mee KAH-*sah ess* SOO-*yah*
My house is yours

NELSON: Tiene Ud. una casa muy bonita aquí.
*T'*YEH-*neh* OOS-TEHD OO-*nah* KAH-*sah mwee boh-*NEE-*tah ah-*KEE.
You have a very beautiful house here.

FERNÁNDEZ: Es suya. Aquí viene mi esposa.—Cristina,
Ess SOO-*yah. Ah-*KEE *v'*YEH-*neh mee ess-*POH-*sah.—Krees-*TEE-*nah,*
Make yourself at home. Here comes my wife. Christina,

quiero presentarte a mi amigo Roberto Nelson.
*k'*YEH-*roh preh-sehn-*TAHR-*teh ah mee ah-*MEE-*goh Roh-*BEHR-*toh*
NEHL-*sohn.*
I want to present my friend Robert Nelson to you.

SEÑORA DE FERNÁNDEZ: Tengo mucho gusto en conocerle.
TEHN-*goh* MOO-*choh* GOOS-*toh enn koh-noh-*THEHR-*leh.*
I am very glad to meet you.

Aquí está en su casa.
*Ah-*KEE *ess-*TAH *enn soo* KAH-*sah.*
Here you are at home.

NELSON: El gusto es mío, señora.
Ell GOOS-*toh ess* MEE-*oh, sehn-*YOH-*rah.*
The pleasure is mine, madam.

SEÑORA DE FERNÁNDEZ: ¿Qué tal le gusta México?
Keh tahl leh GOOS-*tah* MEH-*hee-koh?*
How do you like Mexico?

NELSON: Estoy encantado con este país.
*Ess-*TOY *enn-kahn-*TAH-*doh kohn* ESS-*teh pah-*EES.
I am delighted with this country.

Además su esposo ha tenido la bondad
*Ah-deh-*MAHS *soo ess-*POH-*soh ah teh-*NEE-*doh lah bohn-*DAHD
Besides your husband has had the kindness

de llevarme a muchos sitios.
*deh l'yeh-*VAHR-*meh ah* MOO-*chohs* SEET-*yohs.*
to take me to many places.

(3 niños entran)
(*trehs* NEEN-*yohs* ENN-*trahn*)
(3 children enter)

FERNÁNDEZ: Éstos son nuestros niños.
Ess-tohs sohn NWEHS-*trohs* NEEN-*yohs.*
These are our children.

NELSON: ¡Qué lindos!
Keh LEEN-*dohs!*
How cute!

(a los niños)
(*ah lohs* NEEN-*yohs*)
(to the children)

Hola, preciosa. ¿Cómo te llamas?
OH-*lah prehth-*YOH-*sah.* KOH-*moh teh l'*YAH-*mahs?*
Hello, beautiful. What is your name?

ISABEL: Me llamo Isabel.
*Ee-sah-*BEHL: *Meh* L'YAH-*moh Ee-sah-*BEHL.
Elizabeth: My name is Elizabeth.

NELSON: Y dime, tus hermanitos, ¿cómo se llaman?
Ee DEE-*meh, toos ehr-mah-*NEE-*tohs,* KOH-*moh seh l'*YAH-*mahn?*
And tell me, what are the names of your little brother and sister?

ISABEL: Esta se llama María, y éste se llama Jorge y es muy malo.
*Ess-tah sen l'*YAH-*mah Mahr-*EE-*ah, ee* ESS-*teh seh l'*YAH-*mah* HOER-*heh*
ee ess mwee MAH-*loh.*
This one is Mary, and this one is George and he is very bad.

NELSON: ¡Qué cosa! ¿Por que és malo?
Keh KOH-*sah! Pohr* KEH *ess* MAH-*loh?*
What a shame! Why is he bad?

ISABEL: Porque empujó a María y ella se cayó. Lloró mucho.
*POHR-keh ehm-poo-*HOH *ah Mah-*REE-*ah ee* EHL-*yah seh kah-*YOH.
*L'yo-*ROH MOO-*choh.*
Because he pushed Mary and she fell. She cried hard.

FERNÁNDEZ: Por eso no le daremos postre. (Los niños se van)
Pohr ESS-*oh noh leh dah-*REH-*mohs* POHS-*treh.* (*Lohs* NEEN-*yohs seh
vahn*)
For that we shall not give him any dessert. (The children leave)

 NOTE ON THE FAMILIAR FORM: When Sr. Fernández
talks to his wife or when Mr. Nelson talks to the children
they use *tú* instead of *Ud.* and *te* instead of *le* or *la.*

This is the familiar form of the verb. The verb ending for verb form
with *tú* is usually formed by adding *s* to any form used with *Ud.*
Ex: *Ud. viene....tú vienes. Ud. sabe....tú sabes....Ud. iba....tú ibas*
However, the past form uses the ending *aste* for the 1st. conjugation and
iste for the others. Ex: *tú tomaste, tú aprendiste,* etc.

There is also a pure imperative for this familiar form which is usually
exactly the same as the *Ud.* form in the present indicative.

Ex: *¡Toma! ¡Aprende!* Some exceptions are *¡Ven! (venir), ¡vete! (irse),*
¡pon! (poner), ¡di! (decir).

 CAUTION: The familiar form does not necessarily mean
affection, but only lack of formal politeness. Therefore
remember to be polite, and use the familiar form only
when addressing very young children or animals.

FERNÁNDEZ: ¿Tiene Ud. hijos, Sr. Nelson?
*T'*YEH-*neh oos-*TEHD EE-*hohs, sehn-*YOHR NEHL-*sohn?*
Have you any children, Mr. Nelson?

NELSON: Sí. Tengo dos hijas ya grandes.
See. TEHN-*goh dohs* EE-*hahs yah* GRAHN-*dehs.*
Yes. I have two grown-up daughters.

FERNÁNDEZ: ¡No me diga!
Noh meh DEE-*gah!*
You don't say!

NELSON: Una se casó con un oficial del ejército
*Oo-*nah *seh kah-*SOH *kohn oon oh-feeth-*YAHL *dehl eh-*HEHR-*thee-toh*
One of them married an Army officer

hace tiempo y ya tiene un niño.
AH-*theh* t'YEHM-*poh ee yah* t'YEH-*neh oon* NEEN-*yoh.*
some time ago and already has a son.

De manero que ya soy abuelo.
*Deh mah-*NEH-*rah keh yah soy ah-*BWEH-*loh.*
So that already I am a grandfather.

SEÑORA DE FERNÁNDEZ: **Ud. no lo parece.**
*Oos-*TEHD *noh loh pah-*REH-*theh.*
You do not look it.

NELSON: **Aquí tiene una foto de la más joven.**
*Ah-*KEE t'YEH-*neh* OO-*nah* FOH-*toh deh lah mahs* HOH-*vehn.*
Here is a photo of the younger.

Está comprometida y su novio es abogado.
*Ess-*TAH *kohm-proh-meh-*TEE-*dah ee soo* NOHV-*yoh ess ah-boh-*GAH-*doh,*
She is engaged and her fiancé is a lawyer.

SRA. FERNÁNDEZ: **¡Qué guapa es!**
Keh GWAH-*pah ess!*
How stunning she is!

Le felicito por tener una hija tan bonita.
*Leh feh-lee-*THEE-*toh pohr teh-*NEHR *oo-nah* EE-*hah tahn boh-*NEE-*tah.*
I congratulate you for having such a beautiful daughter.

NELSON: **Gracias, Ud. es muy amable.**
GRAHTH-*yahs, oos-*TEHD *ess mwee ah-*MAH-*bleh.*
Thank you, you are very kind.

SRA. FERNÁNDEZ: **Qué lástima que ella no está aquí en México con Ud.**
Keh LAHS-*tee-mah keh* EHL-*yah noh ess-*TAH *ah-*KEE *enn* MEH-*hee-koh kohn oos-*TEHD.
What a pity that she is not here in Mexico with you.

Tendría mucho gusto en conocerla.
*Teh-*DREE-*ah* MOO-*choh* GOOS-*toh enn koh-noh-*THEHR-*lah.*
I should very much like to meet her.

NELSON: **Ella quería venir pero no pudo.**
EHL-*yah keh-*REE-*ah veh-*NEER *peh-roh noh* POO-*doh.*
She wanted to come but she could not.

Dijo que vendría la próxima vez conmigo.
DEE-*hoh keh vehn-*DREE-*yah lah* PROHK-*see-mah vehth kohn-*MEE-*goh.*
She said that she would come with me the next time.

 MORE NOTES ON THE SUBJUNCTIVE: As you have noticed from the 8th lesson on, the imperative subjunctive verb form is used for direct commands and also after forms such as "I wish that": *Yo quiero que* and "I hope that": *Yo espero que.* Moreover it is used after expression of feeling and emotions. Ex: "I am sorry that you are sick":*Siento que Ud. esté enfermo.* "What a shame she doesn't speak Spanish!": *¡Qué lástima que no hable español!*

LA CRIADA: Señora, la comida está servida.
Lah cree-YAH-dah: Sehn-YOH-rah, lah koh-MEE-dah ess-TAH sehr-VEE-dah.
The Maid: Madam, dinner is served.

FERNÁNDEZ: Vamos a comer ahora.
VAH-mohs ah koh-MEHR ah-OH-rah.
Let us eat now.

NELSON: Este aire de México me ha dado mucho apetito.
Ess-teh AH-ee-reh deh MEH-hee-koh meh ah DAH-doh MOO-choh ah-peh-TEE-toh.
This Mexican air has given me a good appetite.

FERNÁNDEZ: Me alegro que tenga apetito.
Meh ah-LEH-groh keh TEHN-gah ah-peh-TEE-toh.
I am glad that you are hungry.

Después de la comida le llevaremos a pasear un poco.
Dehs-PWEHS deh lah koh-MEE-dah leh l'yeh-vah-REH-mohs ah pah-seh-AHR oon POH-koh.
After dinner we shall take you for a short drive.

Cristina, ¿quieres venir con nosotros?
Krees-TEE-nah, k'YEH-rehs veh-NEER kohn noh-SOH-trohs?
Christina, do you want to come with us?

SRA. DE FERNÁNDEZ: Claro. No creas que me vas a dejar sola.
KLAH-roh. Noh KREH-ahs keh meh vahs ah deh-HAHR SOH-lah.
Of course. Do not think that you are going to leave me alone.

NOTE ON THE CONDITIONAL: The Imperfect endings *ía, ía, íamos, ían,* when added to the future base, form the conditional. It can simply be translated by "would". Ex: "he said he would come." *Dijo que vendría;* "Would you like to dance with me?": *¿Le gustaría bailar conmigo?*

IDIOMS TO REMEMBER: *Está en su casa:* "You are in your house". Said to make friends who visit you feel at ease.
Hermanitos: "Little brothers". The use of the diminutive is widespread in Spanish. Note also that *hermanos* can mean "brothers and sisters", just as *hijos* can mean "sons and daughters".
¡No me diga!: "Don't tell me!" or "you don't say!"

AN OLD SPANISH CUSTOM: Although our Mrs. Fernández insists on going out to see the town with her husband and his friend, it is doubtful that this would happen in some Latin American countries. In a good many of them, it would be considered more discreet that the wife remain at home.

THINKING IN SPANISH
(Answers on page 269)

1. ¿Qué le dice la Sra. Fernández a su invitado?
2. ¿Cómo se llama la esposa de Fernández?
3. ¿ Cuántos niños tiene Doña Cristina?
4. ¿Cuántos hermanos tiene Isabel?
5. ¿Cuántas hermanas tiene Jorge?
6. ¿Es Jorge un niño malo?   7. ¿Por qué?
8. ¿Cuántas hijas tiene el Sr. Nelson?
9. ¿Son casadas?   10. ¿Tiene hijos?
11. ¿Cuántos hermanos tiene Ud.?
12. ¿Con quién se casó la hija mayor del Sr. Nelson?
13. ¿Es abuelo el Sr. Nelson?   14. ¿Parece joven el Sr. Nelson?
15. ¿Cuántos nietos tiene?
16. ¿De quién es la foto que el Sr. Nelson muestra a los Fernández?
17. ¿Es bonita la hija del Sr. Nelson?
18. ¿Está comprometida?   19. ¿Qué profesión tiene su novio?
20. ¿Qué harán los Fernández y el Sr. Nelson después de la comida?

LECCION 38

¡Viva el torero!
VEE-*vah ell toh*-REH-*roh!*
Hurray for the bull-fighter!

FERNÁNDEZ: Aquí estamos en la plaza de toros.
*Ah-*KEE *ess-*TAH-*mohs enn lah* PLAH-*thah deh* TOH-*rohs.*
Here we are at the bull ring.

Es la primera vez que ha visto una corrida?
*Ess lah pree-*MEH-*rah vehth keh ah* VEES-*toh* OO-*nah koh-*RREE-*dah?*
Is this the first time that you have seen a bull fight?

NELSON: No. Cuando estaba en el Perú iba a menudo.
Noh. KWAHN-*doh ess-*TAH-*bah enn ell Peh-*ROO EE-*bah ah meh-*NOO-*doh.*
No. When I was in Peru, I used to go often.

FERNÁNDEZ: De manera que Ud. es ya aficionado.
*Deh mah-*NEH-*rah keh oos-*TEHD *ess yah ah-feeth-yoh-*NAH-*doh.*
So that you are already a fan.

¿Le gustan las localidades?
Leh GOOS-*tahn lahs loh-kah-lee-*DAH-*dehs?*
Do you like the seats?

NELSON: Son excelentes. ¡Qué lástima que su señora
*Sohn ehk-theh-*LEHN-*tehs. Keh* LAHS-*tee-mah keh soo sehn-*YOH-*rah*
They are excellent. What a pity that your wife

no haya podido acompañarnos!
noh AH-*yah* poh-DEE-*doh* ah-kohm-pahn-YAHR-*nohs!*
could not come with us.

FERNÁNDEZ: No importa. No le gustan las corridas. Y ¿a su señora?
*Noh eem-*POHR-*tah. Noh leh* GOOS-*tahn lahs koh-*RREE-*dahs.*
*Ee ah soo sehn-*YOH-*rah?*
It does not matter. She does not like the fights. And your wife?

NELSON: Creo que si estuviera aquí iría con mucho gusto.
KREH-*oh keh see ess-toov-*YEH-*rah ah-*KEE *ee-*REE-*ah kohn* MOO-*choh*
GOOS-*toh.*
I believe that if she were here she would gladly go.

Siempre quiere ver algo nuevo.
S'YEHM-*preh k'*YEH-*reh vehr* AHL-*goh* NWEH-*voh.*
She always wants to see something new.

FERNÁNDEZ: Oiga. Tocan la corneta. Empieza. Ya sale el toro.
OY-*gah.* TOH-*kahn lah kohr-*NEH-*tah. Ehmp-*YEH-*thah.*
Yah SAH-*leh ell* TOH-*roh.*
Listen. They are blowing the bugle. It is starting. The bull is coming
out already.

NELSON: ¿Tiene programa? ¿Quién es el matador?
T'YEH-*neh proh-*GRAH-*mah? K'*YEHN *ess ell mah-tah-*DOHR?
Have you a program? Who is the matador?

FERNÁNDEZ: Es Cagancho. Allí viene.
*Ess Kah-*GAHN-*choh. Ahl-*YEE *v'*YEH-*neh.*
It's Cagancho. There he comes.

Ahora está trabajando con la capa.
Ah-OH-*rah ess-*TAH *trah-bah-*HAHN-*doh kohn lah* KAH-*pah.*
Now he is working with the cape.

NELSON: ¿Qué le parece? ¿Es bueno?
*Keh leh pah-*REH-*theh? Ess* BWEH-*noh?*
How does he seem to you? Is he good?

FERNÁNDEZ: Sí, hombre. Usualmente trabaja bien,
See, OHM-*breh. Oo-swahl-*MEHN-*teh trah-*BAH-*hah b'*YEHN,
Yes, indeed. He generally works well.

pero si viese a Armillita entonces vería algo fenomenal.
PEH-*roh see v'*YEH-*seh ah Ahr-meel-*YEE-*tah enn-*TOHN-*thehs veh-*REEH-*ah*
AHL-*goh feh-noh-meh-*NAHL.
But if you saw Armillita then you would see something phenomenal!

NELSON: Mire. Le ha puesto al toro un par de banderillas.
MEE-reh. Leh ah PWEHS-toh ahl TOH-roh oon pahr deh
bahn-deh-REEL-yahs.
Look. He has put a pair of flags on the bull.

Por poco le cogió el toro.
Pohr POH-koh leh koh-h'YOH ell TOH-roh.
The bull almost caught him.

FERNÁNDEZ: ¡Comó se entusiasma la gente!
KOH-moh seh enn-toos-YAHS-mah lah HEHN-teh!
How enthusiastic the crowd is getting!

Uno pensaría que ésta fuera la primera vez que han visto una corrida.
Oo-noh pehn-sah-REE-ah keh ESS-tah FWEH-rah lah pree-MEH-rah
vehth keh ahn VEES-toh OO-nah koh-RREE-dah.
One would think that this were the first time they had seen a fight.

NELSON: Ya mató al toro con la primera estocada. ¿Ve Ud. allí?
Yah mah-TOH ahl TOH-roh kohn lah pree-MEH-rah ess-toh-KAH-dah.
Veh oos-TEHD ahl-YEE?
He killed the bull with his very first thrust. Do you see there?

Los aficionados están tirando sombreros
Lohs ah-feeth-yoh-NAH-dohs ess-TAHN tee-RAHN-doh sohm-BREH-rohs
The fans are throwing hats

y las muchachas, flores al matador.
ee lahs moo-CHAH-chahs FLOH-rehs, ahl mah-tah-DOHR.
and the girls flowers, to the matador.

FERNÁNDEZ: Y si no fuese bueno le tirarían botellas.
Ee see noh FWEH-rah BWEH-noh leh tee-rah-REE-ahn boh-TEHL-yahs.
And if he were not good, they would throw bottles at him.

NOTE on the Imperfect Subjunctive: The imperfect subjunctive is formed by adding *ase, ase, ásemos, asen* to the root of the 1st. conjugation verbs. Ex: (*tomase, etc.*) and *iese, iese, iésemos, iesen,* to the root of the 2nd. and 3rd. Ex: (*viese, etc.*) In the case of irregular verbs, the past root is used. Ex: (*estuviese*).

ra may be substituted for *se* in the above forms. Ex: *tomase,* or *tomara,* *estuviese* or *estuviera.* Both forms are absolutely correct.

When is the Imperfect Subjunctive used: If you suppose something that is not true, you are supposing a condition "contrary to fact". If for example you say "If Lupita were here, she would sing a Mexican song". You are supposing something contrary to reality, for she is not here. Therefore to express this, use the *imperfect subjunctive* with the conditional in this way: *Si Lupita estuviese aquí, cantaría una canción mexicana.*

Note the use of the imperfect subjunctive and the conditional in the following sentences:

"If I had 1,000,000 pesos I would buy a yacht. *Si yo tuviera 1.000.000. de pesos compraría un yate.*

"You wouldn't talk that way if she were here". *Ud no hablaría así, si ella estuviera aquí.*

EXPRESSIONS to Remember:
la corrida de toros: "*the bull fight*".
un aficionado: "a fan" (a devotee)
la plaza de toros: "the bull ring".
las banderillas: the darts to be stuck into the bull's neck.

fenomenal: "phenomenal". Its colloquial meaning is roughly "out of this world".

THINKING IN SPANISH
(Answers on page 269)

1. ¿Quiénes están en la corrida de toros?
2. ¿Ha estado el Sr. Nelson en una corrida antes?
3. ¿Le gustaría a la Sra. de Nelson ir a la corrida si estuviera en México?
4. ¿Quién es el matador que ven?
5. Según el Sr. Fernández, ¿qué matador sería mejor?
6. ¿Dónde pone el matador las banderillas?
7. ¿Qué tira la gente al torero cuando trabaja bien?
8. Y si no trabajase bien, ¿qué le tiraría?
9. ¿Acompañó a su marido la Sra. de Fernández?
10. ¿Por qué no fué ella a la corrida?
11. Si Ud. estuviera en México, ¿iría a las corridas de toros?
12. Si Ud. tuviera mucho dinero, ¿haría un viaje a Sur América?
13. ¿Qué país le gustaría más visitar?
14. ¿Cree Ud. que el Sr. Nelson se divierte mucho en México?
15. Si Ud. estuviese en este momento en Cuba, ¿podría hablar español?

A PRONUNCIATION TOUR OF SPANISH=AMERICA

THE NAMES of many of the countries and cities of South America are pronounced quite differently south of the Rio Grande from the way we have heard them pronounced in English. For this reason, we have prepared a special chart, containing the phonetic pronunciation of the names of countries, their inhabitants, capital cities, capital city dwellers, and, for good measure, the respective currencies. We have put the adjective of nationality in the masculine singular, but the endings change, as with other Spanish adjectives, in accordance with number and gender.

Concentrate on these pronunciations—Latin-Americans are "touchy" about their national countries. Chileans cringe when we call their country "Chilly", instead of "CHEE-leh".

Here we go:

A PRONUNCIATION TOUR OF SPANISH-AMERICA

Country	Inhabitant	Capital City	Cap. City Dweller	Currency
Cuba KOO-*bah*	cubano *koo-*BAH-*noh*	la Habana *lah Ah-*BAH-*nah*	habanero *ah-bah-*NEH-*roh*	peso PEH-*soh*
la República Domini- cana *lah Reh-*POO-*blee-kah* *Doh-mee-nee-*KAH-*nah*	dominicano *doh-mee-nee-*KAH-*noh*	Ciudad Trujillo S'*yoo-*DAHD *Troo-* HEEL-*yo*	capitalino *kah-pee-tah-*LEE-*noh*	peso PEH-*soh*
Puerto Rico PWEHR-*toh* REE-*koh*	puertorriqueño *pwehr-toh-rree-*KEHN- *yoh*	San Juan *Sahn Hwahn*	sanjuanero *sahn-hwah-*NEH-*roh*	dólar DOH-*lahr*
Venezuela *Veh-neh-*ZWEH-*lah*	venezolano *veh-neh-zoh-*LAH-*noh*	Caracas *Kah-*RAH-*kahs*	caraqueño *kah-rah-*KEHN-*yoh*	bolívar *boh-*LEE-*vahr*
Colombia *Koh-*LOHMB-*yah*	colombiano *koh-lohmb-*YAH-*noh*	Bogotá *Boh-goh-*TAH	bogotano *boh-goh-*TAH-*noh*	peso PEH-*soh*
México MEH-*hee-koh*	mexicano *meh-hee-*KAH-*noh*	la Ciudad de México *lah* S'*yoo-*DAHD *deh* MEH-*hee-koh*	capitalino *kah-pee-tah-*LEE-*noh*	peso PEH-*soh*
Guatemala *Gwah-teh-*MAH-*lah*	guatemalteco *gwah-teh-mahl-*TEH-*koh*	Guatemala *Gwah-teh-*MAH-*lah*	}	quetzal *keh-*TSAHL
Honduras *Ohn-*DOO-*rahs*	hondureño *ohn-doo-*REHN-*yoh*	Tegucigalpa *Teh-goo-see-*GAHL-*pah*	tegucigalpeño *teh-goo-see-gahl-*PEHN-*yoh*	lempira *lem-*PEE-*rah*

NOTE: A person from the capital is often referred to as *capitalino* (*kah-pee-tahl-*EE-*noh*). This is especially useful in the cases where the name of the capital city is the same as that of the country.

Country	Nationality	Capital	Capital resident	Currency
El Salvador *Ell Sahl-vah-DOHR*	**salvadoreño** *sahl-vah-doh-REHN-yoh*	**San Salvador** *Sahn Sahl-vah-DOHR*	capitalino *kah-pee-tah-LEE-noh*	colon *coh-LOHN*
Nicaragua *Nee-kah-RAH-gwah*	**nicaragüense** *nee-kah-rah-GWEN-seh*	**Managua** *Mah-NAH-gwah*	managüense *mah-nah-GWEN-seh*	córdoba *KOHR-doh-bah*
Costa Rica *KOHS-tah REE-kah*	**costarricense** *kohs-tah-rree-SEHN-seh*	**San José** *Sahn Hoh-SEH*	josefino *hoh-seh-FEE-noh*	colón *koh-LOHN*
Panamá *Pah-nah-MAH*	**panameño** *pah-nah-MEHN-yoh*	**Ciudad de Panamá** *S'yoo-DAHD deh Pah-nah-MAH*	capitalino *kah-pee-tah-LEE-noh*	balboa *bahl-BOH-ah*
Chile CHEE-*leh*	**chileno** *chee-LEH-noh*	**Santiago** *Sahn-tee-YAH-goh*	santiaguero *sahnt-yah-GGEH-roh*	peso *PEH-soh*
la Argentina *lah Ahr-hehn-TEE-nah*	**argentino** *ahr-hehn-TEE-noh*	**Buenos Aires** *BWEH-nos EYE-rehs*	bonarense *boh-nah-REHN-seh*	peso *PEH-soh*
el Uruguay *ell Oo-roo-GWIGH*	**uruguayo** *oo-roo-GWAH-yoh*	**Montevideo** *Mon-teh-vee-DEH-oh*	montevidiano *mon-teh-veed-YAH-noh*	peso *PEH-soh*
Paraguay *Pah-rah-GWIGH*	**paraguayo** *pah-rah-GWAH-yoh*	**Asunción** *Ah-soons-YOHN*	asunceño *ah-soon-SEHN-yoh*	guaraní *gwah-rah-NEE*
el Ecuador *ell Eh-kwah-DOHR*	**ecuatoriano** *eh-kwah-tohr-YAH-noh*	**Quito** KEE-*toh*	quiteño *kee-TEHN-yoh*	sucre *soo-kreh*
el Perú *ell Peh-ROO*	**peruano** *pehr-WAH-noh*	**Lima** LEE-*mah*	limeño *lee-MEHN-yoh*	sol *sohl*
Bolivia *Boh-LEEV-yah*	**boliviano** *boh-leev-YAH-noh*	**La Paz** *La PAHS*	paceño *pah-SEHN-yoh*	boliviano *boh-leev-YAH-noh*

REMEMBER: Although proper names are capitalized, nationalities are written in small letters. *Example:* "North America"—*Norte América;* "North American"—*norteamericana.*

ANSWERS

ANSWERS TO LESSON 1

1. Es el libro.
2. Sí, es el libro.
3. No, no es la caja, es el libro.
4. No, no es la mesa, es la caja.
5. No, no es el papel, es la caja.
6. Es la caja.
7. No, no es la lámpara, es la llave.
8. No, no es la silla, es la llave

9. Es la llave.
10. Es el lápiz.
11. No, no es la caja, es el lápiz.
12. No, no es la llave, es el lápiz.
13. Es la mesa.
14. No, no es el libro, es la mesa.
15. No, no es la pared, es la mesa.

ANSWERS TO LESSON 2

1. Es el zapato.
2. Es el zapato.
3. No es la corbata ni el pañuelo, es el zapato.
4. Es el guante.
5. Es el guante.
6. No, no es el lápiz, es el guante.

7. Es el pantalón.
8. No, no es el traje.
9. No, no es el abrigo.
10. Es el pantalón.
11. No, no es el sombrero.
12. No, no es la camisa.

ANSWERS TO LESSON 3

1. No, no es la pluma azul.
2. No, no es la pluma gris.
3. La pluma es verde.
4. No, la pluma no es roja.
5. La pluma es verde.
6. Es el lápiz.
7. Sí, es el lápiz.
8. No, no es el lápiz rojo.
9. No, no es el lápiz blanco.
10. El lápiz es amarillo.

11. No, no es la mesa, es la lámpara.
12. No, no es la puerta.
13. Es la lámpara.
14. Sí, es la lámpara.
15. La lámpara es azul.
16. Es el libro.
17. No, el libro no es amarillo.
18. No, el libro no es negro.
19. No, el libro no es blanco.
20. El libro es rojo.

ANSWERS TO LESSON 4

1. Sí, el libro rojo es largo.
2. Sí, es ancho.
3. Sí, es grande.
4. Sí, el libro verde es corto.
5. Sí, es estrecho.
6. Sí, es pequeño.
7. El libro grande es rojo.
8. El libro pequeño es verde.
9. El traje largo es negro.
10. No, no es rojo.
11. Sí, el traje negro es largo.
12. No, no es corto.

13. El traje corto es amarillo.
14. No es negro ni verde, es amaril
15. La ventana larga es azul.
16. La ventana ancha es azul.
17. No, no es gris.
18. No, la ventana roja no es larga, corta.
19. La ventana azul es ancha.
20. Sí, la ventana azul es grande.
21. Sí, la ventana roja es pequeña.
22. La ventana pequeña es roja.
23. La ventana grande es azul.

ANSWERS TO LESSON 5

1. Yo soy......
2. Sí, yo soy norteamericano. (No, yo no soy norteamericano.)
3. No, yo no soy el profesor.
4. No, yo no soy cubano.
5. Sí, Ud. es el Sr. Berlitz.
6. Sí, Ud. es el profesor.
7. Sí, Ud. es mexicano. (No, Ud. no es mexicano.)

8. No, Ud. no es norteamericano.
9. Sí, Carmen Miranda es brasile
10. Sí, Dolores del Río es mexican
11. No, Maurice Chevalier no cubano, es francés.
12. El general MacArthur es teamericano.
13. El Sr. Churchill es inglés.
14. La Sra. de Perón es argentina.
15. Sí, el profesor es español.

ANSWERS TO LESSON 6

1. Sí, el sombrero del profesor es negro.
2. No, el sombrero de Pablo no es negro, es blanco.
3. Mi sombrero es......
4. No, su sombrero no es verde.
5. No, la cartera de Doña Felicidad no es pequeña, es grande.
6. No, la cartera de Chiquita no es grande, es pequeña.
7. Sí, es azul.

8. No, aquel lápiz no es gris, amarillo.
9. Mi pañuelo es blanco.
10. Mi casa es pequeña. (Mi casa grande.)
11. Sí, éste es mi libro. (No, no es libro.)
12. El sombrero del profesor es ne
13. Sí, la falda de Doña Felicidad larga.
14. Sí, la falda de Chiquita es cort

ANSWERS TO LESSON 7

1. El libro está encima de la mesa.
2. Sí, el libro está encima de la mesa.
3. No, el libro no está debajo de la silla.
   La pluma está dentro de la caja.
4. Sí, la pluma está delante de la mesa.
5. La silla está delante de la mesa.
6. El profesor está detrás de la mesa.
7. No, el profesor no está debajo de la mesa.
8. Sí, el profesor está de pié detrás de la mesa.
9. Sí, yo estoy sentado en la silla. (No, yo no estoy sentado en la silla.)

11. No, yo no estoy de pié delante de la puerta.
12. Sí, el papel está dentro del libro.
13. No, el papel no está dentro de la caja.
14. La caja está debajo de la mesa.
15. Sí, la pluma está dentro de la caja.
16. No, la llave no está debajo de la silla.
17. Ese lápiz es negro.
18. Sí, ese lápiz es negro.
19. Este lápiz es rojo.
20. Este libro es grande. (Este libro es pequeño).

ANSWERS TO LESSON 8

1. El profesor toma el libro.
2. Sí, el profesor toma el libro.
3. No, no pone el libro encima de la mesa.
4. No, el profesor no toma la caja.
5. El profesor está de pié.
6. No, el profesor no cierra la ventana.
7. El profesor abre la ventana.
8. El profesor abre la ventana.

9. No, yo no abro la puerta.
10. No, el profesor no abre la puerta.
11. No, el profesor no va a Nueva York.
12. No, él no va a París.
13. El profesor va a la Habana.
14. La Habana es grande.
15. Yo no voy a la Habana.
16. El profesor va a la Habana.

ANSWERS TO LESSON 9

1. No, encima de la mesa no hay libros.
2. Sí, el profesor cuenta.
3. El profesor cuenta el dinero.
4. No, encima de la silla grande no hay caja.
5. Sí, aquí hay una mesa.
6. Hay una caja encima de la mesa.
   No, no hay cuadros en la pared.
7. No, no hay dos sombreros encima de la silla.

9. 2 y 8 son 10.
10. Cinco por seis son treinta.
11. Este libro cuesta $2.50.
12. Mi sombrero cuesta......
13. La revista Life cuesta 20 centavos.
14. Entre Los Ángeles y Nueva York hay 3.000 millas.
15. Entre París y Nueva York hay 3.000 millas.
16. Yo cuento desde 20 hasta 25.

ANSWERS TO LESSON 10

1. Debajo del brazo izquierdo del profesor hay un periódico.
2. Sí, hay un periódico debajo de su brazo izquierdo.
3. Sí, la pipa está dentro del bolsillo del profesor.
4. El papel está encima de la silla.
5. Sí, la regla está debajo del pié derecho.
6. En la mano derecha del profesor hay plumas.
7. Sí, hay plumas en su mano derecha.

8. Sí, hay lápices dentro de la caja.
9. Sí, encima de la mesa hay llaves.
10. Los libros están encima de la me
11. Sí, en la pared hay cuadros.
12. No, no hay un sombrero en cabeza del profesor.
13. Sí, hay dos perros debajo de mesa.
14. No, no están de pié.
15. Hay cuatro libros encima de mesa.

ANSWERS TO LESSON 11

1. Yo escribo la letra A en el papel.
2. Ud. escribe la palabra "libertad".
3. El Sr. Campana escribe en la pizarra.
4. Yo leo la frase "yo soy norteamericano".
5. En esta frase hay tres palabras.
6. Sí, yo leo este libro. (No, yo no leo este libro.)
7. Sí, el Sr. Berlitz lee en español.
8. No, el Sr. Padilla no habla inglés.

9. Yo hablo inglés.
10. No, el Sr. Cugat no habla franc
11. La palabra "book" es inglesa.
12. Sí, Ud. dice el alfabeto.
13. No, Ud. no dice el alfabeto ruso.
14. En Nueva York se habla inglé
15. Sí, en Buenos Aires se habla español.
16. No, en París no se habla españ se habla francés.
17. En Madrid se habla español.

ANSWERS TO LESSON 12

1. El profesor escribe en la pizarra.
2. No, Doña Felicidad no escribe.
3. Lee "La Prensa".
4. Chiquita lee el libro cómico. (Superhombre.)
5. El profesor escribe la palabra "atención" en la pizarra.
6. El profesor escribe con tiza.
7. No, el profesor no escribe el alfabeto.
8. Sí, Doña Felicidad lee un periódico español.

9. Sí, el profesor habla español.
10. No, su perro no habla español.
11. Sí, yo leo español. (No, yo no español.)
12. Sí, yo hablo inglés.
13. Sí, el Sr. Berlitz habla francés
14. No, Chiquita no habla inglé.
15. Chiquita está sentada.
16. En el alfabeto castellano hay ve tiocho letras.
17. En el alfabeto inglés hay veinti letras.

ANSWERS TO LESSON 13

. Chiquita tiene un peso.
. No, no tiene tanto dinero como el profesor.
. El profesor tiene más dinero.
. Sí, el profesor tiene lápices detrás de su oreja.
. Sí, tiene más lápices que Chiquita.
. No, Chiquita tiene más libros que el profesor.
. Doña Felicidad tiene más libros.
. Chiquita tiene menos dinero.
. No, Chiquita no tiene mucho dinero.
. No, el profesor tiene un libro.

11. Sí, leemos muchas palabras españolas.
12. El profesor escribe más frases.
13. Sí, en este libro hay muchas páginas.
14. Sí, en el diccionario hay más páginas que en este libro.
15. Doña Felicidad tiene 100 pesos.
16. Doña Felicidad y Chiquita juntas tienen 101 pesos.
17. El profesor y Doña Felicidad juntos tienen 600 pesos.
18. Sí, Chiquita tiene sombrero.
19. Sí, Doña Felicidad tiene sombrero.
20. El profesor no tiene sombrero.

ANSWERS TO LESSON 14

. Sí, los alumnos van a la escuela Berlitz.
. Sí, llevan sus libros a la escuela.
. Sí, los profesores escriben en la pizarra.
. Victor y Ud. van al teatro. (Uds. van al teatro.)
. Ellas van a la iglesia.
. Ellos van al cabaret.
. Sí, los alumnos tienen libros de español.

8. Sí, abren sus libros antes de la clase.
9. Cierran sus libros después de la clase.
10. Nosotros leemos español.
11. Nosotros hablamos español.
12. Sí, los libros azules son míos. (No son míos.)
13. Sus libros son verdes.

ANSWERS TO LESSON 15

. Sí, el profesor tiene un cigarrillo en su mano derecha.
. En la mano izquierda de Doña Felicidad hay un libro.
. No, Chiquita no tiene nada en su mano izquierda.
. Ella no tiene nada en su mano derecha.
. Doña Felicidad está al lado del profesor.
. Sí, hay alguien a su derecha.

7. No, no hay nadie entre el profesor y Chiquita.
8. No, no hay libro en la mano izquierda de Doña Felicidad.
9. Nadie está sentado en la silla.
10. No, no hay nada encima de la mesa.
11. Debajo del brazo izquierdo del profesor no hay nada.
12. No, no hay nadie a la izquierda de Chiquita.
13. Doña Felicidad está a su derecha.

14. No hay nada encima de la silla.
15. No, Chiquita no está al lado del profesor.
16. Sí, hay alguien detrás de la mesa.

17. No, el profesor no tiene sombre en la cabeza.
18. El profesor no tiene nada en la cabeza.

ANSWERS TO LESSON 16

1. Elena sale de la clase.
2. Anita no se sienta, está sentada.
3. No, Alfredo no se sienta.
4. Alfredo se levanta.
5. Sí, Roberto entra en la clase.
6. No, Elena no entra; sale de la clase.
7. No, Roberto no sale; entra en la clase.
8. No, el profesor no sale de la clase; entra en la clase.
9. Sí, Roberto y Elena están de pié.
10. Alfredo se levanta.

11. No, el profesor no está sentado.
12. Sí, yo me levanto después de la clase.
13. Sí, yo me siento en la silla.
14. Ud. se sienta en la silla.
15. Sí, los alumnos salen después de lección.
16. Sí, nosotros nos sentamos en el cine.
17. Sí, nos sentamos en el autobús.
(No, no nos sentamos en el autobús.)

ANSWERS TO LESSON 17

1. Sí, el profesor le da un libro a Doña Felicidad.
2. Chiquita no le da nada al profesor.
3. Doña Felicidad le da una pelota a Capitán.
4. No, Chiquita y Doña Felicidad no le dan una corbata al profesor.
5. Nadie le habla a Chiquita.
6. El profesor le da un peso a Chiquita.
7. No, Doña Felicidad no le dice nada a Capitán.
8. Sí, le da algo.
9. Capitán no dice nada.
10. Sí, los alumnos de la clase de

español le hablan al profesor en español.
11. Sí, le dicen "buenos días" an de la clase.
12. Después de la clase el profesor dice "hasta mañana".
13. En la mano izquierda de Doña Felicidad hay una pelota.
14. Yo le digo que en la mano izquier de Doña Felicidad hay una pelo
15. Doña Felicidad le dice "gracias" profesor.
16. Yo le digo "gracias".
17. Mi nombre es......
18. Yo le digo mi nombre.

ANSWERS TO LESSON 18

1. El profesor huele la cebolla con la nariz.
2. No la cebolla no huele bien.
3. Sí, la rosa huele bien.

4. Doña Felicidad huele la rosa.
5. No, no vemos las cosas que est detrás de nosotros.

5. Sí, vemos las cosas que están delante de nosotros.
7. No, no oímos a nadie llamar a la puerta.
8. Sí, oímos hablar al presidente por la radio.
9. Sí, comemos pan.
0. Sí, yo como pan con mantequilla
1. Sí, los ingleses beben mucho té.
2. Yo bebo cerveza. (Yo bebo vino.)
3. Sí, los cubanos beben ron.

14. Sí, yo pongo azúcar en mi café.
15. Yo pongo leche en mi té. (Yo pongo limón en mi té.)
16. Cortamos la carne con un cuchillo.
17. No, no comemos los guisantes con un cuchillo.
18. Sí, hablamos con nuestros amigos por teléfono.
19. Yo escribo con una pluma. (Yo escribo con un lápiz.)

ANSWERS TO LESSON 19

1. Cortamos la carne con un cuchillo.
2. Sí, comemos la carne con un tenedor.
3. Tomamos la sopa con una cuchara.
4. No, no me gusta el café sin azúcar.
5. No nos gusta la sopa sin sal.
6. Comemos la carne en un plato.
7. Sí, nos gusta el olor de la rosa.
8. Sí, a las señoritas les gustan los trajes hermosos.

9. Sí, Dolores de Río es hermosa.
10. No, Boris Karloff no es hermoso.
11. Sí, el profesor habla bien el español.
12. Yo hablo bien el inglés.
13. Sí, yo bailo bien. (No bailo bien.)
14. Yo bailo bien la rumba. (Yo bailo mal la rumba.)

ANSWERS TO LESSON 20

1. Sí, Chiquita toca a Capitán.
2. No, Chiquita no puede tocar la mano derecha del profesor.
3. Sí, el profesor puede tocar el sombrero de Chiquita.
4. No, no lo toca.
5. Sí, la lámpara está baja.
6. Sí, el profesor puede tocarla.
7. El profesor no toca nada.
8. Sí, el profesor lleva anteojos.
9. No, no puede ver sin anteojos.
10. Sí, podemos salir del cuarto.

11. No, no puede escribir.
12. No, no podemos ver las cosas detrás de nosotros.
13. No, los alumnos no pueden tocar el techo.
14. Sí, podemos romper el fósforo.
15. No, no puedo romper la llave de la puerta.
16. Sí, podemos tocar nuestro libro.
17. Sí, los alumnos pueden romper la ventana con una pelota.

ANSWERS TO LESSON 21

1. Chiquita quiere tomar la manzana.
2. No, ella no puede comer la manzana.

3. No puede comerla porque está muy alta.

4. No, el profesor no quiere darle la manzana.
5. No, yo no puedo comprar una manzana si no tengo dinero.
6. Debemos tener dinero para comprar comida.
7. No, no podemos ir al teatro si no tenemos billetes.
8. No, no podemos salir de la clase sin abrir la puerta.
9. No, no podemos abrir la puerta de la casa si no tenemos llave.

10. Debemos tener tiza para escrib en la pizarra.
11. Para escribir en el papel debem tener un lápiz o una pluma.
12. No, los alumnos no pueden escribir si no tienen papel ni lápi
13. Sí, yo quiero hablar español.
14. Sí, yo quiero ir a México.
15. Sí, yo puedo hablar español bie (No, yo no puedo hablar españ bien.)

ANSWERS TO LESSON 22

1. Jorge se encuentra con Ana María.
2. Le invita a ir al restaurante "Buenos Aires".
3. Le invita a comer una comida española.
4. El restaurante se llama "Buenos Aires".
5. Sí, Ana María acepta la invitación.
6. Porque tiene deseos de comer una comida española.
7. En ese restaurante sirven comidas españolas.
8. No, el restaurante no es muy grande.
9. Además de la comida, ofrece musica.
10. La orquesta toca rumbas y tangos.
11. No, no se permite bailar.
12. No, los precios son muy baratos. (No, no es muy caro.)
13. Se sientan en una mesa del centro.
14. El mozo les recibe.
15. El mozo les da un menú.
16. En un menú se ven los nombres de las comidas.

17. Jorge le pregunta al mozo, "¿Q nos recomienda Ud. para hoy?"
18. Éste les recomienda arroz con pollo.
19. Los señores piden arroz con pol y filete con papas fritas.
20. Ana María dice que el arroz co pollo está perfecto.
21. El filete de Jorge está muy buen
22. Los señores piden piña fría y que con guayaba.
23. Después del postre los señores piden café puro.
24. Después de terminar la comida mozo les da la cuenta.
25. El valor de la cuenta es cinco pesos, cincuenta centavos.
26. Al mozo le dan 50 centavos d propina.
27. Después de comer van al teatro.
28. El mozo les dice "gracias" al recib la propina.
29. El mozo se despide de los señor diciendo: ¡Hasta la vista!
30. Yo me despido de un amigo diciendo: ¡Hasta luego!

ANSWERS TO LESSON 23

1. Sí, señor, en este cuarto hay un reloj.

2. Está en la pared.
3. Sí, yo tengo un reloj.

1. Está en mi bolsillo.
2. La mesa es de madera.
3. Sí, mi reloj señala los segundos.
7. Son las doce.
8. Mi lección empieza a las once.
9. Mi lección acaba a las doce.
10. Una hora tiene sesenta minutos.
. Un día se compone de 24 horas.
. Un minuto tiene sesenta segundos.
8. No, mi reloj no está parado.
. No, mi reloj no anda si no le doy cuerda.
. Sí, está adelantado.
. Mi reloj está diez minutos adelantado.
. El reloj del profesor está atrasado.
. El reloj del profesor está veinte minutos atrasado.
. Sí, un reloj de pared es más grande que un reloj de bolsillo.
. Sí, la mesa es más grande que la silla.
. Sí, la pared es más larga que la pizarra.
. Sí, la ventana es tan ancha como la puerta.
. Sí, las señoras tienen el cabello más largo que los señores.

24. Sí, los sombreros de las señoras son más bonitos que los sombreros de los señores.
25. Sí, el agua es mejor para beber que el té.
26. Sí, la violeta huele mejor que el tulipán.
27. Sí, el gas huele peor que la tinta.
28. No, mi pronunciación francesa no es mejor que mi pronunciación española. (Sí, mi pronunciación francesa es mejor que mi pronunciación española.)
29. Sí, yo pronuncio bien el español. (No, yo no pronuncio bien el español.)
30. Sí, el profesor pronuncia mejor que yo.
31. No, yo no escribo tan bien como Ud. (Sí, yo escribo tan bien como Ud.)
32. Sí, yo tengo buena vista. (No, yo no tengo buena vista.)
33. Sí, yo veo bien. (No, yo no veo bien.)
34. No, el Sr. Berlitz no ve bien sin gafas (anteojos).
35. Sí, él ve mejor con gafas.

ANSWERS TO LESSON 24

. Un año tiene 365 días.
. El año que tiene 366 días se llama bisiesto.
. El año comienza el primero de enero.
. El año acaba el 31 de diciembre.
. El primer mes del año es enero, el segundo es febrero, el tercero es marzo, el cuarto abril, el quinto mayo, etc.
. El último mes del año se llama diciembre.

7. Los siete días de la semana son: lunes, martes, miércoles, jueves, viernes sábado y domingo.
8. El último día de la semana es domingo.
9. Estamos en miércoles.
10. No, ayer no fué domingo.
11. Yo estudio los lunes, miércoles y viernes.
12. Sí, el quince será sábado. (No, el quince no será sábado.)
13. El sábado será......

14. Mi cumpleaños será......
15. El lunes próximo será......
16. El jueves pasado fué......
17. No, mañana no será el último del mes. (Sí, mañana será el último del mes.)
18. Ahora estamos en invierno.
19. Una estación dura tres meses.

20. Los meses del verano son juni julio y agosto.
21. La primavera sigue al invierno.
22. No, no estamos en primavera.
23. El sábado precede al domingo.
24. Son las once.
25. Trabajamos el lunes, martes, mié coles, jueves, viernes y sábado.
26. No, yo no trabajo el domingo.

ANSWERS TO LESSON 25

1. Las 24 horas del día se dividen en dos partes: el día y la noche.
2. Hay claridad durante el día.
3. No, ahora no está obscuro.
4. La luz del día viene del sol.
5. El sol está en el cielo.
6. No, el sol no alumbra de noche.
7. Este cuarto se alumbra con la luz eléctrica.
8. Cuando está obscuro encendemos la luz para ver.
9. De noche se ven la luna y las estrellas en el cielo.
10. Los cuatro puntos cardinales son: norte, sur, este y oeste.
11. El sol sale por el este.
12. Se pone por el oeste.
13. A mediodía el sol está arriba en el cielo.
14. En marzo el sol sale a las 6 de la mañana.
15. No, el sol no se pone temprano en verano.
16. Se pone a las 9 de la noche.

17. En verano los días son largos.
18. No, ahora los noches no son m largas que los días. (Sí, ahora l noches son más largas que dos día
19. No, no puedo ver sin luz.
20. Enciendo la luz cuando está oscu
21. El gas se enciende con un fósfo
22. Generalmente me acuesto cuan tengo sueño.
23. Me acuesto en la cama.
24. Por la mañana me levanto, baño, me afeito, me peino, me vis y me desayuno.
25. Me desayuno a las 8 de la mañar
26. Yo trabajo hasta las 5.
27. Sí, me gusta trabajar. (No, no gusta trabajar.)
28. No, la luz de la luna no es t fuerte como la luz del sol.
29. La luna alumbra de noche.
30. No, las estrellas no se pueden contar.
31. Sí, de noche tengo sueño.

ANSWERS TO LESSON 26

1. El cielo está obscuro cuando hace mal tiempo.
2. El cielo está cubierto de nubes cuando llueve.
3. No, ahora no está lloviendo. (Sí, ahora está lloviendo.)

4. En invierno cae nieve del cielo.
5. No, el piso no está bueno cuan llueve.
6. Para preservarme de la lluvia lle un paraguas.

- Ahora hace buen tiempo. (Hace mal tiempo.)
- No, no salgo cuando está lloviendo. (Sí, salgo cuando está lloviendo.)
- Sí, hace mucho calor en este cuarto. (No, no hace mucho calor en este cuarto.)
- Sí, afuera hace frío. (No, afuera no hace frío.)
- Nieva en diciembre, enero y febrero.
- Sí, en febrero nieva mucho.
- No, en abril no nieva a menudo.
- No, en agosto no nieva nunca.
- Sí, tengo frío. (No, no tengo frío.)

16. En invierno la sala se calienta con la lumbre.
17. Nos preservamos del frío con un abrigo.
18. El calor viene del sol.
19. No, el sol no calienta tanto en invierno como en verano.
20. Sí, el piso está siempre malo cuando llueve.
21. Me siento junto a al fuego (al radiador) para calentarme.
22. No, no me agrada salir cuando hace mucho viento.
23. En marzo hace mucho viento.
24. Me pongo vestidos gruesos en diciembre, enero y febrero.

ANSWERS TO LESSON 27

- Los españoles llegaron a México en 1519.
- Hernán Cortés fué el conquistador de México.
- Simón Bolívar fué un general que libertó varios países de Sur América.
- Nació en Caracas.
- No, Alfredo no estudió su lección de historia.
- Porque se acostó tarde anoche.
- Manuel y Alfredo fueron a una fiesta después del cine.
- Sí, fueron a una fiesta.
- En la fiesta estuvieron Elena, Roberto, Vicente y muchos otros amigos de la escuela.
- El profesor preguntó a Alfredo en qué año llegaron los españoles a México.
- Carlos contestó bien a la pregunta del profesor.
- Yo me despierto a las 8 a la mañana.
- Ayer me desperté a las 7.
- Me levanté a las 8.
- Antes de desayunarme me lavé, me peiné y me vestí.

16. Me puse el traje gris.
17. No, no me lavé con agua fría. (Sí, me lavé con agua fría.)
18. Sí, me vestí muy de prisa. (No, no me vestí muy de prisa.)
19. Sí, me desayuné temprano. (No, no me desayuné temprano.)
20. Sí, tomé café con leche.
21. Sí, bebí leche. (No, no bebí leche.)
22. Sí, fuí a dar un paseo. (No, no fuí a dar un paseo.)
23. Sí, recibí algunas cartas. (No, no recibí ninguna.)
24. Sí, las contesté. (No, no las contesté.)
25. Sí, ayer dí un paseo. (No, ayer no dí un paseo.)
26. Fuí al cine.
27. Almorcé a las doce.
28. Sí, tuve buen apetito. (No, no tuve buen apetito.)
29. Sí, tuve mucho que hacer ayer. (No, no tuve mucho que hacer ayer.)
30. Sí, estuve muy ocupado.
31. Sí, yo oí muchos conciertos el invierno pasado.
32. Yo nací en......

33. No, Ud. no estuvo en mi casa el domingo.
34. No, anoche no comimos juntos.
35. No, anoche no fuimos al teatro. (Sí, anoche fuimos al teatro)

36. No, no estuve en la ciudad el invierno pasado. (Sí, estuve en ciudad el invierno pasado.)
37. Sí, reí mucho en el cine ayer.

ANSWERS TO LESSON 28

1. No, las plantas no pueden moverse.
2. Para vivir los animales deben respirar, comer y beber.
3. No, no podemos vivir si no comemos.
4. Sí, las plantas tienen necesidad de agua.
5. Para vivir tenemos necesidad de comer, beber y respirar.
6. Los cinco sentidos son: el tacto, el gusto, el oído, el olfato y la vista.
7. Los ojos son los órganos de la vista, la nariz es el del olfato, los oídos son los del oído, la lengua es el del gusto, y el sentido del tacto se extiende por todo el cuerpo.
8. Los animales se dividen en cuadrúpedos, aves, peces, reptiles e insectos.
9. Los principales animales domésticos son el perro, el gato, el carnero, el burro, la vaca, el buey y el caballo.

10. Las aves pueden volar y tienen d patas; los cuadrúpedos tienen cuatro patas.
11. El águila es el ave más grande.
12. No, no es útil.
13. El pavo real es el ave que tiene plumaje más hermoso.
14. El estómago y los pulmones son l órganos de la digestión y de la r piración.
15. Sí, yo estoy bien de salud. (No, no estoy bien de salud.)
16. Un pez es un animal que viven el agua.
17. La serpiente se arrastra por tierr
18. No; la rana salta.
19. La abeja produce miel y el gusal de seda da seda.
20. Sí, el mosquito es nocivo.

ANSWERS TO LESSON 29

1. El profesor está contento.
2. Está contento porque tiene mucho dinero.
3. Ella llora porque su muñeca está rota.
4. No, ella no se ríe.
5. Porque nadie la quiere.
6. No, el hombre no es superior a los animales en todo.
7. No, yo no pienso en mi lección cuando no estoy en clase. (Sí, pienso en mi lección cuando no estoy en clase.)

8. No, no se puede hablar correct mente sin pensar.
9. Para saber una cosa es necesar aprenderla.
10. En este momento yo aprendo español.
11. Los niños aprenden a leer y escribir en la escuela.
12. Sí, yo sé nadar. (No, yo no sé nadar.)
13. No, no se puede leer sin aprend
14. No, yo no puedo leer sin ver.

No, yo no sé cuanto dinero tiene Ud. en su bolsillo. (Sí, yo sé cuanto dinero tiene Ud. en su bolsillo.)

No, no sabemos cuantas estrellas hay en el cielo.

Sí, yo olvido fácilmente. (No, yo no olvido fácilmente.)

Sí, yo quiero a mi madre.

Sí, yo amo a mi país.

20. Sí, yo admiro la música española.

21. Sí, me alegro de saber que toda mi familia está en buena salud.

22. Sí, si un amigo mío está enfermo, lo siento.

23. Sí, al ver un ratón las señoritas tienen miedo.

24. Un señor español tiene dos apellidos.

ANSWERS TO LESSON 30

El profesor se ha acostado en la hamaca.

Sí, se ha quitado el saco.

Sí, ha leído el periódico.

Sí, ha bebido el vaso de limonada.

Sí, yo he leído el periódico hoy.

El Sr. Rodríguez ha estado en la Habana.

Sí, el Sr. Aja vió al Sr. Rodríguez hace un mes.

Sí, el Sr. Rodríguez ha escrito tarjetas postales.

No, no han llegado.

El mar ha estado malo todo el tiempo.

No, al Sr. Rodríguez no le ha gustado el viaje.

No, el Sr. Rodríguez no se ha divertido mucho en la Habana.

13. Porque no ha tenido tiempo.

14. Sí, yo he estado en la Habana (No, yo no he estado en la Habana.)

15. Yo he estado en......

16. No, el Sr. Rodríguez no ha vendido sus casas en la Habana.

17. Porque no le han ofrecido suficiente dinero.

18. Rodríguez ha traído unos cigarros y un frasco de perfume para Salgado.

19. El frasco de perfume se ha roto.

20. Sí, yo he viajado a España. (No, yo no he viajado a España.)

21. Yo he viajado por......

22. Sí, yo he leído muchos libros en español. (No, yo no he leído muchos libros en español.

ANSWERS TO LESSON 31

Chiquita está pensando: ¿Seré yo un día estrella de Hollywood?, ¿Con quién me casaré?, ¿Me llevarán al teatro esta noche?

Doña Felicidad está pensando: ¿A qué hora iré a la iglesia mañana?, ¿Llegará el profesor a tiempo para la comida esta noche?

El profesor irá a casa de Doña Felicidad.

El Sr. Arango invita al Sr. Sarmiento a ir al teatro.

5. Sí, el Sr. Sarmiento acepta.

6. Almorzarán en casa del Sr. Arango

7. El Sr. Sarmiento irá después a casa del pintor.

8. Si van al teatro sacarán los billetes con anticipación.

9. Durante los entreactos saldrán a tomar aire.

10. El Sr. Santos vendrá a visitar al Sr. Sarmiento.

11. No, el Sr. Sarmiento no podrá ir al teatro.

12. Ellos irán al teatro en otra ocasión.
13. No, la familia de Santos no se quedará en la ciudad todo el verano.
14. Yo iré a...... este verano.

15. Sí, este año muchos norteame canos visitarán México.
16. Sí, vendrán muchos suramerican a Nueva York.

ANSWERS TO LESSON 32

1. Los Sres. Fernández y Nelson están en la Habana.
2. El Sr. Nelson es de Nueva York.
3. Está en la Habana desde hace una semana.
4. El Sr. Nelson está en la Habana de visita y también por negocios.
5. No, el Sr. Fernández no es cubano.
6. El Sr. Fernández es de México.
7. Al salir de la Habana el Sr. Nelson irá a México.
8. No, el Sr. Fernández no se quedará en la Habana.
9. El Sr. Fernández invita al Sr. Nelson a ir con él a México.
10. No, el Sr. Nelson no ha estado nunca en México.
11. Sí, el Sr. Nelson acepta la invitación del Sr. Fernández.
12. Sí, el Sr. Fernández podrá servirle de guía.
13. No, yo no necesito guía en Nueva York. (Si, yo necesito guía en Nueva York.)
14. Para sacar sus pasajes, los Sres. van a una oficina de aviación.
15. No, no es fácil conseguir pasaje en avión para el mismo día.

16. Yo digo al empleado: ¿Puede darme un pasaje para México?
17. Yo pido un billete de ferrocar diciendo al empleado: "Deme billete para......"
18. El primer avión para México sa a las nueve.
19. Porque va directamente a la ciud de México.
20. El otro para en Veracruz.
21. Sí, es más agradable viajar en tren expreso.
22. El Sr. Fernández no quiere un llete de ida y vuelta porque tie su casa en México.
23. Para enviar el automóvil por ell
24. Sí, yo vivo en una ciudad.
25. Mi dirección es ......
26. El automóvil irá por los señores las seis de la mañana.
27. Sí, me gusta dormir la mañar (No, no me gusta.)
28. Porque hay media hora entre Habana y el aeropuerto y hay q pesar el equipaje.
29. Sí, si me levanto temprano ten sueño.

ANSWERS TO LESSON 33

1. Sí, el Sr. Nelson está durmiendo al sonar el teléfono.
2. La telefonista le llama.
3. No, no le gusta levantarse tan temprano.
4. Un muchacho llevará el equipaje al auto.

5. Se levanta, se viste y baja a pag su cuenta.
6. En la oficina del hotel el Sr. N son habla con el cajero.
7. Dejó la llave en la habitación.

8. No le permite al muchacho llevar el maletín porque tiene todos sus documentos.
9. El Sr. Fernández le espera en el automóvil.
10. No, el Sr. Nelson no se despertó temprano.
11. No, en Nueva York no se duerme la siesta.
12. Es costumbre dormir la siesta en Sur América.
13. Sí, los pasajeros tienen que decir su peso.

14. El límite de peso de equipaje que pueden llevar sin pagar es 25 kilos.
15. El Sr. Nelson tiene hambre porque no se ha desayunado.
16. No, no comió nada antes de venir al aeropuerto.
17. No pueden comer en el aeropuerto porque no tienen tiempo.
18. Al saber que no tiene tiempo para comer, Nelson dice: ¡Qué desgracia!
19. Sí, se sirven comidas a bordo de los aviones.
20. Yo hice un viaje por avión en ....

ANSWERS TO LESSON 34

1. Desde un avión veo fincas, pueblos y montañas.
2. Los señores ven el Popocatépetl desde el avión.
3. El inspector de inmigración desea ver sus pasaportes o tarjetas de turista.
4. El inspector de aduana les dice: "Abran sus maletas. ¿Tienen licores, perfumes o tabaco para declarar?"
5. Sí, el inspector de aduana es cortés.
6. No, los inspectores de aduana no son siempre corteses.
7. Sí, generalmente necesitamos pasaporte para viajar de un país a otro.
8. El Sr. Nelson se quedará dos semanas en México.
9. Porque quiere cambiar los dólares a pesos.
10. El Sr. Nelson se hospedará en el Hotel Reforma.
11. El Sr. Fernández recomienda el

Hotel Reforma a su amigo porque tiene todas las comodidades modernas y está céntrico.
12. No, el Sr. Fernández no irá al hotel.
13. Porque tiene su casa en México.
14. El Sr. Fernández vive en México.
15. El Sr. Fernández será el guía del Sr. Nelson en México.
16. Con el dependiente del hotel.
17. Sí, puede conseguir un cuarto.
18. 20 pesos por día.
19. Sí, algunas veces es difícil conseguir un cuarto en un hotel.
20. El Sr. Nelson dejó su equipaje en el taxi.
21. Un muchacho va a buscarlo.
22. Cuando yo viajo por ferrocarril no llevo yo mismo mi equipaje.
23. Lo lleva un portero.
24. Yo le doy una propina al portero.
25. Sí, es fácil olvidar cosas cuando uno está viajando.

ANSWERS TO LESSON 35

1. Los Sres. empiezan su paseo por la avenida.
2. Sí, en las calles hay mucho tráfico.

3. El parque que ven se llama "La Alameda."

4. En las calles de una ciudad grande vemos mucho tráfico.
5. La tienda que vende sombreros se llama sombrerería.
6. El sombrero del Sr. Nelson es usado.
7. No, su sombrero es usado.
8. El Sr. Nelson dice al empleado de la sombrerería: "Quiero un sombrero parecido a aquel gris que está en el escaparate."
9. No, no le gusta el primer sombrero que ve.
10. Prefiere el segundo sombrero porque es más barato.
11. Sí, lo compra.
12. Cuando salen de la tienda van a la calle Francisco I. Madero.
13. El Sr. Nelson quiere comprar estampillas para enviar tarjetas postales.

14. Sí, cuando yo estoy viajando mar do tarjetas postales a mis amigo
15. El gran edificio blanco que ve los señores se llama Palacio c Bellas Artes.
16. Sí, el Sr. Fernández invita al S Nelson a ir al teatro.
17. El Sr. Nelson no quiere aceptar invitación porque cree que el S Fernández quiere estar con s familia.
18. Le invita a cenar en su casa.
19. Deciden dar una vuelta en taxi.
20. El chofer quiere cobrar doce pes por hora.
21. Sí, el Sr. Fernández cree que eso demasiado.
22. Sí, los choferes cobran mucho los turistas.
23. El Sr. Fernández pagará diez pesc
24. Sí, el Sr. Fernández conoce bien ciudad.

ANSWERS TO LESSON 36

1. Los Sres. están en el Zócalo.
2. Antes de los españoles los indios vivían en México.
3. Estos indios se llamaban aztecas.
4. Sí, tenían una ciudad grande.
5. Sí, la ciudad de México estaba en un lago.
6. En lugar de calles había canales.
7. Hace muchos años el Emperador Maximiliano vivía en el castillo de Chapultepec.
8. El año pasado yo vivía en ......
9. Hace 10 años yo vivía en ......
10. Sí, yo tomaba lecciones durante el invierno pasado.
11. No, yo no iba a la playa el invierno pasado.
12. Sí, el año pasado yo tenía automóvil. (No, el año pasado yo no tenía automóvil.)

13. Porque quieren sacar unas fotos.
14. El Sr. Nelson quiere sacar fotos.
15. El próximo día los Sres. irán Xochimilco y al Desierto de 1 Leones.
16. La villa de Guadalupe está cer de ciudad de México.
17. No, Los Ángeles no está lejos México.
18. Sí, Cuba está cerca de los Estad Unidos.
19. El Sr. Nelson irá a casa del S Fernández por la noche.
20. Sí, está invitado a una comida.
21. Cuando un amigo me invita a un comida yo le digo: "Gracias, c mucho gusto."
22. Sí, el Sr. Nelson se divierte en viaje.

ANSWERS TO LESSON 37

. La Sra. Fernández le dice al invitado: "Aquí está en su casa."

. La esposa de Fernández se llama Cristina.

. Doña Cristina tiene tres niños.

. Isabel tiene dos hermanos.

. Jorge tiene dos hermanas.

. Sí, Jorge es un niño malo.

. Porque empujó a María y ella se cayó.

. El Sr. Nelson tiene dos hijas.

. Una es casada.

. Sí, tiene un niño.

. Yo tengo ......

12. La hija mayor del Sr. Nelson se casó con un oficial del ejército.

13. Sí, el Sr. Nelson es abuelo.

14. Sí, el Sr. Nelson parece joven.

15. Tiene un nieto.

16. La foto que muestra a los Fernández es de su hija más joven.

17. Sí, es muy bonita.

18. Sí, está comprometida.

19. Su novio es un abogado.

20. Después de la comida los Fernández y el Sr. Nelson irán a pasear.

ANSWERS TO LESSON 38

. Fernández y Nelson están en la corrida de toros.

. Sí, el Sr. Nelson ha estado en varias corridas.

. Sí, si la Sra. de Nelson estuviera en México, le gustaría mucho ir a la corrida.

. El matador que ven es Cagancho.

. Armillita sería mejor.

. El matador pone las banderillas en el cuello del toro.

. Cuando el torero trabaja bien la gente le tira sombreros y flores.

8. Si no trabajase bien le tirarían botellas.

9. No, la Sra. de Fernández no acompañó a su marido.

10. Porque no le gustan las corridas.

11. Si yo estuviera en México iría a las corridas de toros.

12. Sí, si yo tuviera mucho dinero haría un viaje a Sur América.

13. Me gustaría más visitar ......

14. Sí, yo creo que el Sr. Nelson se divierte mucho en México.

15. Sí, si yo estuviese en este momento en Cuba podría hablar español.

GLOSSARY

A

a to
abierto, a open
abogado lawyer
a bordo on board
abrigo coat
abril April
abrir to open
abuelo grandfather
abuela grandmother
acabar de to have just
accnto accent
aceptar accept
acercar to bring closer
acercarse to come closer
acompañar to accompany
acostarse to lie down
además besides
adiós goodbye
admiración admiration
admirar to admire
adónde where to
aeroplano airplane
afeitarse to shave
aficionado, a "fan"
afuera outside
agosto August
agradable agreeable
agrio, a sour
agua water
ahora now
aire air
alameda alameda
alemán, a German
alfabeto alphabet
algo something, anything

alguien somebody, anybody
algún, alguno, a some, any
alimento food
almorzar to lunch
alrededor around
alrededores outskirts
alto, a high, tall
alumno, a pupil
allí there
amable kind, amiable
amargo, a bitter
amarillo, a yellow
a menudo often
americano, a American
amigo, a friend
andar to walk
animal animal
anoche last night
anteojos glasses
anterior former
antes before
anticipación anticipation
anunciador, a announcer
año year
apetito appetite
a pié on foot
aprender to learn
a propósito on purpose
aquel, -la that
aquí here
araña spider
Argentina Argentina
argentino, a Argentine
arreglar to fix
arriba up, above

arroz rice
arte art
asno donkey
atizar to poke
atrasar to set back
aunque though, in spite of
autobús bus
automóvil automobile
avanzar to advance
ave bird
avenida avenue
aviación aviation
ayer yesterday
azteca Aztec
azúcar sugar
azul blue

B

bailar to dance
bajo, a low
banco bank
banderilla banderilla
bañarse to bathe
baño bath
barato, a cheap
barco ship
barrio district
bastante enough
batalla battle
beber to drink
bello, a beautiful
bellas artes fine arts
bien well
billete bill
bisiesto leap (year)
bistec beefsteak
blanco, a white
blando, a soft
blandura softness
boca mouth
bolsillo pocket
bombilla electric bulb
bondad goodness, kindness
bonito, a pretty
(a) bordo on board, aboard
bosque woods
botella bottle
Brasil Brazil
brasilero, a Brazilian
brazo arm

broma joke
bueno, a good, kind
Buenos Aires Buenos Aires
buenos días good day, good morning
buenas noches good night, good evening
buenas tardes good afternoon, good evening
buey ox
buho owl
buscar to search, to look for

C

caballero gentleman
caballo horse
cabello hair
cabeza head
cada each, every
caer to fall
caerse to fall
café coffee
caja box, case, cash box
cajero cashier
calendario calendar
calentar to warm
calentarse to get warm
caliente warm, hot
calor warmth, heat
calle street
cama bed
cámara camera
camarero waiter, steward
cambiar to change
cambio change
camello camel
caminar to walk
camisa shirt
campo country, rural area
canal channel, canal
canoa canoe
capa cape, cloak
capital capital
¡caramba! good gracious! my goodness! etc.
carbón coal
cardinal cardinal
carne meat, flesh
carnero sheep
caro, a expensive, dear

carta letter
cartera pocket book
casa house, home
casado, a married
casarse to marry, to get married
casi almost, nearly
castellano the Spanish language
castillo castle
catarro a cold
catedral cathedral
catorce fourteen
cebolla onion
cena supper, dinner
cenar to have supper
céntrico, a centrally located
centro center
Centroamérica Central America
cepillar to brush
cepillarse to brush oneself
cerca near
cerrado, a closed, shut
cerrar to close
cerveza beer
cielo sky, heaven
cielo raso ceiling
cien hundred
ciento hundred
cigarillo cigarette
cima top
cinco five
cincuenta fifty
cine cinema, movies
circular to circulate
ciudad city
civilización civilization
civilizado, a civilized
claridad light
claro, a clear, bright
clase class, kind
clasificar to classify
clasificarse to be classified
clavel carnation
cobrar to collect, to charge
coger to catch, to take
col cabbage
coliflor cauliflower
color color
coma comma
comedor dining-room
comenzar to begin
comercio trade, commerce
cómico comic, funny

comida food, meal, dinner
como how, as
comodidad comfort, convenience
compañía company, society
componerse to be composed
comprar to buy
comprobante proof, ticket, check
comprometerse to compromise, to
  become engaged
comprometido, a engaged
con with
concierto concert
conquistador conqueror
conmigo with me, with myself
conocer to know
conseguir to get, to attain
consigo with himself (herself, yourself, yourselves, themselves)
consonante consonant
contar to count, to tell
contestación answer, reply
contestar to answer
continuar to continue, to carry on,
  to last
contrario, a contrary
conversación conversation, tall.
copo flake
corazón heart
corbata tie
cordero lamb
corneta bugle
correcto, a correct
corredor corridor
corrida run, race, bullfight
cortaplumas penknife
cortar to cut
cortés polite
corto, a short
cosa thing
costumbre custom
creer to believe, to think
criado, a bred
criar to breed
cristal crystal, glass
cuadro picture, square
cuadrúpedo quadruped
¿cuál? which?
cuando when
¿cuándo? when?
¿cuánto? how much?
¿cuánto tiempo? how long?
cuarenta forty

cuarto, a fourth
cuarto room
cuatro four
cuatrocientos four hundred
Cuba Cuba
cubano, a Cuban
cubierto, a covered
cuchillo knife
cuello neck, collar
cuenta check, account, bill
cuerda cord, rope, string
cuerpo body
cuesta it costs
cumpleaños birthday
curso course, direction

CH

charco puddle
chileno, a Chilean
Chile Chile
chocolate chocolate
chofer chauffeur
chuleta chop, cutlet

D

dar to give
dar una vuelta to take a walk
de of, from
debajo de under, beneath
deber must, have to, to owe
decidir to decide
decir to say, to tell
dedo finger, toe
dejar to leave, to let, to allow
del of the
delante de before, ahead, in front of
de manera que so as, so that, in such manner as
demasiado too, too much
dentro de inside of
dependiente clerk
de prisa fast
derecho, a right
desagradable unpleasant
desayunarse to breakfast
descansar to rest, to relax
desde since, from

desear to wish
deseo wish
desgracia misfortune, grief
desierto desert
despedirse to say good bye
despertador alarm clock
despertar to awaken
despertarse to wake up
después after, later
detrás behind, after
día day
diccionario dictionary
diciembre December
diez ten
diez y nueve nineteen
diez y ocho eighteen
diez y seis sixteen
diez y siete seventeen
diferencia difference
diferente different
difícil difficult
digerir to digest
dimensión dimension
dinero money
dirección direction
directamente directly
disco disk, record
divertido, a funny, humorous
divertir to amuse
divertirse to enjoy oneself
doce twelve
dólar dollar
dolor pain, ache
doméstico, a domestic
domingo Sunday
¿dónde? where?
dormir to sleep
dos two
doscientos two hundred
dulce sweet
durante during
durar to last, to wear
dureza hardness

E

echar to throw
edificio building
ejercicio exercise
ejército army
el the

él he
eléctrico, a electric
ella she
ellas they
ello it
ellos they
(sin) embargo however
emperador emperor
empezar to begin
empleado, a employee
empujar to push
en in, at, on, upon
encantado, a delighted
encargado, a person in charge
encender to light, to burn
encima de on, upon
encontrar to find
encontrarse con to meet with
enero January
enfermo, a ill
en lugar de instead of
enojado, a angry, cross
enojarse to become angry, to get cross
ensalada salad
enseguida immediately
ensuciar to soil
ensuciarse to get dirty
entrar to enter
entre between, among, within
entonces then
entreacto intermission
enviar to send
equipaje baggage, luggage
es it is
escaparate shop window
escribir to write
escuela school
espalda shoulder
España Spain
español, a Spanish, Spaniard
espárrago asparagus
especialidad specialty
esperar to wait (for), to hope
esposa wife
esposo husband
está he is, she is, it is (position)
estación season
estamos we are
estampilla stamp
estatua statue
este, a this

este east
esto this
estocada stab
estómago stomach
estrecho, a narrow
estrella star
estudiar to study
exacto, a exact, accurate, precise
excelente excellent
expreso, a expressed
expreso express
exquisito, a delicious
extra extra

F

falda skirt
falta lack, fault
faltar to fail, to lack
familia family
favor favor, help
(por) favor please
febrero February
fecha date (of month, year)
felicitar to congratulate
fenomenal phenomenal
feo, a ugly
ferrocarril railway
fiera wild beast
fiesta feast
filete steak
final final, end
finca real estate
flor flower
fonógrafo phonograph
forma form, shape
fósforo match
foto snapshot
francés French
Francia France
frasco flask, bottle
frase phrase
frecuentar to frequent, to repeat
frente forehead
(en) frente in front
fresa strawberry
fresco, a cool, fresh
frijol bean
frío, a cold
frito, a fried
fruta fruit

fuego fire
fuera out
función function, performance
funcionar to function, to perform

G

gafas eye-glasses
gallina hen
gana desire
ganar to gain, to win, to earn
gas gas
gastar to spend
gasto expense
gato cat
generalmente generally
gente people
gota drop
gracias thank you
gracioso, a graceful, funny
gran large, big, great
grande large, big, great
gris gray
grueso, a thick
guante glove
guapo, a brave, handsome
guayaba guava
guía guide
guión dash
guisante pea
gustar to taste, to please
gusto taste

H

Habana Havana
haber to have (auxiliary)
habichuela string bean
hablar to speak, to talk
hace fresco it is cool
hace mucho tiempo a long time
　ago
hacer to do, to make
hacer calor to be warm, hot
hace un mes a month ago
hacia toward, about
hambre hunger
hamaca hammock
hasta till, until, up to
hasta la vista good bye, so long

hay there is, there are
he aquí here is
hermana sister
hermano brother
hermoso, a beautiful
hielo ice
hiena hyena
hija daughter
hijo son
historia history, tale
histórico, a historical
hoja leaf, sheet (of paper)
¡hola! hello
hombre man
hombro shoulder
hora hour, time
hospedarse to stay (at a hotel)
hoy today

I

ida departure
iglesia church
(no) importa it does not matter,
　never mind
importar to import
impuesto tax, duty
incluído, a included, enclosed
incluir to include, to enclose
indicar to indicate, to point out
indio, a Indian
Inglaterra England
inglés, a English
inmigración immigration
innumerable innumerable
insecto insect
inspector inspector
interesante interesting
interrogación interrogation
invierno winter
invitación invitation
invitado, a guest
invitar to invite
Italia Italy
italiano, a Italian
izquierdo, a left

J

joven young, young man, young
woman

joya jewel
judía verde string bean
jueves Thursday
julio July
junio June
junto near, close, at the same time

K

kilo kilogram (2.2 lbs.)
kilómetro kilometer (⅝ of a mile)

L

la the, her, it
lado side
lago lake
lámpara lamp
lápiz pencil
largo, a long
lástima pity
latino, a Latin (adj.)
lavar to wash
lavarse to wash oneself
le to him, to her, to it
lección lesson
leche milk
lechuga lettuce
leer to read
lejos far
lengua tongue, language
león lion
les them, to them
letra letter
levantar to lift, to raise
levantarse to stand up, to get up, to rise
libertad freedom, liberty
libertar to free
libro book
licor liquor
ligeramente lightly, slightly, quickly
limón lemon
lindo pretty, fine
lista list, catalogue
listo ready, quick, clever
lo the, it (neuter)
lobo wolf
localidad place, locality, location
loma little hill

luego later, then next
lugar place, spot
(en) lugar de instead of
luna moon
lunes Monday

LL

llama flame
llamar to call
llamarse to be called, to be named
llave key
llegada arrival
llegar to arrive, to come
llorar to weep, to cry
llover to rain
lluvia rain

M

madera wood
Madrid Madrid
magnífico magnificent
mal evil, harm
mal bad
maletín valise, bag
malo, a bad, evil
mandar to send, to order
manecilla hand (of a clock)
manera manner, way, mode
mango handle, a fruit
mano hand
mantequilla butter
manzana apple, block
mañana morning, tomorrow
mármol marble
martes Tuesday
marzo March
mas but
más more
matador matador, killer
matar to kill
mayo May
mayor greater, greatest, larger, largest, older
media stocking
medianoche midnight
médico physician
medio, a half
medio middle
mediodía noon

mejor better
melocotón peach
menos less, least
menú menu
(a) menudo often
mes month
mesa table
metal metal
meter to put in
mexicano, a Mexican
México Mexico
mi my
mí me
miedo fear
miércoles Wednesday
mil thousand
milla mile
minuto minute
mío mine
mirar to look
mismo, a same, similar
moderno modern
mojado, a wet
mojar to wet
mojarse to get wet
molestar to disturb, to bother
molestia annoyance, trouble
momento moment
mono monkey
montaña mountain
morir to die
mosquito mosquito
mostrar to show, to point out
mover to move (something)
moverse to move
mozo waiter
mucho much
muchos (as) many
¡mucho gusto! much pleasure!
mucho tiempo much time, long time
muelle dock
mujer woman, wife
muñeca doll
museo museum
música music

N

nacer to be born
nada nothing
nadie nobody, no one

nariz nose
necesario, a necessary
necesitar to need, to lack
negocio business
negro, a black
nevar to snow
ni ... ni neither ... nor
nieve snow
ninguno, a none, not any
niña girl, child
niño boy, child
no no, not
noche night
nombre name
norte north
norteamericano, a North American
nos to us, us
nosotros we, us
novecientos nine hundred
novia fiancée, bride
noviembre November
novio bridegroom, fiancé
nube cloud
nuestro, a our, ours
nueve nine
número number, figure
nunca never

O

o ... o either ... or
objeto object, thing
observar to observe, to notice
ocasión occasion
octavo, a eighth
octubre October
ocupado, a busy, occupied
ochenta eighty
ocho eight
ochocientos eight hundred
oeste west
oficial officer, official
oficina office, workshop
oído sense of hearing
oído heard
oir to hear
ojo eye
oler to smell
olor odor, smell
olfato sense of smell
olvidar to forget

THE BERLITZ SELF-TEACHER: SPANISH 279

once eleven
oreja ear
órgano organ
oro gold
orquesta orchestra
oso bear
otro, a other, another

P

pagar to pay
página page
país country, nation
palabra word
palacio palace
pan bread
pantalón trousers
pañuelo handkerchief
papa potato
papas fritas fried potatoes
papel paper
par equal, pair
para for, to, in order to
parado, a standing up
parar to stop
paraguas umbrella
pardo, a brown
parecer to appear, to seem
parecerse to be like, to resemble
parecido, a similar, resembling
pared wall
París Paris
parque park
parte part
pasado, a past
pasaje passage, ticket
pasajero passenger, traveller
pasar to pass, to go by, to move
pasear to take a walk, a ride
paseo walk, promenade, stroll
pasillo corridor, passage
paso step, pace
pata leg (of an animal)
pato duck
pavo turkey
pavo real peacock
peces fish (plural)
pecho chest
pedir to ask for, to request
peinar to comb
peinarse to comb one's hair

pelota ball
película film
pelo hair
péndola pendulum
pensamiento thought
peor worse, worst
pequeño, a little, small
pera pear
percibir to perceive
percha peg
perder to lose
perdonar to forgive
perdone pardon me
perfecto, a perfect
perfume perfume, odor
periódico newspaper
permanecer to stay, to remain
permitir to permit, to allow
pero but
perro dog
persona person
pesar to weigh
pescado fish (when caught)
peso weight
pez fish (when alive)
piano piano
pico beak
pié foot
pierna leg
pintor painter
piña pineapple
piso floor, ground
pizarra blackboard
plata silver, money
plátano banana
plato dish, plate
playa shore, beach
plaza square, plaza
pluma pen, feather
poco, a little, small
poder can, may, to be able
pollo chicken
poner to put
poner en hora to set on time
ponerse to put on
por by, for, through
porque because
¿por qué? why?
portero, a janitor
posible possible
posición position, status
postal postal

postre dessert
preceder to precede
precio price
precioso, a precious, beautiful
precisar to fix, to set
preferir to prefer
pregunta question
preocuparse to worry
preparar to prepare
prepararse to get ready
presentar to present, to introduce
preservar to preserve, to keep
preservarse to keep oneself from
primavera spring
primero, a first, former
principio beginning, start, prin-
ciple
producir to produce
profesión profession
profesor professor
programa program
pronto soon, quick, fast
pronunciación pronunciation
pronunciar to pronounce
propina tip
propósito purpose, intention
(a) propósito by the way
próximo next, nearest
pueblo town, people
puerco pig
puerta door
puerto port, harbor
pues well..., since..., then...,
because...
pulmón lung
punto point, period
punto final period
puro, a pure, clear

Q

que that, which
¿qué? what?
quedar to remain, to stay
quedarse to remain
quemar to burn
quemarse to burn oneself
¿qué pasa? what is the matter?
what happens?
¿qué tal? how do you do? Hello!
querer to want, to wish

querer a to love
queso cheese
¿quién? who? whom?
quien who, whom
quince fifteen
quinientos, as five hundred
quinto, a fifth
quitar to take away
quitarse to take off

R

radiador radiator
radio radio
raso, a flat, plain
rata rat
rato short time, a while
ratón mouse
reanudar to renew
recibir to receive
recomendar to recommend
regla ruler, rule
reir to laugh
reirse to laugh
reloj watch, clock
repaso review, revision
reptil reptile
reservación reservation
reservar to reserve, to retain
respirar to breathe
responder to answer, to reply
respuesta answer, reply
restaurante restaurant
retrato picture, portrait
trait
revisar to review, to check
revistà magazine, review
rojo, a red
romper to break, to tear
ron rum
rosa rose
roto, a broken, torn
rumba rumba

S

sábado Saturday
saber to know
sabor taste, flavor
sacar to extract, to draw out

sacar fotos to take pictures
saco jacket, sack
sal salt
sala living room
salir to go out
saltar to jump
salud health
salvaje savage, wild
sangre blood
se oneself, himself, etc., one another, each other, to him, etc.
seco, a dry
sed thirst
(en) seguida immediately
seguir to follow, to continue
segundo, a second
seis six
seiscientos, as six hundred
semana week
sentado, a seated, sitting down
sentarse to sit down
sentido sense
sentir to feel
señalar to point out
señor sir, Mr., gentleman
señora lady, Mrs., madam
señorita young lady, Miss
septiembre September
séptimo, a seventh
ser to be
servir to serve, to wait on
sesenta sixty
setecientos, as seven hundred
setenta seventy
sexto, a sixth
sí yes
si if
siempre always, ever
siesta nap
siete seventh
signo de admiración exclamation mark
signo de interrogación question mark
siguiente following, next
silencio silence
silla chair
sin without
sin embargo however, nevertheless
sino but, except
sírvase please . . .
sitio place, spot

sobre on, upon, above
sobre envelope
sol sun
solamente only
solo, a alone
sólo only
sombrerería hat shop
sombrero hat
sonido sound
soñar to dream
sopa soup
soso, a insipid, tasteless
su his, her, its, your, their, one's
subir to rise, to climb, to go up
sueño sleep
suficiente sufficient, enough
superior superior, upper, better, finer
sur south
suyo, a his, hers, its, theirs, one's

T

tabaco tobacco, a cigar
tacto touch, tact
tal such, so, as
(¿qué tal?) hello! how do you do?
también also, too
tango tango
tantos como as many as
tarde afternoon
(buenas) tardes good afternoon
tarjeta card
taxi taxi
taza cup
té tea
teatro theater
telefonear to phone
teléfono telephone
telefonista telephone operator
templo temple, church
tenedor fork
tener to have, to possess, to hold
tener gana de to feel like, to wish
tener hambre to be hungry
tener miedo to be afraid
tener sed to be thirsty
tercero, a third
terminar to finish, to end
tiempo time, weather
tienda shop, store

tierra earth, land, soil, ground
tigre tiger
tijeras scissors
tinta ink
tintero inkwell
tirar to throw, to pull
tiza chalk
tocar to touch
todavía still, yet
todo, a everything, all
todos all
tomar to take
toro bull
torear to fight bulls
trabajar to work
traer to bring
tráfico trade, business, traffic
traje dress suit
trece thirteen
treinta thirty
tren train
tres three
trescientos, as three hundred
triste sad, sorrowful, gloomy
trópicos tropics
trozo piece, part

U

⎰ Ud. you
⎱ usted you
Ud. mismo yourself
último, a last, latest, final
uno, a one
usado, a used, worn out
usar to use, to wear, to accustom
usted you
usualmente usually
uva grape

V

vaca cow
valer to be worthy

valor value, price, worth, courage
varios, as several, various
vaso glass
verano summer
veinte twenty
veintidós twenty-two
veintiuno twenty-one
vender to sell
ventana window
ver to see, to look
verdad truth
verde green
vestidos dress, cloth
vestirse to dress oneself
viajar to travel
viaje journey
viejo, a old, ancient
viernes Friday
villa village, town
vino wine
visible visible
visita visit
visitar to visit
vista view, panorama, sight
vivir to live
volar to fly
volver to come back, to return
vuelo flight
vuelta return, turn

Y

y and
ya already
yo I

Z

zanahoria carrot
zapato shoe
zorro fox

Here's your opportunity to make yourself understood across Europe with the *Berlitz Self-Teacher*, a unique home-study method developed by the famous Berlitz School of Languages, and Grosset's *Phrasebook and Dictionary*, developed especially for travelers. Should you also want something more comprehensive, order the 366-page basic dictionary. Geared for students and travelers, the dictionary has over 10,000 entries, selected especially for use in everyday situations. Just call toll-free **1-800-631-8571** or fill out the coupon below and send your order to:

**The Putnam Publishing Group
390 Murray Hill Parkway, Dept. B
East Rutherford, NJ 07073**

The books in the Phrasebook and Basic Dictionary series are also available at your local bookstore or wherever paperbacks are sold.

		Price	
		U.S.	CANADA
___ **Berlitz Self-Teacher: French**	399-51323	$9.95	$12.95
___ **Berlitz Self-Teacher: German**	399-51322	9.95	12.95
___ **Berlitz Self-Teacher: Italian**	399-51325	9.95	12.95
___ **Berlitz Self-Teacher: Spanish**	399-51324	9.95	12.95
___ **El Berlitz Sin Maestro: Inglés**	399-51465	9.95	13.95
___ **French Phrasebook and Dictionary**	399-50794	4.50	5.95
___ **German Phrasebook and Dictionary**	399-50793	4.50	5.95
___ **Italian Phrasebook and Dictionary**	399-50795	3.95	5.50
___ **Spanish Phrasebook and Dictionary**	399-50792	4.95	6.50
___ **Basic French Dictionary**	399-50960	6.95	9.75
___ **Basic German Dictionary**	399-50961	6.95	9.75
___ **Basic Italian Dictionary**	399-51297	6.95	9.75
___ **Basic Spanish Dictionary**	399-50959	6.95	9.75

Subtotal $_____

*Postage & handling $_____

Sales tax $_____
(CA, NJ, NY, PA)

*Postage & handling: $1.00 for 1 book,
25¢ for each additional book up to
a maximum of $3.50

Total Amount Due $_____
Payable in U.S. Funds
(No cash orders accepted)

Please send me the titles I've checked above.

Enclosed is my ☐ check ☐ money order

Please charge my ☐ Visa ☐ MasterCard

Card # _____ Expiration date _____

Signature as on charge card _____

Name _____

Address _____

City _____ State _____ Zip_____

Please allow six weeks for delivery. Prices subject to change without notice.

12